To

`

Reinhard Heydrich
𝕴𝖗𝖔𝖓 𝕳𝖊𝖆𝖗𝖙

The true story of the
German SS General known as
'The Master of Death'

With Love from

Tina Gayle

Fisher King Publishing

Published by
Fisher King Publishing
The Studio
Arthington Lane
Pool-in-Wharfedale
LS21 1JZ
England

This book is dedicated to:

The Latin Teacher at Clapham County Grammar School for Girls in Battersea, South London; who drummed into us the meaning of our old School Motto which has led me through the two year journey of writing this book:

Discendo Veritas
The Truth, by Learning

Many thanks to:

The Wheatcroft Collection for their permission to view and photograph Heydrich's bronze bust statue.

Mark Stretton who has driven me over 12,000 miles around the UK to Military Shows and Militaria Fairs and all across Europe on my trips to Germany and Czech Republic during the research of this book.

Contents

Introduction

This is a book that will challenge the stories about
SS-Obergruppenführer Reinhard Heydrich,
Head of the Gestapo and the man referred to as:
'The Butcher of Prague', 'The Master of Death', 'The Hangman'
and 'The most evil man of the Third Reich'.

Reinhard Heydrich was an accomplished musician on violin and cello,
an Olympic Fencer, an expert horseman, and a qualified Pilot who flew
secret solo missions over France, Norway and southern Russia. He is
described in our history books (56 Titles listed in Bibliography) as: an
effeminate sexual pervert, a ferocious degenerate, dangerous, haughty,
unfeeling, cold hearted, a snake, Hitler's madman, Himmler's brain, the
Beast, a ruthless Nazi, and the most feared man in the Third Reich.
Quite a catalogue of titles and none of them were ambivalent.

I came to be interested in him during some historical background
reading about WW2, for a Fiction Novel I am currently writing. It needs

to make accurate reference to the ideology and discipline of the SS, so my research began with the development of the SS by the man given this task in April 1929 by Hitler.

Himmler was to turn the SS into an elite body of the best men; best educated, most intelligent and highest qualified Germans. He decided that an internal intelligence unit of the SS was needed, a sort of MI5 and MI6.

The Sicherheitsdienst (Security Service), or Sicherheitsdienst des Reichsfuhrer - SS, or SD, was created as the intelligence agency of the SS and the Nazi Party in Germany, and he employed Heydrich as a communications expert to set this up and manage it for him.

Since his Assassination, Heydrich has been blamed solely and uncompromisingly as the Author of The Final Solution and as the most dangerous man in the whole of WW2; more dangerous even than Hitler himself. Heydrich was the only Nazi leader to be assassinated. Why? It was a huge operation funded by the British Government, knowing there would be reprisals.

There are outlandish stories about him and his personal habits, that I cannot find any given facts to support, and they seem out of character and incongruent with the descriptions of him. I have not found any recorded research into whether these accounts of him are true; perhaps no one has thought to question them. So I have taken time out from my novel to investigate the real truth about this man.

The result is the information I give you in this book that will certainly explode some of the myths about him, give you real evidence and real stories about his personal life that shed a new light on his personality and family life. I have even discovered a little known letter from his wife sent to a friend of hers after his death, that there is no reason to disbelieve, which will definitely cause a stir among the historians when I reveal it in this book.

Why rattle the tree? This will be a daunting and much criticised task, but as a professional writer, I am compelled to write it. Writer's write because they have to commit their thoughts to paper, whether or not it will be liked or popular.

My experience of Independent Review Writing for Serious Case Reviews, specialising in Rapes and Murders; where pieces of a complex jigsaw need to be examined and looked at independently has been vital. Using factual accounts from different organisations and different perspectives, to extract and piece together the real story of what happened and why, has been a good background for this piece of work.

My methodology was to look for facts that can be evidenced by people who knew him and to question behaviours that seem at odds with his character traits, with an independent, dispassionate and non-judgemental view. When this type of thinking is applied to the current stories about Heydrich, they just don't make any sense. Hopefully, this book will enable us to make sense of them with the new information that has come to light.

I do not attempt to make any judgements or give any personal opinions about the events of WW2 or condone any of the events that took place. This is simply an investigation into the lifestyle, character and personality of the man that was Reinhard Heydrich.

Chapter One
The Dealer

A Specialist German WW2 Dealer put a Silver Bell into my hand...

If you read any book about the Third Reich, you will find that most of them give a mention or a passing reference to Heydrich. Mostly they all repeat the same stock phrases about him. One or two of them added some interesting facts and I have spent time trying to confirm or deny them by finding other people or stories that evidence them. I used a sort of triangulation process normally used by Builders and Engineers, by trying to match it up with other accounts from different sources.

During this process, I travelled to Re-enactors Fairs, Militaria Shows, and Armaments Fairs across the Midlands, spending whole days talking to people who had an interest in, or expert knowledge of 3rd Reich artefacts: Collectors, Re-enactors, Dealers of memorabilia, Weapons Experts, Militaria Experts, and members of the public who were visiting these shows; all of whom were surprised and slightly bemused by my research.

Without fail, they all quoted the same phrases about Heydrich that appear in the books, with no understanding or knowledge of where they came from. The Blond Beast, The Hangman, The Butcher of Prague, and so on. At an Arm's Fair held at the Motorbike Museum in Birmingham, there were 3 halls of exhibitors; one hall was just Arms but included daggers, knives, and swords, the other halls contained Memorabilia specialists and Dealers in everything to do with WW2.

What better place to find out more about the lifestyle of an SS Officer than here. One of the Dealers traded in original German uniform items and had a collection of original grey SS peaked caps in a glass case. He told me of a black SS cap that he had in the car, original and with a price tag of over £3,000. He asked if I would like to see it but I was more interested in asking him about his knowledge of people, and whether he knew anyone still living that may have known or worked for Heydrich.

"He was a Bastard, wasn't he?" He stated categorically. "He hated Himmler as well".

"Well was he? And did he? That is what I would like to find out", I replied.

A bemused look came across his face. "Well that's what it says in all the books", he said as if to a stupid child.

I started to try to explain why I thought the stories about him were exaggerated and he appeared a little surprised and then dismissive. Clearly none of these thoughts had ever crossed his mind before. I suggested that these stock phrases could have been invented by the film makers to construct a good story, and may well have distorted the truth.

He dismissed the conversation and suggested that I try to find a man called Rochus Misch who was at that time living in Berlin. Herr Misch was in his early nineties, and was one of Hitler's closest aides and was present in the Bunker with him. Hitler's Driver for about 12 years I believe, and a strapping broad shouldered man of over six feet tall.

Misch fled the bunker on 2 May 1945, just a few hours before the Red Army seized it. He was soon captured by the Russians, and taken to Lubyanka Prison in Moscow, where he was tortured in an attempt to extract information regarding Hitler's exact fate. (Strange don't you think, since the bodies of Hitler and Eva were found in the Bunker on 30th April, but that's probably another story).

Misch was released from his Soviet forced labour camp in 1953 and returned to Berlin, arriving home on New Year's Eve 1953, where he lived 3.2 kilometres, or 2 miles from the site of the *Führerbunker*. When the Bunker was rediscovered in the 1990s, Misch stated publicly that the bunker was an important part of world history and should not be completely destroyed, but it was razed and built over with a housing estate.

Churchill's Bunker however, under 10 Downing Street and alongside Horse Guards Parade in St James Park, London, is now a tourist attraction, where you can visit Churchill's War Room, bedrooms, and living quarters for his staff, complete with original belongings and artefacts like radios and maps, so you can see what it was actually like. Not so for the Fuhrerbunker it seems.

On the 1st December 2008, Misch became the last survivor of the *Führerbunker*. He remained loyal to Hitler to the end, and apparently he used to hang around the Bunker site and would talk to people who travelled to (and actually managed to find) the small signboard that marks the spot, now in the car park of an average German Council House Estate in a Berlin back street.

I did go to Berlin in mid February 2013. It was minus three degrees, and snowing. After much walking in between rows of houses, I did find the signboard that just had a location map of what used to be there. I was amazed at how enormous it would have been. The underground complex of buildings and rooms was at least ten times bigger and more sophisticated than Churchill's Bunker. It was almost a small Town. The word Bunker gives completely the wrong impression of what it was.

As expected, no one was silly enough to stand around a signboard in February in three inches of snow; and just six months after my trip to Berlin, I heard on the News that Rochus Misch had passed away on 5th September 2013 at the age of 96.

A great shame, and yet more pressing a reason to find out as much as possible as fast as possible, before everyone who has a living memory of those years and the people involved; pass into history with their stories and knowledge untold.

I still have no idea why this knowledgeable trader suggested I speak to Misch, when I had asked him if he had any contacts who may have known Heydrich, but perhaps he thought that Misch may know other SS Members who had worked with or for Reinhard Heydrich.

Hundreds of people were milling around the stalls which were all tightly packed together around the outside edge of the three halls, and in back to back rows up and down the centre spaces. They were so close together that you could just about get a line of people in front of each stall with enough room to walk or bump from person to person if you wanted to walk past. Seventy five per cent of the items on every table were German, and mainly from WW2 - badges, buckles, documents, ammo bags, books, uniforms, de-activated guns, knives, daggers, hats and pictures.

I was amazed to find that all the German stuff was at least 3 times the price of the British and European items, with a small letter written and signed by Churchill and mounted in a wooden frame, on sale for just £26. Compare that with a copy of Mein Kampf that had a signature from Hitler and the price tag was £2,500.

Apart from one black and two grey SS hats, everything was Waffen SS and not Algemaine, Totenkopf, or Liebstandarte SS, so my eye was suddenly drawn to the corner of the room where a black SS flag was draped over the back of a chair behind a stall, and out of reach of anyone passing by the front of the stall. It was about 2 foot by 3 foot in size. I bumped and barged my way over to it and asked the stall holder if I could have a look at it.

He was a tall gangly man in his early sixties, with once blonde hair a little too long, wearing cargo shorts and a check shirt, open at the neck. His partner behind the stall was a large woman in a knitted cardigan, sitting hunched over a small notebook, pencil and calculator, a hint of a dark upper lip shadow, accenting her non-smiling face. He was standing up and lurched over to me with a loud brash London accent saying; "Its SS luv".

"Yes, I know", I said. The silver SS flashes across the flag were pretty self-explanatory and couldn't be anything else. "It's fabulous", I said. The thick wool or felt material showed signs of age and distress, a few bald patches and a couple of holes – I hoped not moths. The price tag was almost as faded as the flag and I had to look twice to register that it said £700 and not £70.

"You like the SS then Gel?" He said. "Not many people do, that's why I keep it at the back, in case it gets damaged by someone who takes offence at it".

It seemed incredible that anyone would go along to a specialist Militaria Fair like this, and then be offended at any of the original items. I explained that I was a Writer, and wanted to talk to people about Reinhard Heydrich, to find out more about what he was really like.

John then introduced himself, and in a Dell-Boy drawl, invited me to, "Sit down Gel", and thus turned into a willing victim; he began to regale me with stories of how he had collected Third Reich items since he was a ten year old boy. Not exactly conversation about Heydrich, but I listened intently, to see what would be revealed.

According to John, when the War finished and Soldiers returned home; they brought all kinds of souvenirs and spoils of War with them. Lugers, SS Daggers, Hats, Badges, and these ended up shoved under the bed and forgotten about. 10 to 15 years later when the ex-soldiers had married and had families of their own, the children would find the guns and weapons and play with them around the house. This led to a time when such items started to be thrown out for the dustmen. Wives apparently didn't want stuff like that around the house.

I can understand that being true, as one of my friends collects bayonets, and recently found his five year old playing with one in the garden, and is now in the process of selling them, to get them out of the house.

John said that he used to find working Luger's and Daggers sticking out the top of dustbins and he used to collect them up and take them home. This was the beginning of his collection of 'German stuff' which he now keeps in a lock-up somewhere in South London.

John said that he used to buy German stuff from a famous South London dealer by the name of Bill Tobin. He used to visit Bill's damp Lockup, lit only by one single light bulb where he rummaged through boxes of badges and other stuff, looking at it and buying pieces when he had enough pocket money.

John emphasised that none of his vast sixty year collection was ever kept at his house – I couldn't work out whether this was from fear of burglars, or from a Sméagol-like desire to keep it all to himself and hidden from the world. I have since discovered that it is the latter and secret hoarders of Third Reich items do seem to be the norm. Anyway, my investigation of Heydrich was about to be thrown into total confusion.

Chapter Two

𝔗𝔥𝔢 𝔇𝔦𝔫𝔫𝔢𝔯 𝔅𝔢𝔩𝔩

John rummaged under the table at the back of his stall and placed in my hand a small silver hand bell, badly tarnished and pitted. It had Reinhard Heydrich's name engraved on it with a faint date and some other words written in German.

He told me it was Heydrich's Dinner Bell, since a man of his rank would be waited on at table, and to call over a waiter he would simply ring this bell.

'All the high ranking Officers', he said, 'had a bell like this at dinner for this purpose.'

I was surprised that I had never before heard of this or seen one; but he was adamant that a man of Heydrich's rank would certainly not be so undignified as to shout to a Waiter, and would use this bell to summon a serving staff at dinner. Seems a little odd for a man whose job it was to give orders to other people all day, being undignified to give orders to a butler or waiter, but I supposed it could be possible.

Let's imagine it might be feasible, especially as the higher ranks of the elite SS had silver plated platters and serving dishes, all engraved beautifully with the SS runes and sometimes the name of their Regiment. I have seen plenty of these changing hands quietly through the specialist dealers. I have even seen a silver-plated and monographed salt and pepper set, so a monographed silver plated dinner bell could certainly be possible.

John asked if I wanted to buy it for a special bargain price (just to me of course) of £2,000. I asked him if I could take a couple of pictures of it and do a bit of research before I made up my mind, and he promised to keep it for me until I could let him know.

Over the next few weeks I scoured every book for a picture of any SS Officer at dinner, and found nothing.

I searched the internet looking for images of any SS Officers at dinner, and again found nothing.

Not one single picture that showed anything like a dinner bell, or a silver bell of any description with any SS officer or in any dinner scene.

The bell clearly had age. I held it in my hand and it does exist, so it must have a purpose. If there was one thing I had learned about Heydrich thus far, it was that everything he did or owned had a reason and a purpose. So, on with my search.

The fact that a small-time collector and dealer in South London had an item that had clearly been a personal possession of Heydrich really started to bother me. How did he come by it? And why was it in England? Was it authentic? If not, why would anyone invent it? Why did no-one know about it? And what on earth was it for?

Even though I had no idea of the answers to these questions, I decided I had to buy it from him, and a meeting was set up one afternoon for us to meet at Reading Services on the M4 about forty miles west of London. John and his surly wife Jan, sat with their coffees while John told me all about some of the 'stuff' he was hoarding in his secret lockup. It seems he has boxes of uniforms, enormous swastika hangings, too heavy to lift or move, folded up on the ground and going mouldy. Silver platters, Candelabra, dishes, and even named silver fruit bowls complete with Regiment name, runes, and dedications.

This should all be in a museum and not hidden in secret locations, but this appears to be normal practice for Third Reich collectors.

John said he had bought it from Bill Tobin in the 1960's for his personal collection and after having it for over fifty

years, he now thought he might like to sell it; but only to someone who would appreciate it, since he wasn't a Dealer; but simply, a Collector!
I did a little searching on the internet, and did find a reference to someone called William Tobin, and here is the site reference:
www.britishbadgeforum.com/forums/archive/index.php/t-4509.html
details of Bill Tobin German Militaria Dealer in the 50's and 60's.

So the provenance checked out from wartime to present day, but the purpose of the bell still needed to be found. The deal was done and I

drove away with the small
silver bell bearing Heydrich's
name, and the mission to find
out what it was now began in
earnest.

To Berlin

I spent a weekend in Berlin
and went to the new Museum
called – rather unnervingly – Topography of Terror. An outdoor and
indoor collection of historical pictures and documents built over the
place where the SD and SS Headquarters used to be, when it was called
Prinz-Albrecht-Strasse (now called Niederkirchnerstrasse) where
Heydrich worked every day managing the operations of the SD while a
few corridors away, Himmler was managing the operations of the SS
from 1933 onwards.

It is worth a marker in the sand here that these two organisations
were in fact separate, and had completely separate offices, staff and
lines of Hierarchy below them, while Heydrich's role was as a direct
report to Himmler, but more about that later on.

The actual buildings that housed the SD and SS headquarters were
destroyed by Allied bombing during early 1945 and then after the War,
the remaining ruins were demolished. The area then became a part of
the cold war no-man's-land where the boundary between the American
and Soviet zones of occupation in Berlin ran along the Prinz-Albrecht-
Strasse, turning the whole street into a fortified boundary, with the
Berlin Wall running along the south side of the street, which was then
given the Soviet name of Niederkirchnerstrasse, from 1961 to 1989.

This section of the Berlin Wall was never demolished and the section adjacent to the Topography of Terror site is the longest surviving segment of the outer wall and is a startling reminder that the aftermath of WW2 still has an effect on us today.

After studying every single picture in the building, and buying every book and piece of literature they sold; you may not be surprised to discover that there was no trace of anything that resembled a Silver hand bell anywhere.

To The Castle

The next best place to look was Wewelsburg Castle in Germany, the ideological home of the SS. It is now a Museum that displays historical artefacts from when it was an SS Officers Training Centre and Himmler's 'Camelot' style Castle.

I can't resist quoting an article by Allan Hall printed in the Daily Mail on 23rd March 2010:

'Spiritual castle home' of infamous SS opens to public with £8m exhibition

An £8million exhibition chronicling the empire of the SS within the Nazi state opens next month in Germany at the Renaissance castle that was once its spiritual home.

Organisers of the exhibition say its principal aim is educational rather than glorifying the regime.

The display will be the largest in the world devoted to the history of the Third Reich's murderous elite - and a poignant warning never to allow it to happen again.

Read more: www.dailymail.co.uk/news/article-1259803/SS-castle-Nazi-murderer-Himmler-round-table-knights-open-public.html#ixzz2zAgPxRAV

Surely an £8 million exhibition of the *'murderous elite'* would reveal something about the history or purpose of Heydrich's silver bell?

The main Tower still houses the (rebuilt) Black Sun Swastika, and the Crypt with 12 Plinths for the 12 Tutonic Knights of the elite SS, but more about this and Himmler's 'Devil worshipping' Ceremonies later.

I scoured the whole of the exhibition in every area of the Castle: the exhibits, the pictures, the written history of the SS; looking for any mention or picture that showed a Dinner Bell. The main part of the Castle was used for training the elite Officers and also as a holiday camp for SS Officers' families to spend time together, where the children played together, the wives made friends and supported each other, and the Officers had time to relax and enjoy time with their loved ones, in an environment that was informal, encouraging and (SS style) enlightening.

You would have thought that a dinner bell with an engraved message on it and beautifully embossed Sig Runes on the tiny circular top of the handle would have been captured in a picture or a mention somewhere. But none were to be found. No one I spoke to had ever heard of this item or this particular use for it.

In truth, I was rather disappointed at the contents of the Museum. Perhaps they have a lot more artefacts hidden in their archives? But there was nothing to show the pomp and ceremony of the elite SS. Perhaps it isn't politically correct but it is real history. There wasn't one silver platter or engraved Regimental salver, dish, or even a knife or fork engraved with its Regimental badge and Divisions. I have seen more items like this at a Militaria Fair in Stoneleigh (and in cardboard boxes in the back of a Dealer's Range Rover at a Motorway Services) than there were in the whole of Wewelsburg Castle. If you haven't seen the items I have seen held in these secret collections, then you would never know such things ever existed. Can that be right?

The only Totenkopf Honour Ring on display in the Castle is said to be a copy and not an original. I don't know how true this is, but since a real one will sell for around £30,000 and usually then disappear to America; this could be a prudent decision by them.

Luckily I had written down the German inscription that was still readable on the Bell, not daring to take the bell itself across to Germany and asked a German friend who is a Business Lecturer what it actually said, hoping that this may give me a clue as to its use.

What an incredible discovery it was when I realised the meaning and the significance of what it said. It wasn't a Dinner Bell at all.

Chapter Three

The Honour Ring

Before I tell you what the Bell was for, I need to give you some background information about the Honour Rings.

Most interesting at Wewelsburg Castle, was the stone circle in the middle of the Crypt, where the eternal flame used to burn over the casket of Totenkopf Rings that had been presented to SS Officers by Himmler, and then taken back to the Castle on their death.

Heydrich of course had one of these rings and we presume that his ring was indeed returned to the Castle after his Assassination in 1942, although strangely, I cannot find any record of this – which is very odd as the record keeping of the SS was extremely regimented and detailed, and thousands upon thousands of card index records were found after the War. Each Member of the SS had everything recorded on one of these cards. The regiment they served in, the dates, their rank, promotions, awards, Military Honours and Medals awarded, and the date of the SS Honour ring presented by Himmler.

The significance of these rings in the context of Heydrich now needs to be explained for two reasons. The first concerns the date that Heydrich received his Honour Ring from Himmler, and the second concerns the hand on which it should be worn.

I began to research the date that Heydrich had been presented with his Honour Ring and failed to find it recorded anywhere. The book that is currently used as the expert witness for all things to do with these rings is:

Don Boyle author of 'SS Totenkopf H. Himmler Honor Ring 1933 – 1945'.

I did not manage to find a copy of this rare and expensive book anywhere in the UK, although there are copies of it in America. The book lists all the Honour Rings known to have been presented by Himmler, in date order, since 1933, so I searched for the date that Heydrich received his ring.

Nothing!

If it wasn't for the famous portrait picture of Heydrich wearing his ring on the wrong finger (as all the books say) then I would never believe he had a ring at all.

Each ring had an inscription inside it and I quote directly from Don Boyle's book:

The full inscription reads: 'S.lb. Meyer 21.12.41 H. Himmler'. The 'S.lb.' means 'seinen Lieben' or in English 'to dear' followed by the recipient's last name, date of presentation and a facsimile of Himmler's signature.

These awards were normally presented at promotion ceremonies and were worn on the ring finger of the left hand with the Totenkopf or skull facing up toward the wearer.

Note that Germans customarily wore their wedding rings on the ring finger of the right hand. The only known exception to the correct wearing of the award is with SS-Obergruppenführer Reinhard Heydrich who insisted on wearing his SS Honor Ring on the ring finger of his right hand, this is known to have infuriated Himmler which was probably Heydrich's intention.

Here you can see the familiar derogatory comments about Heydrich, in any and every comment about him. There is no evidence at all that Heydrich wished to infuriate Himmler, and here is a blatant off-the-cuff remark that just doesn't match his character. I address his relationship with Himmler in great detail further on.

Heydrich's life was ruled by the letter of the Law, detailed precision in everything he did, including the way he dressed. I have seen a letter written by Lina Heydrich, his wife; that said he hated to be dressed incorrectly.

Lina wrote many letters to an English lady called Jean Vaughan, a Writer, who wanted to write a book about the real character of Reinhard Heydrich and agreed to spit the proceeds 50:50 with Lina, if she helped her with the research. Unfortunately the book was never finished or published and Jean suddenly and unexpectedly died.

All her notes, papers, and letters from Lina were then sold by Auction and once again we see valuable history being sold off to the highest bidder, and disappearing from public view or knowledge.

Luckily, just before this Auction, some of the letters were read by David Irving who uploaded them to a website at www.fpp.co.uk the provenance can be found here:

http://www.fpp.co.uk/Heydrich/Vaughan_provenance.html

The collection includes photographs and a folder of documents including scores of private letters written by Lina describing her late husband, his work, his relationship with Wilhelm Canaris and Heinrich Himmler, and other matters of historical importance.

Photo: Reinhard Heydrich,
winter 1932, Munich

Inventory of the Vaughan Collection of Reinhard Heydrich, prepared by the current Owner, William Rasmussen -

1. Forty-four original unpublished photos of Heydrich, his family, SS personnel and top leaders etc.

2. Invitation by Kriegsmarine to SS

Gruppenführer Heydrich (1936).

3. Set of four postcards - one of a town, one of his father's music theater, 3rd is a large building, 4th showing his father Bruno at an opera. All are written by Heydrich? Two are signed Reinhard and 1 believed to be sent to wife signed Reini.

4. Fourteen envelopes from Mrs Heydrich.

5. Approximately 60 pages written by Mrs Heydrich.

6. Eleven miscellaneous pages of correspondence written about Heydrich from different persons to Jean Vaughan, who was writing a book.

7. Also a dozen or more items related about Heydrich.

8. One of Heydrich's calling cards - S.D.

This collection has now been sold to an American collector, and has never been seen or heard about since. Here follows a section of one of Lina's letters to Jean that tells of Heydrich's passion for correctness and attention to detail:

Letter from Lina Heydrich to Jean Vaughan, December 12, 1951.

Today I am going to tell you something about the character of my husband.

The most characteristic trait was that he was a man of few words. He never talked about something or discussed something [just] for the love of talk. Every word had to have a concrete meaning, or purpose, had to hit the point. Therefore he never said even one word more than necessary. My husband was vain. He hated nothing more than to be dressed inadequately. He also was ambitious, ambition meant work and efficiency, it meant, 'don't seem to be more than you are'. [Website comment: Mehr Sein als Scheinen: Generalstabsdoktrin]. The fact that he spoke so little made him seem a ruffian [philistine, boorish?], but his refined and exquisite manners charmed every one.

He required absolute obedience as he himself obeyed without questioning. Order was order, and a soldier had to have no personal meaning [Meinung, opinion] as to an order. His life was the conditionless [unconditional] devotion to his task and that was what he expected from everyone. Once a newly engaged assistant asked quite harmless[ly] what his wages would be. 'Wages', my husband asked him. 'You ought to ask what your work is going to be. Until now nobody is starved in my resort.'

Orders from Hitler were obeyed absolutely. My husband saw in him the one great man. I sometimes ask myself what his thoughts would have been if he had seen the bitter end. He thought him to be the one and only being who could lead the German nation to greatness and glory. Therefore it is good that my husband died in 1942. He has kept his faith and ideal.

I wrote you these items today because they just came to my mind. I am not always able to write, there are too hard and woeful memories connected with this.

The symbolism of the Honour Ring was that each Officer who wore it was in effect 'married' to the SS. The Citation that was presented with each ring by the Reichsfurher-SS Heinrich Himmler, translates as follows:

I award you the SS Death's Head Ring.

The ring symbolises our loyalty to the Fuhrer, our steadfast obedience and our brotherhood and comradeship.

The Death's Head reminds us that we should be ready at any time to lay down our lives for the good of the Germanic people.

The runes diametrically opposite the Death's Head are symbols from our past of the prosperity which we will restore through

National Socialism.

The two Sig-runes stand for the name of our SS. The Swastika and Hagall-rune represent our unshakeable faith in the ultimate victory of our philosophy.

The ring is wreathed in oak, the traditional German leaf.

The Death's Head Ring cannot be bought or sold and must never fall into the hands of those not entitled to wear it.

When you leave the SS, or when you die, the ring must be returned to the Reichsfuhrer-SS.

The unauthorised acquisition of duplicates of the ring is forbidden and punishable by law.

Wear the ring with honour!

H. HIMMLER

More than 14,000 of them were given by Himmler between 10th April 1934 and 17th October 1944, when no further rings were issued. Presentation only happened on particular days that were noteworthy to the SS, and these were:

30th January – the NSDAP assumption of power anniversary,

20th April – the Fuhrer's Birthday

21st June – Midsummer's Day Pagan Celebration and SS Festival

9th November – Munich Putsch anniversary

(A good way to spot a fake is if the date inside is not one of those four days.)

The ring was full of symbolism as you can see from the citation.

They were all made in Munich by Otto Gahr, who also sculpted some very fine busts of Hitler (one of which I was shown by John, who calls himself a collector and not a dealer. It was on loan to him from the real owner and was an original Gahr, about 18 inches high, hollow bronze, and so valuable that John could not even guess at a price that the owner of it might sell it for. So it was not for sale) and every ring was hand finished by particular Companies that were supervised by Otto.

The Honour Ring was the most highly coveted award that any SS Officer could achieve and was so sought after, that some SS Officers who had not been chosen to receive one; had a copy made by a Jeweller in a Concentration Camp and some of these still survive today, although they change hands for a very high price. Possibly the only 'copy' that is also 'real'; and they are needless to say, very collectible.

Every presentation was entered in the Officers' Seniority List (Dienstaltersliste), and a further notation was made in their SS personnel file. When any ring holder died, his next of kin was entitled to the notation as a keepsake, but the ring had to be returned to the SS Personalhauptamt for immediate return to Himmler's castle in Wewelsburg, where it was preserved in memory of the holder.

Accordingly, if a ring holder was killed in combat, it was removed from his person and handed to the unit commander, who would send it to the SS Personalhauptamt and then onwards to Wewelsburg Castle.

In many cases, the Americans, or Russians, actually cut the finger from a dead SS Officer to take the ring for themselves as spoils of war; as well as to prevent it being returned to Himmler, which is why so many of them have since turned up in USA and Europe, although they are now very rare indeed. Whoever currently owns these original rings, they are quietly holding on to them like Sméagol.

The rings of fallen SS officers were all kept in the crypt inside a shrine called the Schrein des Inhabers des Totenkopfringes or Shrine to the holders of the Deaths' Head Ring, which was treated with extreme respect, care and reverence.

I believe there was an 'eternal flame' over them, which although we cannot evidence with any surviving photographs, I did see evidence of what might have been a gas supply pipe under the floor of the centre of the Crypt, inside the raised stone ring of about 8 feet across. It is now just rough stone.

Authors note: If anyone still living has first-hand knowledge of what this room was like and would like to describe it to me, I would love to interview you.

On October 17th, 1944, as a result of the hardships of war, the Reichsfuhrer-SS cancelled manufacture and presentation of the ring for the duration of the conflict. Official SS statistics show that during its ten year life, approximately 14,500 rings were presented. By January 1st, 1945, 64 per cent had been returned to the shrine, 26 per cent were in the possession of their holders, and 10 per cent had been lost in the battlefield.

This means that a little over 3,500 rings were in circulation outside the shrine at the end of the war.

In the spring of 1945, with the Wehrmacht in full retreat, Himmler ordered that the rings cared for in the Shrine be blast sealed into the side of a mountain near Wewelsburg, in order to prevent their capture by the Allies.

It was Joseph 'Sepp' Dietrich who carried out this task and even to this day, they have never been recovered. I would guess that it wasn't only the casket of rings that were buried into the mountainside that day; and highly likely that other treasure such as gold ceremonial goblets, priceless paintings, and even Nazi gold was also buried to be retrieved one day by the offspring of the 4th Reich.

But back to a mystery that we can solve; the hand that Reinhard Heydrich wore his Honour Ring, and what does this have to do with the strange silver bell?

Chapter Four
By Accident or by Design

The symbolism of the Honour Ring was that each Officer who wore it, was in effect 'married' to the SS. Accepting the ring was to accept a responsibility that you, your family, and your future family would uphold the SS motto of "My Honour is Loyalty" to the Reich, to the Fuhrer, and to your family; and I believe that Heydrich took this promise very seriously indeed.

This would not have been questioned by his wife Lina, as she was a model German good wife, and was devoted to the Fuhrer, her husband, and the 3rd Reich. In fact it was Lina who introduced him to the SS soon after they met, but more about her later.

Prior to Heydrich being made Reichsprotektor of Moravia and Bohemia, he did wear his ring on the left hand, as I found a picture showing this in a book called: Men at Arms. 266, The Allgemeine-SS by Osprey Publishing on page 46. This can be viewed online on this link: http://ww2visual.blogspot.co.uk/2011/04/allgemeine-ss-osprey-men-at-arms.html

And the black and white picture shows Heydrich at his desk in 1937 with a pencil in his right hand, and the Honour Ring very clearly on his left hand:

SS-Gruppenführer
Reinhard Heydrich at his
desk in 1937. Note the
single shoulder strap,
finely embroidered collar

patches, and the bullion
cuff title of a
Hauptamtschef. The SS
Death's Head Ring can
clearly be seen on his left
hand.

armband. The cuff title on the right sleeve com-
memorates Schaub's membership of the Stosstrupp
Adolf Hitler in 1923, and his Old Guard status is
reinforced by the Alte Kämpfer chevron, Coburg
Badge, Golden Party Badge and the Blood Order
ribbon stitched to the right breast pocket flap.

E2: Ehrenführer Dr. Lammers, 1942

The Head of the Reich Chancellery, Dr. Hans
Lammers, was a wily civil service lawyer who had
solved many legal tangles for the Nazis during their
formative years. He was subsequently rewarded by
Himmler with honorary SS rank, and rose to
Obergruppenführer on 20 April 1940. As an Ehren-
führer he did not have operational authority over any
SS forces but, nevertheless, was entitled to sport the
insignia and accoutrements of a full SS general. The
Reichsführer's Sword of Honour hangs from his left

46

side, and the brocade belt, embroidered with oakleaves and runes, was worn on ceremonial occasions.

E3: SS-Standartenführer Graf Strachwitz; evening dress, 1944

The aristocratic Hyazinth Graf Strachwitz von Gross
Zauche und Camminetz was a Standartenführer
attached to the staff of Oberabschnitt Südost, and the
first SS member to win the Knight's Cross of the Iron
Cross with Oakleaves, Swords and Diamonds. He
earned the award in April 1944, while serving as an
army (not Waffen-SS) Panzer commander on the
Eastern Front. Here he wears the sparkling decoration to good effect with regulation SS evening dress.
The jacket sports full insignia, complete with its
distinctive breast badge comprising a death's head
over a scroll bearing the SS motto, 'Meine Ehre heisst
Treue'. The ornate buttons are embossed with SS
runes surrounded by a wreath of oakleaves.

F1: Senior NCO, Security Police, c.1943

During the war, members of the Security Police
serving in the occupied territories were afforded the
protection of the grey uniform of the Sicherheitsdienst, irrespective of whether or not they were
members of the SD or, indeed, of the SS. The
regulation grey Allgemeine-SS tunic became increasingly difficult to find from 1942 onwards, however,
and this senior NCO has had to make do with an army
field blouse. The blank right-hand collar patch and
the 'SD' sleeve diamond, originally denoting attachment to the old SD-Hauptamt, eventually became
universal throughout the Sipo and the SD, while the
rank insignia combines the collar patch of an SS-
Hauptscharführer with the shoulder straps of a Police
Hauptwachtmeister or Kriminaloberassistent. The
ribbon of the War Merit Cross 2nd Class, often
awarded to the Security Police for their 'special
services', extends from the second buttonhole, and
this man has also been awarded a Police long-service
decoration and the SA Sports Badge in Silver.

F2: Oberwachtmeister, SS-Police Regiment, 1944

From 1943, German Police formations serving as
security troops in the occupied territories were
known as 'SS-Police' Regiments, to distinguish them
from the recently raised native auxiliary 'Police Rifle'

This is the only picture I have found that shows his ring, other than
the posed pictures that were taken during his time as Reichsprotektor

and acting Head of State, which show him wearing the ring on his right hand. So what caused him to make the change? Here are some logical suppositions:

Germany and many other Catholic European countries still wear their Wedding rings on the right hand from a long standing tradition. The Catholic Church deemed that the left hand was unholy or sinister, whereas the right hand stood for dexterity and goodness, so wedding rings have been worn on the right hand for hundreds of years. When England broke away from the Catholic Church and became Protestant, it was decided to switch to the left hand as a sign of defiance to the Catholics and to have a tradition that was different from Roman Catholic Tradition.

Himmler did his best to remove all Catholic Church Traditions from the German people, and replace them with Pagan, Mystic or ancient Germanic traditions and rituals wherever he could. One of these was to order that the Honour Ring should be work on the left hand, thus separating it from all religious meaning and symbolism.

Interestingly, it is an ancient Custom for Monarchs to wear a Wedding Ring on their right hand during a Coronation; to show that they are married to the State. Heydrich as Reichsprotektor of Moravia and Bohemia (now known as the Czech Republic and Slovakia) was certainly an 'Acting Head of State', ruling over both these areas on behalf of the Reich.

If you look a little more closely at every picture that Heydrich has 'posed' for a Portrait, since his promotion to SS Obergruppenfuhrer and Reichsprotektor; you will notice the position of his hands and fingers, with the right hand forward to camera, the knuckles slightly lifted, left hand pulled back over his wrist, and the ring prominently displayed as a gesture of Head of State, status and duty.

SS-Obergruppenführer Reinhard Heydrich

So why would Reinhard Heydrich break a Military Order by wearing his Honour Ring on the wrong finger, in public, for everyone to see and hold him to account?

Would he really go against an order and flout it in public, just to annoy Himmler?

Would behaviour such as this sit well with a man whose life is governed by precision and attention to detail?

Being installed as the Acting Head of State for Moravia and Bohemia meant that Heydrich would now answer directly to Hitler himself, not Himmler. As a devoted follower of Hitler, would he really concern himself with any public act as petty as trying to annoy Himmler?

We have already heard from his wife Lina that anything other than following orders, carrying out his duty and being correctly presented was of vital importance to him. My view is that he would not have worn his ring on his right hand unless he believed it completely and utterly, to be the correct hand to wear it on in the absolute performance of his duty.

These are the reasons that I firmly believe that Reinhard Heydrich purposefully and symbolically wore the Totenkopf Ring on his right hand.

Not to annoy Himmler, not by accident, and not in defiance of an order.

Myth: *Heydrich wore his Honour Ring on the wrong hand (his right hand) to annoy Himmler.*

Busted: *So how is all this connected with the silver Bell? Time to explain.*

Chapter Five

A Present from Himmler

The inscription engraved on the little silver bell is exactly this:

SS

SS BRIGDEF
REINHARD HEYDRICH
ICH SCHENKE IHNEN DE
TOTENKOPFRING DER SS
24 Dezember 1933

Translated that means:

SS

SS BrigadeFuhrer
Reinhard Heydrich
I present to you
The SS Totenkopf Ring
24th December 1933

This was earth shattering news. This proved a whole raft of things as yet unknown:

1. That it wasn't a dinner bell.

2. That it was a personal present from none other than Himmler.

3. That it provides the ONLY hard evidence of the date Heydrich received his ring ever found by anyone.

4. It provides crucial evidence – so far eluded by all the Ring Historians that the first rings were given as personal presents by Himmler, long before they turned into an award.

Questions needed to be answered and fast.

Why didn't anyone know about the date?

Why didn't anyone know about the existence of the bell?

Were there more bells out there somewhere in a private collection that provided evidence of other rings being presented by Himmler, before the official records were started?

How had this slipped from any form of official record keeping by Himmler's office or the SS?

Could I evidence that Himmler did give presents on this date?

Could I evidence that any of his presents were Totenkopf Rings?

Could I find anyone else who had been given either a present or a Ring by Himmler on the same date?

Where on earth to start on such a task?

No point telling everyone what I thought the bell was, unless I could prove it with second and third forms of evidence from other independent sources. So it was time to trawl through my ever growing pile of books for inspiration.

Nothing!

I went to more Militaria, Memorabilia and Arms Fairs, scouring the piles of old books and Military History books, along with my now usual chat to the stall-holders, who asked me how my research was getting on. Then on a table filled with specialist Military History books, I found it!

A book called: The SS Totenkopf Ring

An illustrated History from Munich to Nuremberg

By Craig Gottleib

Published by Schiffer Military History in 2008

I paid the US $59.99 equivalent of £45 Great British Pounds and couldn't wait to get it open:

Using modern tools not available to previous authors on this subject,

Craig Gottleib paints a comprehensive picture of the Totenkopf Ring and the man who was behind it - Reichsfuhrer SS Heinrich Himmler. Contains over 200 examples to document currently believed notions about the ring. Never before seen photos and documents that covers the pre-history of the Death's Head Ring, placing its appearance onto the SS scene in historical context.

Perfect, just what I needed. There must be something in here that will evidence Heydrich's ring on this date, and back up the authenticity of the bell; after all, he was a major figure in History.

1933 Christmas Presents from Himmler – 24.12.33

A heading on page 39 says:

The Totenkopf Rings began as Christmas presents from Himmler in 1933, marked with the date of 24th December which is the traditional day for present giving in Germany.

At the same time Ernst Rohm was making presents of engraved daggers to senior SA men; another Christmas gift that would, coincidentally, later become an award.

1933 had been a year of astonishing success for Himmler, becoming Police President of Munich, then political Police Commander in Bavaria, giving him (and Heydrich) control over the entire security apparatus in Germany's second largest state.

In early 1934 Himmler was appointed Head of the Police in all the remaining States of the Reich – except Prussia, where Goring ruled as Minister President with his own secret Police force called the Gestapo.

So at Christmas 1933, Gottlieb believes that Himmler's Christmas presents were: *to reward the loyalties of those who had travelled with him this far, and to bind them to his side for the year ahead. Although no list of the original recipients has been found, we can piece together a partial list from existing rings, ring documents, and archive files. To date, here are the only known recipients of the Christmas 1933 rings:*

Franz Xavier Schwarz: SS Obergruppenfuhrer

Treasurer of the Nazi Party and second only to Himmler. His ring survives and is in the personal possession of Gottlieb

Karl Wolff: SS Sturmbannfuhrer

Chief of Himmler's Staff; Member of the Reichstag and Himmler's personal Adjutant. His ring existed until the 1990's when it was lost.

Fritz Schlegel SS Brigadefuhrer

Philosopher, Gold Party Badge Holder and SS number 907. He died in 1936 and a letter in his records from Himmler stating the Reichsfuhrers' desire to attend his Funeral means that they were obviously friends; which explains why he was on Himmler's 1933 Christmas list. We know he was a 1933 recipient due to the document presented elsewhere in this book.

Erich Von Dem Bach Zelewski: SS Obergruppenfuhrer

Member of the Reichstag. We know he received a Christmas ring because his ring conferral document – one of only 2 1933 dated documents ever found and observed – is retained in a private collection and is pictured in the Chapter on award documents.

Wilhelm Reck SS Standartenfuhrer

Employed at SS Headquarters in Berlin and on Himmler's personal staff. We know that Reck received a 1933 ring because it still exists and the only surviving example of a 1940's style re-issued ring that bears the original Christmas 1933 conferral date.

Walter Darre: SS Obergruppenführer

Reich Minister of Food and Agriculture from 1933 to 1942. We know he received a Christmas ring because his conferral document bears a 24th December 1933 date.

Ulrich Graf

Hitler's personal bodyguard from 1920 to 1923 who shielded Ah with his body and received 16 bullet wounds, saving Hitler's life. His receipt of the Christmas 1933 ring is confirmed in a letter written by him to the SS Personnel Office in which he mentions his ring date. Graf held Party Number 8. The whereabouts of his ring is unknown.

While one would like to draw a concrete conclusion from this short list of confirmed recipients of the Christmas 1933 ring, the tiny amount of data make such an effort impossible and meaningless. However we do observe that several SS Officers on this list were members of the Reichstag. Additionally, most achieved the rank of General later in their careers and would go on to play pivotal roles in the SS and in the NSDAP.

Only one thing seems certain – all of these Officers were well known to Himmler, and it is reasonable to assume that these men would have received a personal Christmas gift from him.

Was that it?

No mention of Heydrich?

Not even a mention that it was odd that he wasn't in this Christmas list?

I was almost beside myself at this point. No one thought that this was a serious omission by Himmler?

So I *can* evidence that rings were given out on 24th December 1933

I can also evidence that they were *all personal Christmas presents*, and as this Author stated 'probably would have been part of a personal Christmas Present from Himmler'. But nothing about what the personal present may have been.

Nothing about a Silver Bell with the Totenkopf Ring slipped over the engraved handle and engraved with the owners name and, 'I present you with this Ring'.

Was Heydrich the only recipient of a silver Bell?

It was back to the drawing board. There MUST be something somewhere that gives solid secondary evidence to confirm the ring and the Bell presented to Heydrich, and I was determined to find it.

Chapter Six
An Email from Prague

A trip to Prague seemed the next sensible thing to do; perhaps a visit to the Church where Heydrich's Assassins were found, to find the place where the Assassination took place, and if possible, to visit the village where the Heydrich family lived, in a large Manor House or Schloss, or Chateau, that was surrounded by a small village on the outside of the grounds. This would be also about twenty miles outside the centre of Prague, in the direction of two o'clock on a watch face.

Perhaps I might find someone who knew something about him as a family man, although this was probably doubtful as Heydrich was assassinated seventy two years ago, so anyone with a living memory would be very elderly by now. Another consideration was that Heydrich kept to himself and didn't make friends with any work colleagues in case he needed to reprimand or have them arrested at a later date. So that severely reduced the chances of finding anyone currently alive who would be in a position to comment on his private life. No wonder that there were so many stories about him, with the truth so difficult to discover.

In Skorzeny's Autobiography (Skorzeny's Special Missions – The Memoirs of Hitler's Most Daring Commando – Otto Skorzeny) on page 31, where he talks of his promotion to Captain in the summer of 1943, with orders to set up an elite Commando Force called Section V1S. This was a full year after Heydrich's assassination, and the new Director of the State Security Department (Heydrich's previous role) was Dr Ernst Kaltenbrunner.

Skorzeny says: *Nor was the then Director of the State Security Department, Dr. Ernst Kaltenbrunner, any stranger to me, as I had known him in my student days. He had been a member of a Student's*

Club in Graz, which was associated with mine, and we had seen a good deal of each other up until 1938. Now he was apparently one of the most important men in Germany. I had to present myself to him and was agreeably surprised to find that we were soon on the old footing. It struck me that even with all his glory, this man was not feeling quite at his ease.

He surprised me greatly by telling me about his worries during one conversation: 'I took over this difficult department a year after the death of Obergruppenfuhrer Heydrich', he said. 'During the interregnum, Reichsfuhrer Himmler added it all to his other ministries and jobs and during that period my seven departmental chiefs achieved quite a degree of independence. They always went straight to Himmler himself, and even today, I am often side-tracked, and there is much that I only find out afterwards. Your new chief, Schellenberg, and the Gestapo Chief, Muller, are too fond of short circuits. Heydrich certainly knew his business, and built up his department in a cold, impersonal fashion, which we Ostmarkers don't like.'

(An Ostmarker was an Austrian Nazi, in favour of Austria becoming a German Province)

A comment that certainly evidences the fact that Heydrich had a good reason not to make friends with work colleagues or direct reports; as we all know the subterfuge that Schellenberg was involved in later. Heydrich did not like or trust Schellenberg, according to a letter from Lina Heydrich to Jean Vaughan on, December 12, 1951:

TODAY I am going to tell you something about the character of my husband. The most characteristic trait was that he was a man of few words. He never talked about something or discussed something [just] for the love of talk. Every word had to have a concrete meaning, or purpose, had to hit the point. Therefore he never said even one word more than necessary.

He never wasted a minute of his time. Every minute had to have his aim and purpose. Therefore he simply hated to go for a walk. Gymnastic exercise was not meant for a past-time or leisure, but for discipline, a training to reach the highest possible record in it. Therefore he always chose such sports to which he did not take naturally, but which required a hard training, self-discipline. For instance, he was not at all gifted for fencing, but the end of its hard and enduring training was that he became German champion.

The only exception in this respect was perhaps hunting. But even that was not only and simply pleasure and past-time. He knew he had to get away from his office, his work, once [in] a while, that he had to relax; and going hunting meant recreation and activity at the same time.

His memory was astounding. He never needed a telephone directory. He knew by heart all the numbers he needed, he never forgot a single report that he had read. In this respect the most surprising stories are told about him.

Neither in his youth nor later on had he any personal friends. He also tried to avoid every social contact with neighbours or fellow workers. That was very hard on me. When I once asked him for the reason, he answered, 'How can I be friends with any one, as I never can tell whether there might not perhaps arise the possibility of having him arrested one day!'

He distrusted every one and he was hardly ever mistaken in his judgment of persons. How often did he not say to me, 'I don't know, there is something about this person that I don't like, if I would only know what's wrong with him.' So my husband who seemed to be guided only by his logic and intelligence was in the end led by intuition. There was an immense danger in his development, that of human isolation.

It was very interesting for me to hear from you that in foreign countries there is the rumour of Walter Schellenberg's death. Now, to make it entirely clear, I speak of that Schellenberg who was sent into Sweden to [Count] Bernadotte by Himmler in 1945, who stayed there until the Allied forces had him given up to them, who then was kept in Great Britain in order to write and who then came to Nürnberg into the Justizpalast.

His comrades look upon him as a traitor for he is said to have disclosed much at that time and to have written in the tendency of putting the whole blame on my husband, while he pictured himself without any blame. Here he is called the crown witness against the SD (there is no such institution as crown-witness in the German justice)

In 1950 he wrote a book: Die geheime Front (the secret front) under the name of Walter Hagen.

[Walter Schellenberg schrieb unter dem Pseudonym 'Walter Hagen', sondern Wilhelm Höttl.]

In his early time Schellenberg was the fellow worker of my husband, he entered the SD as a Referendar then he was advanced quickly and at the time of my husband's death he was the head of the Section 6 [Amt VI] (spies in foreign countries).

In June 1942 people wanted to know that he was very eager to get the place of my late husband to become chief of the SD. Later on, when Kaltenbrunner had become chief of the SD, he always kept close to him, to this politically untrained man, and knew how to attain the favour of Himmler.

Therefore it is no wonder that Schellenberg became the successor of Canaris. Whether Sch. is to blame for the death of Canaris, I don't know, but I know for sure that if my husband had been living, Canaris never would have been hanged. Experts also say, that there never would have been a July 20th, on the one hand nobody [would have] had dared it, and on the other hand my husband had mentioned to me the people of the 20th July [1944 plot] as politically suspicious years before the actual happenings. It was my husband's opinion that only very few officers were able or willing to think politically. For too many years they had been educated as 'unpolitical soldiers.'

The accounts in their own words, from Lina Heydrich and from Ernst Kaltenbrunner via Otto Skorzeny, are both in agreement with each other. Both views are given by people that actually knew him very well, and both reveal good reasons for Heydrich to have adopted this kind of persona. People who possess a very logical mind are often able to keep all emotions separate from their work, and examples of this are easily seen today in high ranking Policemen, First-on-Scene Services, Health Professionals and Social Care decision makers who deal with the outcomes of particularly nasty criminals, major incidents, and of course, the outcomes of any war zone activity. Indeed, training to enable them to do this successfully is an important part of their professional instruction.

A good friend of mine has a colleague who lives on the outskirts of Prague, and who had served in the Czech Military as a Naval Officer and was now working as an electronics designer for the car industry in the Czech Republic. He was duly approached by email to see if he could help by sparing some time to point out the places I needed to visit.

When the reply arrived, I could hardly believe it. He said, (and I quote his English exactly):

I know perfectly where Heydrich was assassinated, but the locality itself is covered by new buildings and highway crossing. The original Road isn't there, but you can get close to about hundred metres, where also a memorial for the commandos stands. My friend in Paratroopers who is now a Chief of Police, did his Thesis on an analysis of the

*Atentate (*assassination*) if you would like to speak to him.*

*Heydrich was living in a Castle in a village where my Grandmother side of family and my Mother comes (*from*). My Grandmother was a sort of serving girl at the Castle when she was about 14 years old. She is still alive and still lives in the same village.*

On my Father side, the family very nearly perished, being all in underground resistance and seven sisters of my Grandfather were executed in one sweep. When I was young boy, the old man shown me the sewer drain where he was throwing leaflets and weapons that night. He was also quite young, which is one of reasons he survived. Thinking of which, best you come and listen to my Grandma, she is one of few people who knew Heydrich personally and is still alive. I can translate for you and the old Lady likes visitors.

It's just a coincidence that I have visited my Grandma about month ago, and she was in talkative mood; no wonder, when she is whole day alone at home and has nothing to do. So lots of family history came up. For example, one of my other uncles (which I never met) was Nazi hunter and agent in post-war Germany, working directly for General Exner and he found over 300 Czech children who were taken for 'reformation' which was basically to make them good little Germans during the War. In 1952 two men in long leather coats came to him from behind on the street and shot him in the head. He obviously knew too much being intelligence officer and was the type of man Commies feared the most.

On the subject of Heydrich, he was sent to Czechoslovakia to actually crush the (until 1940) very effective resistance. He claimed that he was going to cobble Wenceslaus Square with Czech skulls. He very nearly did it. Nevertheless, if you want to come and get some first-hand information, I can organise it for you. My Grandma being 88 years or something, is still very sharp thinking woman, you have to be prepared for the fact that she doesn't sugar-coat things – in fact being a farm girl originally, she speaks like an old Irishman.

As for Czechs in War, we had undoubted military advantage against Germans in 1938. If we didn't submit to the Munchen betrayal, we could have won the general battle and eventually prevail for short time. Hitler, who had not support of Army brass in 1938, would likely fail face to face to the catastrophe. France and England would have to keep their promises and the whole history would be very much different, the world war two, being fought in 1950 against Joe Stalin.

In 1938 the spine of my nation was broken. When Gestapo took over the Prague, people were denouncing their neighbours, old enemies and virtually anybody to Gestapo at rate which caused Chief of the Prague Central, to write to Berlin to double his amount of people, because Germans were unable to cope with the amount of collaboration in progress. Also Germans printed in Czech newspapers, formal notices: 'Czechs do not denounce so much,' quite a difference to a million men in arms absolutely resolute to die standing, with best training and equipment only six months before the final occupation.

See there is six months from Munchen when Sudetenland was taken to March 1939, when the rest of Republic was finally occupied. It's called 'Second Republic'. The occupation was bad enough, but these six months is the darkest time in the modern history of State, because morals, spine and consciousness of the nation were destroyed, so it could be occupied easy. Some scars will never go away.

My Grandmother actually went to School with the Heydrich's boys, she also saw Karl H. Frank visiting there and was sent to castle to deliver things and such. There was also a German Solider housed in every house in the village.

Also family history is that when they executed K.H. Frank, there was one of my Great-Uncles present at the execution in some capacity. If you come on Friday and stay till Monday, then we probably can visit my Grandmother during the weekend.

What were the chances of this?

What an unexpected reply. The chances of finding someone who had such family connections was probably a million to one so there was no time to be lost. This coincidence had been thrown into my path, and I now made immediate plans to take advantage of it.

- A true account of what it was like for an ordinary family to live in an occupied country, told by a person who has a living memory will be priceless.

- The fact that the family would have suffered some kind of trauma with deaths of some family members was inevitable as an occupied nation, and this would certainly lead to a view that would not be impartial in any way.

- Her personal knowledge of Reinhard, Lina, his wife of 11 years, Marte, Silke, Heider and Klaus, his 4 children would be totally unique and unrepeatable, because of the rarity of the experience, the age of the people involved, and their willingness to talk about it to a complete stranger from another country.

- All these factors increase in their unlikelihood with every passing day, as the passage of time relentlessly takes away the people concerned along with their capacity to remember and their willingness to speak.

This first-hand account of everyday life: evenings, weekends, habits, visitors, parties, lifestyle, clothes they wore, and how the Heydrich family behaved as a family, would be totally unique, unknown to the current history books, and irrevocably true.

The down side to that would be the expected hatred of Heydrich, his family, and everything that happened to the Czech people while he was their acting Head of state. I fully expect her to have extreme anti German views about the Heydrich family based on the trauma of living through a War as an occupied citizen with the resultant implications of life and death that brings to any family, any village community and any overthrown Nation. But in a way, this would also act as a safeguard against any further fantasy or fiction being expounded about the Heydrich family and their personal lives.

The facts she could reveal would be first-hand knowledge and therefore priceless and irreplaceable, as no one else is still alive who has the same knowledge or is able to recall and tell it.

The importance of whatever she was able to tell me was without doubt and her story needed to be told in whichever way it was revealed, and I vowed to take the information she chose to disclose, and to deliver it truthfully and accurately.

The only problem was that this lady was already 86 years old and was a Diabetic who was in and out of Hospital for dialysis and other treatments, it was the middle of winter and temperatures were falling, along with the driving conditions getting more treacherous with snow and ice expected for the next 3 or 4 months, and so planning a trip to coincide with when she was well enough to cope with it would be almost impossible.

The remaining task was to get there quickly, as soon as she was next out of Hospital. Diaries would need to be cleared with a few days' notice, ready for a journey at top speed by car, across the channel, through Belgium, straight across Germany, and into the Czech Republic.

Chapter Seven
The Race to Prague

Over the next 6 weeks, Anna was in and out of Hospital several times and we waited for news from Jaroslav, her Grandson, who visited every weekend. Anna came out of Hospital again in the middle of December and Jaroslav told us that if she felt up to it by the following week, we could be on for an interview. His Grandmother still lived in the same village on the outskirts of Prague, vPanenske Brezany which surrounded the Chateau where Heydrich lived with his family: Lina his wife of 11 years, Marte, Silke, Heider and Klaus, his 4 children.

Heydrich served directly under Himmler as Reichsprotector of Moravia and Bohemia (now known as the Czech Republic), a title given to him by Adolf Hitler when he moved to Prague to replace the previous title holder in September 1941. Heydrich held the title for just nine months until his death by Assassination on June 4th 1942 at the age of thirty eight.

Jaroslav said that Anna was keen to meet me knowing that I was a Writer from England. According to Jaroslav, she can't remember her children's names' or whether she had any lunch; but she can remember everything that happened during the war years with great clarity. She wanted to tell someone about her experiences of living in the same village and going to School with Heydrich's children from the age of thirteen.

Anna and her family worked for the Heydrich household during Occupied Czechoslovakia during the War years. Anna has stood 6 feet away from Heydrich on many occasions, and wants the world at large to know what it was really like for her and her family, growing up through this difficult but historic time.

The problem is that she has no one to tell, being confined to her house unless her brother or daughter take her out, and restricted to constant hospital visits, and the occasional visit from her Grandson Jaroslav.

So began a 3,000 mile drive across Germany, from Leicester to Prague a week before Christmas in 2013 and just 4 days after Anna came out of hospital; to spend an afternoon with Anna and hope that she felt well enough on the day to tell us all she wanted to say. I did have some very specific questions that could only be answered by someone who knew about the personal habits of the family, if indeed she knew any of the answers.

We left Leicester at 11pm on a Thursday evening and drove to Dover to catch the 4am ferry crossing to Dunkirk. Landing at 6am, we started across Belgium in the dark, with driving rain but luckily no snow or ice.

By Lunchtime we had crossed into Germany. Looking at the map Germany suddenly seemed much bigger than it had done on the kitchen table at home, but we reckoned that we should cross into Czech Republic at around tea time and be in Prague by 10pm.

The rain had cleared and although grey and dull, the scenery as we followed the Moselle valley past Koln was spectacular, even in the middle of winter. Traffic during the afternoon started to build and the usually efficient German Autobahn became unusually full of traffic that was all going the same direction as us, and we were getting slower and slower.

As we came close to Nuremburg at 4 o'clock, the fast lane turned into a slow stroll, and then stopped altogether in a most inefficient and uncharacteristic German traffic jam. To our horror we realised that the day was Friday 20th December, the last working day before the Christmas break and we were in the middle of a major Bank Holiday style departure. After another hour of moving a few hundred yards, we pulled in to the next service area and took a two hour sleep until it was all over.

Back on route, we travelled with no further issues into Czech and arrived at the Prague ring road at 10pm which we needed to circumnavigate from a clock-face entry position of five o'clock, up and around to an exit position of two o'clock and then another twenty kilometres to Jaroslav's Village.

The Road signs in Prague are quite unbelievable showing a plethora of complicated place names that you can't even find on the road map, so you have no sense of direction. The Junction numbers are not consecutive either, with exit numbers jumping two or three numbers at a time ; most confusing. It took us 2 hours to find our way through Prague and to Benatky Nadjizerov and we finally arrived at 1am after twenty six hours of driving.

The next day we awaited news of Anna to see if she was well enough to receive us and her daughter – Jaroslav's Mother – decided it would be best to leave it for another day, so we just had to wait.

Chapter Eight
An Encounter with the Czech Police

The next day Jaroslav took us to meet a friend of his, who had served in the Military with him some years ago, and was now a very Senior Officer in the Czech Police. He served in the Paratroopers with Jaro, while on National Service and then stayed on, rising to a high strategic rank and specialising in the psychology of performing special tasks. When he came out of the Military, he went into the Czech Police with a rank something like a Chief Inspector we think in translation. This man (we will call Ivan) had completed a dissertation on The Atentat, or Operation Anthropoid (Heydrich's Assassination) as part of his Post Graduate qualifications taken in the Military where he rose to be head of Special Forces and was an expert on every detail of how it was carried out by Gabcik and Kubis.

So an unexpected interview took place with this man, who didn't speak or understand a single word of English, translated both ways by Jaroslav which I will relay after Anna's story, for reasons that will become clear when you read the shocking stories of what Anna told us.

Chapter Nine
Family Secrets Revealed

The next day we were to arrive at Anna's house at midday. It was minus 10 degrees and snow was in the air. The car windows were covered in ice and when we sprayed them with a can of de-icer; it too froze into a solid sheet of ice on the windscreen. Twenty minutes later we were on route to the village of Panenske Brezany twenty kilometres from the centre of Prague where Anna still lives; in the village that surrounded the large country estate where the Heydrich family lived.

The house was on the edge of the village and looked over open fields towards Prague. The small garden was overgrown and Anna's son, who is close to sixty years old and lives in the ground floor flat, came out to greet us. He looks after his Mother as best he can, with some help from his sister who is Jaroslav's Mother. He gets the shopping and makes sure she is alright on the days when she is home from Hospital.

We were told to take off our shoes at the door, and were given some pairs of old worn out slippers to wear, before being taken up the bare wooden staircase to meet Anna.

Anna was sitting in a large armchair by the window and clutching her walking stick, pushed herself up in the chair to greet us in Czech. She didn't speak or understand any English at all and gestured to us to sit at the small dining table in the centre of the room. She spoke in Czech to her Grandson in a loud and commanding voice, telling him that she would sit next to us at the table, while she slowly stood up using her stick and took three or four steps at great effort on her own to reach the nearest chair to her at the small table and lowered herself into it with great concentration. Jaroslav said: 'She wants to do it on her own; she doesn't want to look helpless in front of you'. She sat with Jaroslav on her left and me on her right and spoke to us for the next five hours while

I asked questions in English to Jaroslav, he asked them in Czech to Anna, and then after thinking for a time; Anna spoke to Jaroslav in Czech, which he then relayed to me in English, all the while I wrote in my notebook.

The first question to take her back to the time concerned and to start her thinking process was to understand the everyday way of life then, and get some background on how any of that changed when they became an occupied nation. I now relate everything Anna said, using exactly the words she used to tell me, as translated first hand by her Grandson who relayed both my questions, and her answers

A few times he became deeply moved during this process, hearing stories about his family that his Grandmother had never told anyone until today. These are all presented in this book with as much detail as I had time to collect during the five hour interview. I am very grateful for her time and her honesty and I hope I have portrayed everything she said with accuracy and sensitivity.

Following this information, I will then suggest how it is now possible to re-write some of the outlandish stories about Reinhard Heydrich, based on this first-hand account of his home life at the Chateau in the village of Panenske Brezany on the outskirts of Prague. This will undoubtedly burst some of the American film script style myths surrounding him and finally reveal some first-hand truth that can now be added to our history books.

What changed for you in the village when the Germans took over? Anna replied:

There were twenty nine small farms and four big farms in the village. All agricultural and the families there were considered to be well off as they had work to do which earned money for their families. Others in the village had no work and there were lots of beggars. In German

occupation, everyone had to work so they all had to report to the nearest munitions factory and into industry, so it gave jobs to people who didn't have any before. It was not possible or acceptable to stay as a beggar or stay without work, so it was a big change for the village not to have the local beggars hanging around waiting for us to help them. They were not members of our local village, this was post crisis and lots of them were just roaming the country. The German occupation changed all that because of their 'Total Einsatz' policy where everyone had to work for the war machine or they were just disposed of, so the beggars pretty much disappeared.

The Castle here was owned by a Jewish man called Bloch. It was a well-known magnate family, although not as rich as the Rothschilds. I don't really know what he did, but he had a lot of money and when the Germans arrived, he flew to America and never came back. The Germans took over the Castle.

The first Reichsprotektor was Konstantin Freiherr von Neurath, he was a Freemason and by all accounts was a decent man. His Grandfather comes from this area and owned the Castle in the 17th Century. The original Nobleman is buried in the next village and he wanted to live in the family Manor House. When Heydrich took over, it was Lina who decided she wanted to live in this Castle, and Neurath had to move out, but all the furniture stayed, the Heydrich's just brought their clothes and personal effects with them from Berlin.

We all noticed a difference when the Heydrich's moved in. The first Reichsprotektor was a decent Nobleman. Next they started a ration system.

Some of our fields were taken by Lina for her business of selling roses in Prague and all the farm owners had to give a sizable part of everything they produced to the German War Office. I don't know exactly how much that was, but you can guess that it was a lot. We were given ration Cards to get grain for bread and we had 30 grams of meat per month each.

At this point, Jaroslav, relayed the translation to me, and said, 'Hang on, I must have got that wrong, that is just one ounce, so maybe half a sausage per person for a month. That can't be right. Let me check.' Then went back to his Grandmother and after a very loud Czech conversation, the response came back that indeed, 30g per person, per month was the right amount of their allowance. Jaroslav commented that he probably throws away that much per person every day, and he started to look visibly shocked at what he was hearing for the first time in such detail.

Everyone in the village had to have a German soldier live in their house. We had to feed him as well with whatever we had. In winter, we had to take all our winter coats and hand them in at stations, to the Germans. The soldiers were all poorly equipped and had no winter coats. We couldn't get away with keeping anything for ourselves, because if any of the Germans caught you wearing such things, they would shoot you.

The German Army were all dirty when they arrived. They had lice, parasites and insects. Most of them were returning from Russian fronts when they were sent into Chechoslowakia.

What work did you do in the Castle?

I didn't do any work in the upper Castle where Karl Frank lived. After Heydrich's Assassination, all security was increased and no one was allowed in there. No Czechs anyway, only the Germans went in there. But in the lower Castle, where the Heydrich family lived, I went there quite often because my Uncle was the Shoemaker and had to repair all the shoes for the Germans, but he never had the nerve to go there himself, so he used to send me.

I was 13 to 17 years old during this time and I hated going there. I would have to carry all the pairs of boots and then find the right Soldiers by asking for them in perfect German. They had their names inside their boots. If I didn't say it right, the SS Guards would keep me there for hours until I did.

When I found the right soldier, I would have to address him in perfect German to give him his boots, and sometimes they would give me a coin as a tip, but only if my German had been perfect. .Lina always told me to do jobs for her in the garden before I went home so I never knew how long I would be kept there.

I dreaded having to go there, because I was scared of what might happen to me, but I had no choice. When my uncle was told to collect a pair of boots to repair, I had to go and get them, and when they were repaired, I had to go in again and take them back. I never went inside the main house, only to the Barracks which were full of SS Units. All around the main house were the out buildings where the SS Protective Unit was for Heydrich and where the horses were kept in the stables. All the staff that went inside the house were specially chosen. There were a lot of Soldiers living in the outbuildings of the Castle, not the Castle itself, that was just the Heydrich's and their house staff.

All the grown-ups in the village hated having to go to the Castle; it was another risk to their lives that they would rather not have to take. No one ever really knew if they would come out again, or if the work they had done was considered not good enough for any reason. I think that's why my Uncle used to send me, it was probably less likely that a teenager would come to harm than an adult; but can you imagine what it was like for my Mother, sending me in there and not really knowing when or if I would come back?

I think people just get used to the amount of risk they have to deal with every day and gradually come to terms with it. As a child growing up in in an occupied country, it is all you know and you are not old *enough or knowledgeable enough to make comparisons; you just do what you need to do every day.*

What was Heydrich like? Did you see him in person?

Yes, loads of times. He and Lina would ride through the village every day on a pair of white horses. Sometimes he rode alone, and sometimes during the day, when Heydrich was in Prague, Lina would ride on her white horse on her own. Lina used to have us horse whipped if we didn't greet her properly in German.

When Heydrich passed someone from the village, we would just stop dead and keep our eyes down until he had gone past, and he would say Dopriden as he went past us. That is Hello in broken Czech, a bit like you would say pigeon English.

But Lina would stop her horse and make us greet her properly in perfect German and we had to say Heil Hitller perfectly as well, but when Heydrich was on his own, he never stopped and made us do that; he just said hello and went past.

What Social Events did you see or know about at the Castle when Heydrich lived there?

He received visitors and colleagues at the Castle most every week. They usually arrived at 5pm for Dinner. They always arrived with a protective detail of 2 Motorbikes, one in front and one behind and a Mercedes car with the visiting Officer.

Heydrich wasn't one for big parties or events though, it was always just one visitor, or one car anyway.

Lina liked to be a model German woman and didn't waste money on things like parties. She didn't even dress well, just wearing frugal dirndl dresses.

What do you know of Heydrich's daily habits, like Laundry or food?

Well he didn't ever wear uniform when he was here. We used to see him wearing a silk cream shirt – even when he was riding his horse – and he didn't wear a cravat either. He was always dressed casually in the village but you could tell the clothes were expensive and good quality. I never saw him in uniform around the village at all.

All his laundry, for the whole family, was done in the village by the village laundry service. None of it was done in the Castle. Why would it, when we had a laundry service in the village? They collected all his clothes, laundered them, and returned them to the castle. They were paid to do it.

I have read in some English History books, that Heydrich never wore a shirt twice, and that he tossed his worn shirts in the bath to pile up, and got a new one out of the packet the next day. Was this true?

No such nonsense, Said Anna vehemently. *If that was true, everyone in the village would know it, because the Laundry service would know it, and people in the village talked to each other every day. Anyway, he had house staff that got his Uniform or clothes out for him, and took away the laundry, replacing the clean clothes in his drawers for him.*

He had nothing to do with all that, Lina ran the household staff and arranged all that. How would he have a bath if it was full of dirty shirts?

That doesn't make any sense; anyway Lina was a perfect German wife and that kind of wastefulness wouldn't have been acceptable to her. As well as that, it was the middle of a War, so where would he get such a supply of brand new shirts? It's nonsense.

What did Lina do during the days?

Lina spent her days ordering people to do work. She had a typical Roman approach to Slaves. She had a Housemaid at the Castle and treated her quite well, but used her to get information about the village and what people were doing or not doing. When the Heydrich's first moved in, she ordered the Guards to send her all the women in the village who could speak German, to be interviewed for a job as her Housemaid. No one wanted the job, but there wasn't any choice. If you were chosen, you were chosen. Lina chose the person that looked the most presentable and who could speak the best German. She also had a good German name which was Reitmayer. She was a good Czech woman who came from Sudetenland and spoke very good German. I think Lina probably thought that she was of German pedigree, which is why she was considered acceptable to be in the private household.

What was Lina Heydrich like as a person?

Anna replied: *She was a skinflint who destroyed the winter gardens and turned them into vegetable fields. She made us grow roses that she sold in Prague and she kept the money for herself. It was her private business. The older children were not allowed to go to School, we had to tend to her fields instead and there were German soldiers who watched us and beat us with a horsewhip if we broke any of the plants that we were planting, or if we stopped.*

What were the children like?

I went to school with the two eldest Heydrich boys. They were sent to our Elementary School in the village along with a Nanny and with two SS Guards who carried machine guns. I think it was a Machinenpistolle MP-40, not the big MG 42 with the belt drive. All lessons had to be given in German. The boys were little brats. The older ones realised that nothing bad could ever happen to them, whatever they did, or however they behaved so they were quite cruel to the local children. The young boy wasn't, he was kind to the village children. I think he just wanted to have friends. It's a bit like 'Little Princes' behaviour. The first time they arrived at the School, the old Schoolmaster ordered us all to greet the Germans, then he had a stroke or a heart attack or something and fell down and died on the spot. It was a terrible experience for a room full of children, we will always remember it.

When he died, one of the refugees from Sudetenland after it was annexed stood in as Schoolmaster. We had many refugees arrive with only their children and the clothes they stood up in. All their possessions had to be left behind. If I remember, the Mayor of London read about this in his Newspaper and was so shocked by the sorry state of ordinary people who were on the run from the Wehrmacht front lines, that he organised a big Charity and people in London collected blankets and old clothing for them and sent it to Czechoslovakia.

He was either a Captain or a Colonel in the Army and was a highly educated man who left everything behind to run away with his wife and little child. I think he was probably a Captain because he was a relatively young man; even though he had the appearance of an older man because he has suffered so much physically, that it turned him into looking like an old man with pure white hair, even though he was quite young in years.

He masqueraded as the Schoolmaster, but was in fear of his life if the Germans found out that he was a high ranking Army Officer. They would shoot him instantly if they ever found out.

But someone needed to teach the children in School and he just as much needed a role in the village to allow him and his family to stay. He was so stressed when he was teaching while the German guards were there, that when the Guards went for the day, he hit the children. He just used to flail right and left, hardly knowing what he was doing – he just couldn't take it.

The Heydrich boys used to go and skate on the village pond. They were aggressive and behaved arrogantly and with the same air of superiority as the German adults and Soldiers. They used to beat the other children for fun and we couldn't do anything because they had two SS Guards with them who had machine guns.

There was a freak accident the year after Heydrich died. Klaus was cycling towards the main gates of the Castle grounds one afternoon – it was a Sunday I think – and the Guard acting as watchman on the gate saw a lorry coming down the hill and told him not to go out. But he ignored the Guard and rode straight out the gates onto the road and was knocked over by the lorry.

It was coming back to the village with a group of villagers who had played a football match that afternoon. It was illegal to carry people on a truck, but there was no other way to get the football Team to the match, so everyone turned a blind eye to it, until the driver ran over the Heydrich boy that is.

It just happened that both Karl Frank and Von Neurath were both visiting Lina at that moment and Karl Frank stopped Lina from having the driver shot instantly. Lina was shouting and screaming for everyone to be shot on the spot, but Frank imprisoned him instead as it wasn't his fault, I think it was von Neurath who used his influence over Frank and stopped the carnage, because he could see that it was just a bunch of villagers who were coming back from a local football match and the driver was helping them by letting them pile onto his truck to take them and bring them home again. It wasn't anyone's fault that the boy rode out on his bike at that moment. Klaus was buried in the village and his grave is still here.

Did Heydrich call in his Officers for meetings in the evenings? The English History books say that he worked every evening till late, and summoned his Officers to meetings as late as 10pm in the evenings...

No, when he got home, he took his uniform off and was off duty. He didn't have evening meetings. My Grandfather worked in the gardens of the Castle and would have known if there was any unusual activity in the evenings. He would definitely have known if any cars arrived in the evening with Officers in them. In fact he would be looking out for things like that because if there was any unusual activity in the evening, that would mean a great possibility of danger, it would mean that something was happening or about to happen and this would be immediately known by my Grandfather and word would be spread around the village.

Was he rude or polite to people in the village?

He was different to Lina and was never rude to me in the village or as far as I know, to anyone else he met when out riding his horse. He sent his children to the Village School and wanted them to make friends and have some sort of normal life. He let them go into the village and to the local pond to play – we used to play on the ice when it was frozen in winter. That is not the actions of a barbarian. I would say he was like a Medieval Ruler; seemingly humane – even though people knew bad things happened, no one really knew what his job was or really anything about what he did. It never affected people in the village.

Did he have any extravagances or any secret pastimes?

Well if he did, word would soon spread around the village from his house staff, Gardeners, and others. We used to keep a watch on what was happening in the Castle so we could warn the village if we thought anything big or dangerous was about to happen, so we would definitely know if he had any strange visitors, or had any strange habits. He was just a family man when he was here.

Did Lina spend money on finery and frippery? The History books say that she lived like a Princess when she was here.

Anna listened to the translation of this question and then laughed uproariously, waving her arms around to add emphasis to her words: *Certainly not! Lina was a skinflint and a model German woman. She wore Dirndl dresses – not silk and finery. She was obsessed with money, making money any way she could, but certainly not spending any of it! Lina had Jewish prisoners from the local Concentration Camp to cut down trees and do work for her. She had her own business, growing roses and selling them in Prague. She was industrious and money oriented and sold whatever she could to make money, which she kept for herself. She was always rude to everyone in the village. She rode about on her white horse every day and everyone dreaded crossing her path because she would stop and make you greet her in perfect German and if you didn't say Hiel Hitler at the end, you were punished. Everyone was scared of her.*

She used to stand on her balcony all day and watch everyone. She watched us through binoculars and if we were in the fields not working, we would be punished. There is this little story about somebody hiding the grain crops and Lina sending troops to retrieve them and punish the culprit – because she saw it through her binoculars.

What changed after Heydrich was assassinated?

When Heydrich was killed, two SS Units moved into the village, One moved into the Lower Castle where the Heydrich family lived, and the other moved into the upper Castle [Manor House]. The soldiers in the village were all Wehrmacht and not SS.

Karl Frank moved into the Upper Castle with his family after Heydrich died, but he never went into the village, he was too afraid. We never saw him or his wife or children. They had a German Tutor in the Castle and were not allowed to go into the village to play with us.

We stopped talking as Anna's daughter – and Jaroslav's Mother – brought lunch for us all. It was a traditional meal of Czech Duck, with dumplings and red cabbage which we all ate together on the small dining table. It was only a little larger than a card table, but big enough for the four of us there. After dinner we exchanged presents, since it was so close to Christmas. We had brought a silver necklace for Jaroslav's Mother and a warm shawl for Anna in a smart 'London store' plastic bag. Anna presented me with 2 beautifully embroidered place mats made of thick white linen, that she must have spent many hours working on. They will be treasured.

After coffee we carried on and Anna told her Grandson something in Czech that visibly shook him and his Mother. An emotional few minutes passed and I could see that whatever had been said, was something of note, clearly something shocking about the '*most evil man of the Third Reich*' and I waited for the translation.

Chapter Ten
𝔄 𝔖𝔥𝔬𝔠𝔨 𝔱𝔬 𝔱𝔥𝔢 𝔉𝔞𝔪𝔦𝔩𝔶

Anna had been talking non-stop for two and a half hours and talking easily and quickly about everything that happened seventy years ago. It was hard to believe that these experiences were so long ago as the authority and conviction she spoke with made it seem as if it all took place only last week.

Her replies to Jaroslav were fast and furious, her language was clear and definite; no pondering or pontificating. It was as if all this information had been kept tightly sealed in a box for all this time, never opened and never diluted, but sharp and accurate, and waiting to be lifted out and passed over, in its entirety, to whoever had been chosen to receive it. I could see that Anna was getting tired, as was Jaroslav, who was coping with me asking questions in English, translating them in his head into Czech, saying them again to this Grandmother and then taking in the answer that was fired back at him with information that he could barely take in and understand for himself about his family and the way they managed to survive; before translating and retelling it to me in another language.

But I knew that this chance would not happen again and although my better nature would rather have allowed Anna to rest for the afternoon, and for me to come back the next day, I knew that this wasn't possible and so pressed ahead as fast as I could, to get as much of her story as I could knowing that I was really pushing her too hard at eighty eight years old.

But Anna herself wanted to carry on, and my questions became fewer, as she remembered other things she wanted to tell, which I had no questions about, but which turned out to be priceless.

Anna Continues with her story

One day my Grandmother, Anna Petru who was then 58 years old, was out picking mushrooms for us to eat, when she met two men sitting on the edge of the forest. They were sitting in a spot that had a good view of Heydrich's Castle and looking at it through a pair of binoculars. She hadn't realised they were there, as they were in cover of the trees, and was scared in case they were going to harm her. It seems as though they were just as scared to have been discovered and both parties stood and looked at each other for a time, waiting to see what would happen. My Grandmother said they were both very badly dressed and didn't look like anyone from the village, but they said 'good day' in Czech and my Mother went somewhere else to look for mushrooms and didn't give it another thought.

My Grandmother was a clever woman. She was educated and wanted to be a Schoolteacher, but there was a Widower in the village who wanted a new wife, and as he had a cow of his own, my Grandmother was forced to marry him. This was considered to be a good match for her, so she was not able to become a Schoolteacher. She had to marry because that was the way of things then.

I am telling you this because when Heydrich was Assassinated, the pictures of the men they were looking for was printed in the Newspaper and when my Grandmother saw it, she said out loud: 'Oh my dear God!' because they were the two men that she had seen in the forest that day.

Jaroslav and his Mother were almost unable to speak at this point. They spoke at once in very fast and loud Czech and I just had to wait until they had both come to terms with what they had just heard from Anna. It seems that Anna's Grandmother had seen Gabcik and Kubis doing their reconnaissance a short time before the assassination took place. Gabcik and Cubis are now celebrated icons in the Czech Republic and there are statues to them erected in Prague and a memorial inside the Church where they were hiding in the underground crypt, before they shot themselves to prevent being captured by the Germans.

Jaroslav and his Mother were on the edge of tears at the thought that their Great Grandmother had played a very small part in the outcome of Operation Anthropoid; even though it was by default, by not telling the Germans about them watching the Castle.

After some time of animated conversation, Anna carried on:

My Mother told me that they had been watching Heydrich out riding on his horse that evening, and she thinks that they could have killed him right here in the village, any evening when he was out on his horse. She believes that the reason they chose not to, was because of the reprisals for everyone in the village. Everyone would most certainly be shot without question, and because the two Soldiers were actually Czech, it seems that even they couldn't bear the thought of that happening and so ruled out this location as a place where they could perform his assassination.

There followed an emotional conversation in Czech between Anna, her daughter, and her Grandson Jaroslav. The story then told to me in English was astonishing.

It seems that one of Jaroslav's Great Aunt's was responsible for the Paratroopers Gabcik and Cubis actually escaping from the Germans when they were being chased through the streets of Prague.

They ran into a blind alley way that led off a Street called 'Na rokosce' and the only way out was by running through a very large Butcher's shop, but it didn't have a back exit. The next door flat was lived in by Anna's Aunt by the name of Hartman, a German name. The Butcher's name was Browner. He led the 2 fleeing men into the flat next door where they ran through her apartment, and they both helped them to jump out of a back window into the garden and then run off. This is the point where the German Soldiers chasing them lost track of them, having to go around and clamber over fences and through hedges that formed an effective obstacle course for the time being at least.

There was another story about the Butchers shop. After the war, the shop was empty and Anna's Uncle decided to buy it, so it could once again belong to a Czech citizen. Anna said that her Grandmother warned him not to buy it, but he went ahead with the purchase so that it would not be confiscated by Germans. Some-time after the War, he was arrested by the Czech's and sent to prison to do fifteen years hard labour for buying the house from a German, when the previous owner was a Czech citizen who had been shot by Germans.

My conversation with the Chief of Police the day before suddenly came to mind, because he had told me of the Butchers Shop incident which I had no idea would be evidenced the following day by Anna herself.

Details of the Police conversations follow after the rest of Anna's Story: Cups of coffee were brought by Anna's daughter, along with a cardboard box decorated in blue and gold paper that was presented to me along with the coffee. I opened the box and saw rows of delicate pastries laid out in little paper cases. Star shapes, circles and balls. All were decorated differently with icing, with sugar and with nuts. A traditional Czech Christmas treat and I nibbled my way through half the box over the following 2 hours, while I listened to Anna speaking in Czech to her Grandson as I waited for the English translation to the rest of Anna's story.

The Music Teacher

In 1938 and 1939, the School had two classes of 56 children each. Class one was for the Elementary years of 5 to 9 years old, and Class two, was for the children aged 10 to 13 years. In 1940 a High School was opened, but the School Master was a Nazi.

The other Teacher in the Village School was a very good organist and the Chapel next to the Castle had a wonderful old organ that he used to play. When the German Soldiers moved in, we weren't allowed to go anywhere out of our houses, except to work and back, he wasn't allowed to play the Organ anymore. But he used to slip away and creep into the Chapel, risking his life to go and play the organ there. He would sit and play Czech Folk songs until late into the evenings, in total defiance of the rules. Luckily for him, Czech Folk music sounds very much like German music and one by one, the German soldiers crept into the Chapel to sit and listen to him playing. The Soldiers never spoke to him or questioned him, they just sat and listened. He was never stopped from playing, but he did it at risk of his life. His name was Vlastimil Bohous.

He used to warn all his children that one day they might be taken in the night and sent off to live with German families in Berlin. He prepared them, especially the younger children, and told them all: 'Remember who you are', and he made sure that they all knew their family name and the name of their village, so that if they were taken away, then one day they might be able to get back again, if they knew where they came from.

The implication of the Schoolteacher knowing this information, is that he was in contact with someone from the Resistance, otherwise there was no way that a 'local' Schoolteacher in a small village 9 miles from Prague, in occupied territory, would have known. Anna had no information about this, which would be expected as telling his pupils anything about where he received his information, would certainly increase his chances of being found out by the Germans.

This also adds weight to his behaviour to the children when the

Germans were not around, and the stress he was under not to be discovered.

Anna continued:

Work in the Village

As I said before, everyone in the village had to work even the children. We had work to do after School and at weekends. Working in the fields for a normal day, after School, was just normal for us. We had to plant potatoes, Turnips, and we even had to scythe Barley. At 13 years old that was very heavy work, now in these days, not even full grown men do that anymore. They have machines to do it.

In the War, all the work usually done by men had to be done by the women and children instead for the War effort. We had to put a parasite on the Barley by hand and we had scratches all up our arms from doing it. We had to get a piece of cloth, put the parasites on it, and then walk through every row scraping the cloth along each barley plant to infect it with the poison. It was poisonous to us as well, but that didn't matter.

Drugs were made from this parasite Rye Ergot, a sort of mushroom and in the War, it was planted deliberately to get the drugs for the front line. The Germans wanted it for Anaesthetics and amphetamines – all medicinal purposes, not for the Barley to be a food crop. So we couldn't eat any of the Barley, or give any of the straw to the animals because they would die from the poison. We got it all over our fingers while we were doing it.

If you were really good at it, you could separate some good straw from the poisoned, but it wasn't easy and it was very dangerous. We could have easily died doing it there was a boy in the village who was really good at it, he was about 4 years older than me at the time.

It was the German's instructions; they needed it for the Troops so we all had quotas of how much of the land had to have this on it, and how much had to have Poppies. When the crop started to bloom, we had to drag contaminated rags along the rows with our bare hands until we had contaminated it all. There were sheets of fabric but eventually everything becomes contaminated – hectares of fields of it!

The Poppy fields were grown for morphine for the Soldiers. They took every bit of the plants, seed heads, leaves, stalks; they took everything to make morphine. It was Lina who made us turn all the fields into medicine crops for the War effort. The Farmers were paid a measly rate for growing it in comparison to what they would get for growing a health crop in peacetime.

A Soldier in every house

The German Soldier living in our house had been to Russia. When he walked in I remember my Father saying: 'Give him some soup or I can't eat', and he put a bowl of soup on the sofa for him. We got used to him being around every day and he showed us how to use his RPS Rifle. I used to go out with him and shoot rabbits with it to eat. Otherwise we only had soup every day, so you soon learn to shoot straight pretty quickly if you need to.

My Father had a Radio, and if you dared to listen to Moscow or London broadcasts, it was punishable by death. My Father used to listen to them, but our soldier said it was OK. He used to listen to it as well, but he told us not to tell the soldier living next door, who was a very strict Nazi, who would have shot my Father right there on the spot.

The Lorry Driver

The Driver of the flatbed lorry that killed Klaus was a strange story. He was put in prison but not killed after the accident. It was a stupid accident and was a shame because he was the eldest boy and the kindest. He never tried to hurt any of the Czech's; he was just a normal boy and was the same age as me.

The Truck Driver was a tall blond man with pale blue eyes, he looked very German. He was never seen again and there are some strange stories about him. Some say that he was killed by accident because he looked German, some say that he used his looks to escape after 1945, some say that Lina took him out of Prison when she had to evacuate because the Russians were coming, and used him to drive her and her children away to safety. Some say that she did finally take revenge on him for killing her son, and had him killed after he drove them to safety. I suppose we will never know the truth, unless someone can be found who knew him. So many stories will never be told now because no one can be found who lived through it and is still able to tell their story – or able to find the right person to tell for it to be recorded and told to the world.

I am glad that I can say these things at last, and that the truth of what I lived through will be remembered. I was born in 1932 on the 4th of May and even though I am 82 years old, my memory of those years is sharp and clear.

Jaroslav was concerned that his Grandmother was looking and sounding very tired and said we should bring the interview to a close. It was 4 o'clock and getting dark outside very quickly and I still had to visit the old School, the Churchyard, and of course, the Chateau where Heydrich lived with his family to see what it looked like 72 years later. But there were still questions that I wanted to ask Anna, and asked Jaro if I could ask just one last question. Reluctantly he agreed:

Did Heydrich have a Nickname from the SS Officers or from the Villagers?

This was an important question as many books about WW2 mention that he was called by many nicknames, so I wanted to find out what the word was in the village. If the SS Officers referred to him by a nickname; they would certainly know, and if the villagers called him by some code name, I would like to know what it was.

Anna's reply was therefore unexpected:

Oh no, nobody dared call him any name and it was the same for the German soldiers, neither did they. The SS in the barracks of his Chateau didn't ever refer to him by any kind of nickname. They wouldn't dare. My Grandfather would have known because he was working as a Gardener in the grounds and would have heard their conversations. Actually let me say that in a different way: he used to listen to their conversations because that was the only way to protect the villagers. Finding out about anything that was about to happen, so that we would have some warning of any danger to the village. So it didn't happen by accident, he tried to listen to as much as he could. He would have told us about any different names he heard.

As we were getting ready to leave, Anna told Jaro about what happened to the Manor House that Heydrich had lived in since the War. It seemed that the Villagers had taken care of it for many years, keeping it repaired and maintained as a beautiful feature of their village, until the 1970's. A Research Company took out a ninety nine year Lease on the Castle, for one Czech Crown (1 penny) from the Local Council on the understanding that they took over the maintenance of the building and paid for its repairs and upkeep.

The Problem was Anna told us, that they had not maintained the building at all. The grounds were not restored to their former beauty and the gardens were overgrown and unkempt. The building itself she said, was now falling down and is serious disrepair. The roof had fallen in and the perimeter was now boarded up with a tall wooden hoarding that you can't see over the top of. You can't get in as it is always locked up and there are no signs telling you who to contact, or which research company it is. It is a disgrace, she said. We looked after it for years, and they have let it fall down, with no one to hold them to account.

Anna said it is impossible to do any kind of research there or even any kind of office work, without a roof, so what on earth were they doing there? What did they want it for? And why was it left to fall down while being boarded up and hidden from view? And what were they hiding?

Anna explained that the village members were too scared of what might happen to them, if they made any complaints about it to the Council, so she asked if I could include it in my book, so that someone would be able to do something about it, before the beautiful old Chateau was gone for ever.

The Chateau at the top of the hill, where Karl Frank lived, was also boarded up now and empty. It was used as a care home for a while, but is now vacated and abandoned, with the gates firmly padlocked.

I promised Anna that I would try and find out all these things for her, and would let her know what I discover. After all, it was December 2013, the age of Google Earth and mobile Wi-Fi, so it must be possible to find out who was renting it, and how to report them to the Czech Authorities.

With my head already spinning from all the information after five hours of top speed writing, and in a bit of a rush, as it was getting darker and colder by the minute; we said goodbye's and I got into the car with Jaroslav driving and his Mother in the front seat, to point out all the places that had been mentioned by Anna. So we set off to see them in real life and to take a few pictures.

If only we had known what was about to happen next.

Chapter Eleven
Chased by Armed Guards

We drove through the village at 4pm, three days before Christmas on 22nd December as the afternoon gloom started to change rapidly into twilight. We decided to go straight to the main Chateau to see as much as we could before dark. Rounding a  bend in the main street, we passed the little School building looking beautifully tidy and clean, a square building painted white with a happy bright yellow sun painted on the wall. It had surprisingly small windows for a School, which is usually wall-to-wall windows, in the UK at least.

If there was enough daylight, we planned to stop there on the way back from Heydrich's Chateau, so I contented myself with a few pictures  on my Blackberry through the car window as we went past.

A little further along the small village Road, a tall wooden fence appeared on our right, blocking all sight of the Chateau, which was somewhere behind it. We continued until we reached the main driveway and big gates, that Heydrich had driven in and out of in his black open topped Mercedes every day all those years ago. It wasn't hard to imagine the SS guards on patrol along this road as there were no other cars or people to be seen.

We went just past the gates and stopped at the side of the road. I was eager to jump out and walk briskly towards the main gates to see if we could get in. I stood just two feet into the driveway, staring at the large statues on tall plinths at either  side of the large double gates. The statues were of large animals, I think, but were in such a sorry state, dirty and with pieces missing from them, that it was hard to identify what they might have been.

They were originally hunting dogs biting on a deer and a boar and stood easily as tall as me. Unloved and uncared for now, they would certainly have looked magnificent and very daunting when the Chateau was in use seventy five years ago.

Darkness was descending fast now and I stood to take in the slightly gothic filigree iron work of the gates and the impregnable stone wall that had stood up to a World War and survived. The large pillars of stone behind each statue were standing firm, but had cracks running across their surface and large chips missing here and there, telling a tale of distinct sadness and woe.

I took a picture of the gates themselves; and estimated that we probably had about 20 minutes to go before being plunged into total darkness, so had no time to waste. Out of the corner of my eye, I saw a man striding towards us and shouting something in Czech. I ignored it –

we weren't doing anything wrong – and tried to see what was written on a sign on one of the gates. I craned up as high as I could but couldn't see anything of the entire Mansion, or what was supposed to be left of it, behind the gates.

I tried to re-set the flash on my Blackberry to get one or two more photos as the darkness was settling fast, Jaroslav who was standing next to me and talking to someone in Czech, started raising his voice and the conversation began to sound as though they were shouting at each other. I began to feel uneasy.

The man was wearing a Guards Uniform (known as black sheriff style, used by private security companies, not any statutory body) and noticed that he wore a gun attached to his waist belt with his hand over the handle of it, as if he was about to draw it on us.

The Guard raised his other arm and pointed at me and by instinct rather than logical thought process; I shoved my phone inside my coat and down the top of my dress, making it disappear as fast as possible while keeping it safe in case he tried to grab it from me.

The Guard stepped forward towards me and Jaro stepped sideways in front of him with his legs apart and braced and his shoulders squared. He lifted one arm outstretched across me and the other he held about chest height and from a fleeting glance, looked braced for action.

Jaro had been in the Military for some years, a Naval Officer I believe, and also a proficient War-bow Archer, drawing Longbows with a draw weight of up to 130lbs, so I had no doubt of his strength, agility, and combat training if needed. Even under his woollen greatcoat I was sure that he could move quicker than the guard could think which was reassuring. I didn't believe that the guard had been employed for his strategic thinking skills, and hoped that he didn't suffer from a short temper.

I stepped backwards onto the Road in the direction of Jaro's extended arm movement when he suddenly turned to me and shouted in English: 'Get in the car, now!'

His voice left no suggestion of challenge or argument and I fled past him as quickly as I could, my hand holding the place where my phone was on the inside of my clothes, so that it wouldn't fall out the bottom of my dress onto the floor, or get broken. Jaro started walking briskly behind me towards the car and through all this, the Guard was shouting at us in Czech, pointing at the sign on the gate and then pointing back at us, with his other hand still holding the handle of his gun, which could be pulled on us in seconds.

Jaro's Mother, who had been sitting in the car all this time, had opened the car doors and I threw myself inside, slamming it shut behind me. I pulled out my Phone and hid it under the driver's seat in front of me.

Jaro had reached the car now and hurriedly got in still shouting in Czech and gesturing to the Guard who was now walking towards us. Doors slammed shut, we drove off up the hill at great speed.

The road twisted and turned its way uphill, round and up with the fence on our right of the Chateau boundary, and woods and trees on our left as we climbed up towards the Manor House at the top of the hill, where Karl Frank lived as Secretary of State with his family until 1945. Jaro parked at the gates and we sat there for a while collecting ourselves, wondering if we should get out of the car or not, and trying to figure out what on earth had just happened.

Jaroslav was incensed and a stream of English phrases poured out all at once, without the aid of many pronouns:

'He can't do that! I am Czech citizen and allowed to stand on any Czech street. We were not even in driveway of Chateau, what on earth they trying to hide in there? How dare he threaten me with gun for standing on street, I shall report him, I will go straight to Czech Police and make complaint'.

It was pretty dark now and we were parked at the top of the hill outside the locked gates of the upper Castle or Manor House, We gathered ourselves and got out of the car wondering what on earth would happen now?

Chapter Twelve
𝕷𝖔𝖈𝖐𝖊𝖉 𝖚𝖕 𝖆𝖓𝖉 𝕬𝖇𝖆𝖓𝖉𝖔𝖓𝖊𝖉

When we finally decided to get out of the car, we did so quietly and without talking walked towards the second set of locked gates. They were large and ornate double wooden gates set underneath a brick archway that had been painted in salmon pink

and with ornamental white painted plaster features and overgrown shrubs encroaching onto the once beautiful frontage. I could imagine that the shrubs were once well kept and shaped but were now sprawling

and shapeless. It represented a dim reminder of days gone by and a grandeur that was now lost in time. We couldn't quite see the grand house beyond about 200 yards away in the gloom, but there was a sealed sign board with pictures of it and writing in Czech that I photographed as best I could in the darkness with the limitations of a Blackberry Flash.

The Guards down the hill didn't appear to have followed us, and we were alone, no cars within earshot, no people, just us and an empty house, locked up with all its history and memories.

The sign board was lit up and showed pictures of a very ornate building with statues, beautiful gardens and a golden winged female statue set on the roof of the triangular Chapel, wearing a golden robe, long hair flowing

and arms outstretched to the sky possibly an Angel or a Saint as the building used to be a Priory and Nunnery back in the 17th Century.

But none of this was visible to us from this side of the gates and the last of the daylight disappeared leaving us standing in the dark, still shell shocked from the unbelievable happenings with the armed guard at the lower Castle, just a mile away; three days before Christmas in the digital age of Google maps and Sat Nav's of 2014.

Both Baroque Castles, the upper and the lower, became the property of the State in 1945 and were looked after by the local villagers until the lower castle was rented out to the mysterious Research Company, and the upper Castle was used as a residential home for old people. The old people's home was now closed and the

house stands again unused, and as far as I can find out from research, still owned by the Czech State.

Chapter Thirteen
Interview with the Police

Now is the perfect point to return to the interview with the Commissary of the Czech Police.

After some introductions we sat down in his lounge and I found out that his Paratrooper training was a similar training to what the members of Operation Anthropoid would have received with the SOE in Britain.

Unlike the punishments though, because instead of painting stones white on the drill field, they were given tasks to develop their thinking skills like writing a 10,000 word thesis.

Jaro met him when he was Drill Sergeant at the Military Academy some years ago. After Jaro and he had swapped news, Ivan invited me to ask him anything I wished about the assassination attempt of Heydrich and decided to ask about the military techniques and physiological issues of the men involved. I started with a scene setting background question:

Why was Heydrich was targeted for assassination, since there had been a Gentleman's Agreement by all the Governments involved, not to assassinate – or attempt to – any of the Political Leaders, so why was this different?

His response was: *The Czech people had no active resistance who were giving any fight back to the Germans by 1940-41 because being organised by the military, it was easier to uncover. The only operational resistance group was a trio of former military officers who were known as the 'Three Kings' who continued to carry out random acts of sabotage, like blowing up an Italian light cruiser in an Italian harbour with a smuggled bomb. The Three Kings were pretty much the only target for the Gestapo to squash at the time.*

Benes the Czech President who was in exile in Britain was firmly against them carrying out any further actions that year and it was only the persuasiveness of Colonel Moravec (Head of the Czech Secret Service) to get British backing that finally made Benes agree to give the Moravec plan a green light.

The British Government had given only provisional recognition to Benes as the Czechoslovakian Government – in exile, whereas they had granted full recognition to the French and Polish exiled Governments who were also hiding out in Britain.

The Allies seemed quite happy to allow Germany to annexe Moravia and Bohemia (now Czech Republic and Slovakia). The Czech President Benes was hiding out in Britain and wanted his people back in Czechoslovakia to do something memorable that would have an impact on the War and raise the profile of Czechoslovakia as an effective allied partner instead of a sacrificial lamb to the growing German Reich.

Ivan explained:

The partial recognition from Britain was because after the Munich betrayal, the Czech Government could not withstand the international pressure, and asked the Germans formally for a Protectorate. (Hence the Reichsprotektor role of Heydrich). The Polish and French continued to fight the Germans although their military force was very feeble.

When the Germans agreed to the Protectorate of Moravia and Bohemia (then Czechoslovakia and now Czech Republic and Slovakia) they also planned to completely replace the inhabitants of the Czech nation with native Germans within five years.

In fact, when Heydrich took on the role of Reichsprotektor, he stated that his primary goal was the *'de-politicisation of the Czech population'*

This meant that he would integrate the provinces of Bohemia and Moravia into Germany. This would be achieved by a 'Germanisation' process of most of the population; German culture, German money, German business practices, German language, German Schools, and any undesirables who didn't want to adapt to this way of life would be identified and deported to make room for ethnic Germans to spread into their new lands. That was the plan, and to make his point, Heydrich reopened the old German Concert Hall in Prague, built back in the 19th Century, and renamed Smetana Square after the German composer Mozart.

More about what Heydrich did after taking up his post further on, meanwhile back to the Police interview.

During 1940, the SOE or Special Operations Executive was created in Britain by none other than Churchill with a 5 lined directive: for the sole purposes of using any means against Germany, to achieve three goals: to get behind enemy lines and sabotage, subvert and destroy the German enemy.

There was an infamous spy known as A54 who was sending information through, he was an Abwehr Agent who sold information to the three kings, who then 'somehow' tried to radio it out to England and Moravec. The British were looking for a way to get more first-hand information so that they could send in some SOE teams to create as much havoc as was possible. only they didn't know anything at all about what was happening in Czechoslovakia. Unlike the other occupied territories, there was an information blackout. The reason for this was that Holland, France and Poland were occupied against their will, and the Germans lived among them just keeping the peace, but Czechoslovakia had become a Protectorate of Germany and was therefore more or less turned into a Police State and totally ruled (owned) by Germany.

Benes was keen to win favour with the British to raise his exiled Government position to full recognition, and to try to tempt the British forces to go into his country to create some anti-German activity.

Benes had no special teams or troops he could send in, and no access to the supplies, resources or equipment that this would take; apart from his access to the Czech Gold Bullion, so his only chance of building any resistance activity in Prague was to hope the British would agree to do this using their equipment, resources and men in return for an amount of Czech gold. An agreement was reached for an amount of the seventy tons of Czech gold that was already stored inside the Bank of England. The British charged him forty tons of gold after the war and he was presented with a comprehensive Bill that included: uniforms, shoes, shoelaces and every meal itemised.

Benes was also concerned about the Communist underground in Czech, who were supplied by the Soviets and who might be able to win the support of the Czech people, away from Benes and his half recognised Czech Government hiding out and rendered powerless in Britain. He did not want to alienate them and speed up his own deportation if the Soviets were to seize power. He was known to have passed information to Stalin before the onset of the war and would be keen to retain as little antagonism as possible with the Soviet power.

To give testament to this, on July 18th 1941, both the Soviet Union and Britain granted full diplomatic recognition to the Benes Government with a proviso that every country needed to give their full support to the total Allied War effort and great pressure was put on him to play his part.

I can imagine the conversations. If I was a British Commander, I would not be happy to send in any of my men to a protectorate German

State without the vital information about the situation they would find themselves in when they got there. But I would be happy to send in someone else's men.

Imagine how tempting it was to the British, for Benes to suggest taking a team of Czech Soldiers, training them in SOE techniques, and sending them in with a mission that would deliver enough information for the British SOE to be able to know where and how to move in behind enemy lines and take action. A Czech team would speak the language, understand the culture, know where to find supplies, and be easier to hide than a British team.

There were already Czech Pilots flying in the Battle of Britain as well as Polish and other nationals, who formed about one third of the British Air Force in the air on most days, so the plan from Moravec to start training Czech's in the SOE would not have been out of place.

A large group of Czech Soldiers were immediately enrolled into the specialist SOE training to see how they would match up; fourteen Officers and twenty two NCO's. They were kitted out at Cholmondeley Park near Chester, and then moved up to Scotland for training in combat, explosives, survival, boats, and weapons, then on to Wilmslow for parachute training with the RAF. The few men that passed all these tests were then sent on to either Dorking or Hertfordshire to the Sabotage Schools at Brickendonbury Manor, and Villa Bellasis.

There are two different accounts currently in the history books that the Czechs received just six weeks of total training, or the full six months that was for British commandos. But however long it was, they were then sent to wait with their 'home' units until the drop. Assassination options would have been worked out in several variants during the British SOE training, although they would have no idea who it might be possible to get to, and how they might be able to achieve it at this stage.

Lots of operations were then planned by Moravec – the military man- to present to Benes- the non- military Politician President in exile who was under pressure to prove to The British and Soviet Governments that the Czechs really could be an equal allied partner in the War effort, and were not passed over as unimportant or of no use to the allies.

The biggest fear of Benes was that if the Allies won, they would be content to leave Czechoslovakia as a German territory in whatever treaty might be drawn up in the aftermath where it was annexed by them on 15th March 1939. So in effect, they would lose their country whether Germany won or lost the war. Not a great prospect for the Czechs either way and this called for desperate measures before their nation was swallowed up for ever and disappeared from history.

Chapter Fourteen
Accident or design?

Operation Anthropoid was named and was given to a group of men who had passed through the SOE training (after either 6 months or 6 weeks depending on which books you read). They were divided into four groups. Group Anthropoid, group Silver A and group Silver B, along with an outlying group appropriately named 'Out Distance' whose role it was to provide radio communications for the operation.

Curda was a Radiographer in this group, and he later became the Czech traitor who betrayed the paratroopers hiding out in the Crypt of the Church in Prague. Sergeant Josef Gabcik and Sergeant Jan Kubis were the Anthropoid named group.

There was another Paratrooper who later turned traitor, William Gerik a Slovak who after unsuccessful activities on the Czech and Slovak borders, managed to get back to Prague but then found himself with no one to help or harbour him, and with no further resources, available to him – no food, money, shelter or papers; he gave himself up to the Gestapo. His group was called Zinc (we guess from the name that it was a less important group than Silver A or B) He knew the men from the 'Out Distance' group and gave the Gestapo all the names of the men who had been killed in the Church Crypt siege, and also the names of all the Czech people who had helped or sheltered him. Of course we have no idea what the Gestapo threatened him with, or promised him in order to get these names, but I think it is safe to assume that with everyone else dead except Curda, this was their only chance of backing up the information that Curda had given them, to find out whether it was corroborated, or had been a bunch of lies.

After the War, both Gerik and Curda were executed.

Here are the only names I have managed to track down for the Czech

Paratroopers and the Teams they belonged to:

Group Anthropoid

Josef Gabčík

Jan Kubiš - Who replaced a Soldier called Karel Svoboda who injured himself during the training in Scotland)

Group Silver A

Josef Valčík - (He didn't shoot, but he was the man who signalled to Kubiš with a pocket mirror that the Staff car containing Heydrich was coming)

Group Out Distance

Adolf Opálka - Who didn't shoot, but covered Gabčík with his wide coat when he was assembling his stengun.

Curda - The Radiographer who turned traitor

In all, there were seven paratroopers from all these groups hiding out in the crypt of the Church, including of course Kubiš and Gabčík, so this was a desperate attempt to make an impact on the Germans, the British and the Soviets in order to save their country.

The result of their mission is now famous, but it started out as a rather vague assignment from the British SOE which was worded thus:

'At the right time and in the right place and under ideal conditions, perform sabotage or terroristic activity, important enough that it will become well known, *even outside* of Czechoslovakia'.

Colonel Moravec however, knowing that much was at stake with this mission; made a private suggestion directly to Gabcik that they might try to kill either Karl Frank the Secretary of State or Reinhard Heydrich the Acting Reichsprotektor as this would certainly achieve the goals of their mission. So on 29th December 1941, Gabcik and Kubis were parachuted into the outskirts of Prague.

It was the third planned attempt with the first two dates probably scrapped due to weather conditions as it was late December. The drop point was near Plzen, ninety four Kilometres from the centre of Prague, but a place where there were some known Czech contacts that could help them. Plzen was the centre of military industry in Bohemia, so there would also be access to necessary equipment around this area that could be provided by the Czechs to help them.

It is described as a navigational error that they were in fact dropped very close to Prague in a small village called Nehvizdy which was 125 Kilometres from Plzen, and just north or the city of Prague (or Praha) and a lucky escape for one of the three Halifax Planes that the British owned at that time. It was the only plane that had the power to get there for the drop and get home again without having to land and it was a huge risk for the British to send this precious plane on such a mission that was most probably doomed to failure anyway.

Nevertheless Gabčík and Kubiš found their way down to Pilsen, which is about one hundred km from where they landed, and they were eventually able to establish contact with their support in a very minimal and very underground Czech resistance.

When they found their way to Heydrich's Castle in Panenske Brezany, it was the Teacher Jan Zelenka, who furnished them with information about Heydrich; his usual movements through the village and his usual security arrangements. Here the information from the Czech Police Superintendent and the Stories from Anna actually meet up and evidence each other. We have already heard Anna tell about the Schoolteacher who was an incognito Captain and about how he had information to warn the children that they may be taken away to Germany, and now we can see that he did indeed have links with the Czech resistance. We also note Anna's story about seeing two men with binoculars in Panenske Brezany forest when they were watching the village and the Castle.

The Schoolteacher also managed to get transportation and some papers for Kubis and Gabcik to get to Prague, however, he and most of this resistance cell later perished in the Lager concentration camp.

Let us think again about the Allied Agreement not to assassinate any of the Political Leaders of each nation, we can now see that although the British Government trained these men and used their valuable resources to fly them in, looking at the vague orders from the SOE, the actual nature of their mission does not appear to fall foul of this Gentlemen's Agreement.

I wonder exactly how much Churchill and the British Military Leaders actually knew about what Operation Anthropoid might achieve, other than sabotage and subversion, and whether the vagueness of the orders was to protect them against any recriminations should this mission be successful. There is no doubt that authorising one of their only three Halifax planes, and an experienced Pilot could not have been done by any junior ranks and would certainly have needed Churchill's approval.

I wonder if such papers exist and have been released from the Official Secrets Act quarantine of fifty years. But I suspect any such paper did not survive. The fact that it was only Czech people, who would pay the penalty if it were to be successful, is something for the consciences of those involved and not really a primary concern of this book. Perhaps Benes and Moravec decided that such a sacrifice to save a Nation was a worthwhile risk, and shows how complex a single decision can be in a time of War.

Another thought is that as far as the British Government was concerned, Heydrich was not really one of the major Political leaders. He was Head of the German Police Force and was 'acting' Head of State in a country that always used to be a part of Germany anyway. Heydrich's rank was Gruppenfuhrer, rising to Obergruppenführer when he was made Reichsprotektor of Czechoslovakia; the equivalent of being a Major-General and Lieutenant-General. Hardly a rank that would convey senior political status during the war, until he was given the role of 'Acting Reichsprotektor'.

There were many other Gruppenfuhrers and Obergruppenfuhrers most of which you would need to look up in a book, not memorable and important figures, and the Allied equivalent rank holders would equally not be considered as key leaders that would be threatened by the non-Assassination agreement. Just senior military ranks that all countries had many of.

Once Heydrich took up the post of Head of State over Moravia and Bohemia, he was suddenly the head of a major military and industrial complex, unmatched in size by anything apart from the Rhineland industry or Russia's industrial magnitude.

All the ships were built with Czech steel – even British ships used Czech steel that was bought before the start of the War. The armoured deck on the Aircraft Carrier Victorious was made from the famous Poldi steel and it received nine direct bomb hits during the War, and still stayed afloat.

Heydrich also inherited hundreds of trained engineers although when he arrived they were all on strike from the factories, unpaid, underfed, and desperate. Von Neurath was put on sick leave by Hitler – what we now know of as 'Garden Leave' as he was failing to keep the factories working, failing to quash the resistance, and failing to affect any control over the Czech Political Leaders and Council Leaders. Heydrich was expected to make changes to this situation very quickly, and with his usual attention to detail and efficiency.

The other important consideration in the decision making of this operation is the Chronology and timeline of what happened to all the parties concerned in the same timeline. It is always important when viewing in hindsight, to remember exactly what each party concerned knew at the time and what they came to know at a later stage. It is very easy for us to make a judgement when we can see everything that happened all at the same time. - At least everything that has been revealed anyway. The rest we can then make informed suppositions about based on the characters involved, which is the purpose of this book.

Date	Activity
18th July 1941	British give full diplomatic recognition to Benes as President of the Czech Government in Exile
July 1941	Option A: Group of Czech Soldiers begin a 6 month training programme with the British SOE with the objective of sabotage
27th September 1941	Heydrich replaced von Neurath as Acting Reichsprotektor of Czechoslovakia
Mid November 1941	Option B: Czech Soldiers start 6 weeks training in sabotage, and 2 of them were told they were to kill Heydrich or Frank
29th December 1941	After 6 months or 6 weeks training the Czech Paratroopers are dropped into Prague
27th May 1942	The Atentat (Czech name for the event known as the Assassination of Heydrich)

The assassination attempt took place on 27th May 1942 – 5 months after they landed. The British Government and Czech Government under Benes would have been more and more concerned that nothing had been achieved in 5 months. They would have had a very low expectancy that anything would come of sending a bunch of Czech Soldiers back into their own country, with no experience of carrying out any special operations as Soldiers under the command of an experienced Officer, much less coming up with their own plan and carrying it out by themselves. So back to the Ivan the Police Superintendent to explain.

Chapter Fifteen
Five Months Underground

Why did it take so long for anything to happen? They were dropped in late December and the assassination attempt didn't take place until the end of May. Five months to remain hidden from the Germans was certainly no easy task, and during that time, much was changing in Prague as well as in the other Czech Cities as Heydrich started to Germanise the two new colonies of Moravia and Bohemia, bringing in German laws, culture, language, and work ethics.

Ivan had plenty of information to tell me about these five months:

First was the problem of finding any Radio's that worked. All the Radios dropped with them did not survive the fall. The British expected this to be the case, as they were finding it impossible to make a Radio that would survive a parachute drop.

They all believed that the resistance on the ground would provide the paratroopers with radios, but the infamous 'Three Kings' had been reduced to just one remaining, and he was by then living as a homeless gunman on the run. The activity of the 'three kings group' was probably the major contributor for Von Neurath being stood down by Hitler. They were very effective at subversion and sabotage and he was blamed for not being able to dispose of them.

They are important in our story; because they were supposed to furnish the Anthropoid group as well as other (Silver A, Silver B) groups with documents and local visas. The information blackout in German controlled Czechoslovakia was so tight that nobody in England had any idea of what these documents were supposed to look like, so they had no possible way of furnishing the men with them before the drop.

During the five months, both groups met at least once and photos taken of paratroopers which were to be used for their documents. During these months, the German net closed in on the three kings, and all of them were killed with the photos of the paratroopers falling into the hands of the Germans; making life even more difficult for the Anthropoid Teams.

Back in England during these months, with the three kings dead, there was no information getting out of Czechoslovakia at all. The British had no idea about how the Germans were operating, living or protecting themselves, numbers of troops, weaponry they were using, or locations of any factories that were making military equipment. They had no possibility of planning any kind of reprisal or attack on Czechoslovakia.

Does all this evidence the current History book stories that say Heydrich was removed because he was next in line to take over from Hitler?

Does it back up the stories that this was a James Bond like plot to take out the most evil and dangerous man in the whole Third Reich?

Does it show that the British had classed Heydrich as a Senior Party Leader since he was made Head of State?

Does it prove that the British went against their Gentleman's Agreement not to take out any of each other's Senior Leaders and purposely targeted Heydrich?

Or is it more probable that they were so desperate to find out what was going on in Moravia and Bohemia that they agreed to Moravec's crazy plan, believing that it wouldn't succeed anyway?

Is it probable that Churchill just wanted to cause as much trouble as possible for Germany inside their own territory and didn't want to send any of his own men?

Is it likely that the Czechs had settled themselves too easily into the welcoming arms of Germany and so Churchill saw them as part of the enemy and therefore more disposable for any retribution should the mission be successful?

The Czech nation has made Gabcik and Kubis into legendary Hero's, but was the success of their mission more of a lucky accident than a well-planned operation?

Back to the story told by Ivan the Czech Police Superintendent, who had showed me his Thesis on the subject – all written in Czech so not understandable by me, but he did his best in the course of about five hours, to tell me everything that he had found out from military sources, while he was in the paratroopers. Pretty much none of this information I had ever seen before in English or American history books, but what he told me did make sense, so let's look at it in detail here:

As far as the British story goes, the original operation was just to cause as much havoc as possible, but their suggestions were naive. One of them was to 'Set fire to Pilzn fields to navigate the British bombers towards the Skoda heavy industries factory' and this would clearly be a suicidal mission. The British also told them to make all radio transmissions for at least fifteen minutes and preferably for 45 minutes, when the Germans only needed five minutes – and later just 3 minutes – to triangulate the position of the radio signal.

Before they left England, the two paratroopers received some rather special VIP treatment. Only Gabcik and Kubis – none of the others were invited. They had private meetings with Benes and Moravec prior the drop, and were also taken into a private meeting with Churchill, who awarded them with British Military Medals before they had even set off on their mission. This is indicative of the fact that they were not expected to return.

Another indicator that this was a higher profile mission than was alluded to in the History books, is that Churchill approved the use of one of his three Halifax planes. It was the only plane capable of getting there and back without landing, and a seriously expensive risk. It could easily be shot down, losing a vital and expensive resource along with an experienced and trained pilot that would be difficult to replace.

On the way back from their meeting with Churchill, Anthony Eden was waiting for them in the corridor, and invited the two chaps 'for tea' before they set off on their mission

There was clearly more to this mission of sabotage than met the eye. Were Churchill and Eden in on the special instructions given to Gabčík and Kubis? Was this a plot to cause mayhem to the SS and the Gestapo to allow the resistance to regroup? Or was it a very definite plot to assassinate a key member of the higher echelons of Hitler's war machine now that he was separated from the safety of Berlin and alone in the wilds of occupied Czeckoslovakia?

Sending the Czech's into Prague with a vague mission of sabotage would certainly vilify the British Government of going against their agreement of assassinating key figures and would also vilify them against any possible retribution should the 'mission within a mission' be a success.

Perhaps Churchill thought that even an attempt on one of the German Leaders would draw the eye and the resources of Hitler into his 'own territory' like the eye of Sauron and perhaps cause more of the German War machine to be redistributed, thinning out his central layers of protection in Berlin.

All of these considerations form a backdrop of opportunism rather than premeditated plot, and a result of unexpected luck rather than military strategy to remove 'the most evil man in the third Reich'. This was a title given to Heydrich in the History books that were written after the War and a long time after his assassination.

I asked the Police Superintendent a further question about the operation and have to say that I was totally shocked by his answer.

Chapter Sixteen
Traitor, Coward or Soldier?

A question still puzzled me about operation Anthropoid. Why did Curda tell the Germans where his team members were hiding?

He was out and free, and could have re-joined his wife and child and carried on with his life or he could have joined his team mates in the Church crypt, and taken his chances with the rest of them. So what made him take the decision to betray them?

The films made about the assassination of Heydrich show him as a weak willed coward who set out to save his own skin above that of his team mates or the needs of his country. But was this a true representation?

Was this the likely response of a man who had been through the same SOE training as the rest of them and had passed each test, physical, emotional and psychological that was given to him? Would the British have risked the success of operation Anthropoid by allowing a weak willed coward to be an integral member of the team?

How could they have got their assessment of Curda so wrong, when he had been intelligent enough to join the team, or were the British just making the best of a bad group of unsuitable Czech and Slovak Soldiers that they didn't much care whether they came back or not?

Ivan listened to these questions and laughed out loud.

Curda did exactly what he was told to do. He Said.

None of them were supposed to escape because then the Germans would find out who exactly had facilitated the operation, and Churchill and the British Government would find themselves in serious trouble from Hitler.

Ivan carried on: *In special Op's, it is vital that the source of the operation as well as the reason for it is never found out. It is standard procedure to give one member of the team the responsibility of making sure that they never get back.*

I was shocked. Here was a man who had been trained as a Paratrooper in special operations, and knew the internal strategy of secret operations. These are procedures that are never spoken about outside the ranks, or told to the men carrying out the operations, and are certainly not generally known by the public.

Do you mean that his mission was only to make sure that his team was killed by the Germans, or committed suicide before being captured? I asked.

Yes of course, said Ivan. *If the mission failed, they would have been captured or shot; and if the mission succeeded, the outcome needs to be the same to prevent the enemy from knowing who sent them and for what reason. It is standard procedure and is always the mission of one of the professional soldiers in every team.*

Ivan explained that he had contacts in the Paratroopers Vet's Club and the oldest British trainer in this club who was now ninety two years old actually knew the men. He also explained that the training course they received was the same now as it had been then, and had not been changed.

The Trainer in the Vet's Club had told Ivan that Curda was a well-motivated soldier, who had 'no bad bones in him'. He knew full well what he was doing. All the men had been out drinking before they went on their mission, to celebrate (if that is the right word) never being able to return.

Ivan also said that until the moment comes, one can never really tell if they will be able to carry out their orders. There is a large amount of serendipity involved. However, for any professional Soldier there is another angle to it: Do it and everything is clear – you die – and your mission is complete. Your country has a large-scale benefit. Surprisingly, it is always easier to do it, than to not do it. If you 'bottle-out' of your mission, your existence cannot be justified. Not to yourself, your colleagues, or your superiors. It is then almost impossible to sustain yourself in any arena. Living with the dishonour and guilt for the rest of your life would be unbearable, and most soldiers that fail to carry out their orders end up by committing suicide at some point afterwards. Judas Iscariot is the most famous example of this.

Consider the expense of an operation like this; the cost of training 5 men and shipping them out was the same cost as training a Brigade of 20,000 men. Normandy showed that the cost to the country of men lost in fighting vastly outweighed the cost of ten to fifteen men who were sent to carry out a one way mission.

However shocking this information was, it certainly explains the way they were treated before setting off, and the reason that Churchill presented them with medals before they left, in the certain knowledge that under any circumstances, they were never coming back alive.

Does this make Churchill, Benes, and Moravec into 'butchers' and 'evil men'? No, it just makes them good leaders, good strategists and good soldiers, looking after the interests of their own country. A philosophy that is only excusable for the winners of great battles; but never to the losers.

Myth's Busted

1. **It was a plot to kill the man destined to take over from Hitler** – No; this is like taking out the Head of Interpol or MI5, in case he becomes Prime Minister.

2. **It was a plot to kill 'the most evil man of the Third Reich'** – No; it was an operation to kill whoever they could get to between Frank and Heydrich; the higher the rank, the better the score, and to

try and kick start the Czech resistance back into action instead of their passive acceptance of turning Czechoslovakia back into a German territory.

3. **Curda was a Traitor and a Coward** – No; he was carrying out his own mission instructions to protect the British Government. It was always supposed to be a suicide mission, whatever the outcome. There were never any plans to send in a Halifax to get the men back out again.

These myths appear in all the history books and won't be let go easily. But looking at who knew what, when, and with evidence of special-operations training procedures; these conclusions fall naturally from the facts although they will be intensely disliked by patriots of the Czech Republic and of Britain.

While we let this thought settle in our minds, let us look at the other side of the fence, and recount what Heydrich had actually done to the Czech's and Slovak's during the nine months of his tenure as Acting Head of State before his assassination.

Chapter Seventeen
A Job Description to Die For

What did Heydrich do when he took up his post as Reichsprotector in Prague? Industry was in tatters, the best engineers in Europe were on strike, underpaid and their families were starving. The most advanced engineering factories were barely operational. Skilled people refused to work for meagre wages, so that their goods could be sold for vast profits on the black market. They had no meat to eat, and no money for beer or cigarettes. Moral was low, the Czech Government was in hiding somewhere in London and politically unrecognised by the British Government. They had no visible Allies, they had no hope. A black market was in force, the Czech Politicians were profiteering, German factory bosses were losing money and bad feeling was everywhere.

This didn't happen overnight, it took two and a half years from March 1939 when Czechoslovakia surrendered itself and willingly restored itself as a part of Germany. It always used to be a region of Germany and part of the Austro-Hungarian Empire, but was taken away from them after the Great War. It was territorially a significant place and Germany now controlled the Baltic, the Danube, South East Europe and the Central European waterways; as well as the Skoda works in Pilsen which was making weapons and the small arms factory in Brunn (where the British Bren gun was designed).

By September 1941 Czechoslovakian industry were producing one third of the Tanks for the Wehrmacht, a quarter of its trucks, forty per cent of its machine guns and most of its steel for Ships, U Boats and Submarines. Germans were moving into this 'bomb free zone' to open more and more industrial factories. It was too far for any British plane to fly, drop bombs, and be able to return without refuelling. – Apart from the Halifax that is, but the British only had three of them and couldn't risk getting them shot down. Over 3,000 German civil servants and office workers had moved in with their families to manage and run these industries. Set against that backdrop, was the BBC overseas Service broadcasting a message to the Czech people every hour which said:

'POMALU PRACUJ' which translates as: **'WORK SLOWLY'**

Czech workers began to go on strike and worse, to set light to their factories. In August 1941, one hundred thousand tons of fuel was purposely burnt, wagons of finished goods were blown up and telephone lines were cut. Production in this new German territory began to fall first by eighteen per cent and then still further until it reached rock bottom at thirty five per cent. Word spread about a general strike being planned across the whole of Czechoslovakia that was planned for 28th October 1941, so something had to be done and fast. Hitler was now sending vast numbers of troops to the Russian front, the need for the production of weapons, tanks and trucks was growing by the day. Any threat to the efficient production and delivery of these made the situation in Czechoslovakia completely untenable for Germany. Hitler was angry, his Generals were screaming for supplies and only excuses were coming back from Von Neurath, the existing Head of State for Germany, and Reichsprotector of Moravia and Bohemia.

This was the background of events that led Hitler to summon the thirty seven year old Reinhard Heydrich to his first ever face-to-face meeting in September 1941, and ask (tell probably!) him to take on the additional task of Acting Reichsprotector. His sole purpose was to restore order and get a complete country back to work to supply the German War Machine with its desperately needed weapons, bullets, tanks and trucks; and to do it fast. This was no small task, not just a couple of factories, or a city or two; but two enormous regions the size of two of our current complete countries!

Here are two very important things to note

Firstly, this was noted in all the current history books, as the first time that Heydrich – Head of the Reich's internal Police Force – had ever been summoned to appear before Hitler himself, and yet stories in these same books maintain that Hitler had already earmarked him as his natural successor. It does seem a little far-fetched when you consider his top team of:

- Reichsmarschall **Hermann Goering** Head of the Luftwaffe, and the founder of the Gestapo.
- Dr. **Paul Josef Goebbels** Reich Minister of Propaganda,
- **Heinrich Himmler** Reichsfuhrer of the SS
- **Ulrich Friedrich Wilhelm Joachim von Ribbentrop** Foreign Minister of the German Reich
- Field Marshal **Wilhelm Keitel** Chief of the High Command of the Armed Forces (OKW)
- General **Alfried Jodl** Head of the Operations Section of OKW. Jodl and the brains behind all of Hitler's campaigns except for the invasion of Russia
- Admiral **Erich Raeder** Commander in Chief of German Naval Forces
- Admiral **Karl Doenitz** Commander of the German Navy's U-boats until 1943 then subsequently Commander in Chief of the Navy. Doenitz was respected and trusted by Hitler and became Head of State after Hitler's death in 1945.

With a list like that of top Generals and Advisors, why on earth would anyone conclude that Heydrich, a mere Obergruppenführer, leading the internal Police Force, was destined to succeed Hitler?

MYTH BUSTED
Heydrich was already earmarked
by Hitler as his successor

The second thing to note was that this was not an appointment into a sought-after position. Not the dream job of a lifetime, or a chance to be noticed as a superior military leader. If I had been Hitler in this position, I would have gathered my top 3 Generals, for a discussion about the process for selecting someone for this role; and with my 'Serious Case Review Independent Observer' head on; my key criteria would be something like this:

- Who is fairly unimportant enough to be 'missing' from Berlin without unsettling the War effort?
- Who has a highly ethical and disciplined nature that will be able to resist being dragged into the bribery and corruption culture?
- Who is intelligent enough to negotiate with and win the allegiance of the German businessmen running the factories?
- Who has been educated to a standard that will enable him to act as a credible Head of state for the Czech people?
- Who is a true 'company man' that will go willingly and without question into this nest of vipers and barbarians; (non-Germans) and may or may not be devoured by them?
- Who is expendable to the War effort if they do not survive or succeed?

There was clearly only one man who fitted these criteria, and Himmler would have nominated him.

The Man with the Iron Heart...

Chapter Eighteen
𝔍𝔯𝔬𝔫 𝔥𝔢𝔞𝔯𝔱

Can you now imagine the meeting between Hitler and Heydrich? I don't think it was a cosy fireside chat with tea and biscuits, but more of a Dictator issuing orders to a subordinate.

Hitler was not known for his diplomacy and my guess is that he would have barked out the urgency of the job in hand, and the importance to the Reich of achieving total and uncompromising success. He would also have emphasised the honour and trust that he (Hitler) was personally placing in Heydrich to stop at nothing (I repeat, NOTHING!) to deliver the desired outcome. It is very likely that Hitler would have accented the important phrases with accompanying thumps of his fist on the table adding force to his demands and directives

Now does that sound like the Hitler we have heard on old recordings and read in old transcripts? This is a much more believable process.

Would Heydrich have had any choice in deciding whether to accept this new commission? Refusing it would have meant a certain end to his career and possibly his life. It would most probably have resulted in a posting out to some far flung and desperate front line or a move sideways into the oblivion of history.

Would Heydrich have dared to refuse this task given to him by 'The Prince' himself?

Heydrich has been quoted by Lina his wife, in a letter to Jean Vaughan in the 1950's as saying: 'Don't ask for an audience with the Prince, if he hasn't called for you'. When one of his SS Officers asked if he could speak directly to Hitler about something.

I think we can safely assume that refusing Hitler was totally out of the question.

So now we have:

- The Job Description from hell.
- A (so far) impossible task to achieve.
- A posting away from comfortable and familiar Berlin into a hostile and barbaric (because 'non-German') territory.
- No back-up whatsoever apart from Karl Frank as Secretary of State.
- Hitler demanding he succeeds at all costs and as fast as possible.
- The whole German War Machine relying on Heydrich for the constant production of Tanks, Trucks, Guns, Bullets and Steel for U-boat's and Submarines.

That is the kind of pressure under which most men would buckle. No wonder that Hitler called Heydrich, **'The man with the iron heart'** to complete this mission. This phrase is recorded in pretty much all of the current history books in a derogatory way; implying that Heydrich was without human feeling, cold-hearted and cruel. Most of the books even add words like that as a description to the phrase.

The phrase and the description seem completely incongruent to me. Iron is usually associated with being strong, strong willed, physically strong, never giving up. Indeed there is a famous Triathlon competition that is commonly known as 'The Iron Man' in which only the strongest, toughest, fittest, and most motivated ever complete the course – much less win.

If you want to describe someone as cold, heartless and unfeeling; you would be more likely to choose phrases such as: cold or hard as stone, as ice, or as steel.

Hitler was a master in the use of words. If there is one thing on which every history book and historian agrees, it is that Hitler was a fantastic orator. He chose his words carefully and often used adjective phrases and adjective clauses to add powerful visual pictures to his speeches. He captivated crowds of people with the motivating images he created in his speeches. I firmly believe that if Hitler had wanted it to mean cold-hearted and unfeeling; he would have used completely different words such as ice, stone or steel.

There is a good chance that Hitler took this phrase directly from the Writer Alexandre Dumas from his famous book 'The Count of Monte Cristo'. Here is the well-known excerpt that contains it:

*Monte Cristo endeavoured also to leave, but Maximilian would have died rather than relax his hold of the handle of the door, which he closed upon the count. Julie, Emmanuel, and some of the servants, ran up in alarm on hearing the cries of Maximilian. Morrel seized their hands, and opening the door exclaimed in a voice choked with sobs, 'On your knees - on your knees - he is our benefactor - the saviour of our father! He is', - He would have added, 'Edmond Dantes,' but the Count seized his arm and prevented him. Julie threw herself into the arms of the Count; Emmanuel embraced him as a guardian angel; Morrel again fell on his knees, and struck the ground with his forehead. **Then the iron-hearted man** felt his heart swell in his breast; a flame seemed to rush from his throat to his eyes, he bent his head and wept. For a while nothing was heard in the room but a succession of sobs, while the incense from their grateful hearts mounted to heaven.*

The Count of Monte Cristo by Dumas, Alexandre

Nothing derogatory there…

Consider also the symbolic use of Iron in German Mythology which was used everywhere in the Third Reich. What was the highest honour and award for valour, bravery and courage?

The IRON CROSS

- The Iron Cross was awarded for one act of bravery.
- The Iron Cross First Class was awarded for many acts of bravery.
- The Knights Cross was an even higher award, and was an iron cross worn on a ribbon around the neck.

Silver and gold were totally insignificant compared to the stature and kudos of the awards made of iron. I am astounded that so far, no one has ever made this connection, or at least considered the high esteem that the Third Reich placed in the use of Iron.

Therefore it seems we need to bust another of those myths and stories about Reinhard Heydrich, in fact we have shattered it beyond all recognition and any book claiming to be recounting history that uses these descriptions needs to be re-written:

MYTH BUSTED
The Man with the Iron Heart is a Derogatory
Term for a Cold and Unfeeling Bastard

On 23rd September 1941 Heydrich and his pregnant wife Lina, moved to Prague. He took his new office as Head of State very seriously; the outcome of the War and Germany's future depended on it. Three days later he began a 'death or glory' plan to create order.

As it turned out, it was death.

Chapter Nineteen
𝔚enceslas 𝔖quare 𝔓aved with 𝔠zech 𝔖kulls

Heydrich summoned the German leaders and delivered his famous harsh speech where he told them that the Czech people had no future in the new Europe. They would be 'Germanised' and those that refused to comply would be sterilised or put against the wall. The Czech people will tell you even today that Heydrich threatened to 'line Wenceslas Square with Czech skulls' although I cannot find any hard evidence of that particular quote, or that a single Czech skull was ever used in this way.

That is not to say that I disbelieve he said it, because using such an emotionally charged phrase would certainly gain the attention of the Czech people. Strange how such a powerful emotional phrase has gone down in history against the man who supposedly had no emotions? Another incongruent example.

It is inbuilt in small boys in the School playground to use phrases that are designed to instil fear in their childhood opponents; my Dad is bigger than your Dad; and this technique was famously used to dramatic effect by Mohammed Ali. He was the boxer who made shockingly violent threats to his opponents in the media before each fight, to create fear and an expectation that they were going to lose. The purpose was to de-motivate the opponent without the use of physical force. I repeat for emphasis – to instil fear without the use of physical force.

The world thought this was a brilliant and very clever way to win a battle before going to fight when Ali used it. The difference is that Mohamed Ali was American and Reinhard Heydrich was a Nazi.

Interesting that Heydrich spoke of the concept of a 'new Europe' and if you imagine that in 1942 there seemed no possibility of Germany failing. It was all just a forgone conclusion with just the how and when to be decided. This big-picture thinking by Heydrich has now come into being and his actions just before his assassination may have influenced the way Europe is organised today, but back to his first weeks in Prague for the moment.

Heydrich declared Martial Law and the Gestapo (SS Police) arrested and convicted 400 people who were then sentenced to death. 215 of them were Politicians convicted for political crimes and 189 were Czech people who were convicted for black-market activity. A very severe start to his reign as Head of State, but throughout history this is a standard practice for any nation taking over another nation by force of War. The top echelon of the previous ruling organisation is always removed to enable the incoming rulers to establish their own law and order systems on the deposed country.

They were not tortured or starved and none of their skulls were used to line Wenceslas Square. Harsh yes - but barbaric - no. It was War. This resulted in two new nicknames for Heydrich that are probably familiar: *The Butcher of Prague and The Hangman.*

Heydrich's other measures and actions towards the ordinary people of Czechoslovakia are very difficult to find reported with quite the same enthusiasm. Most books with an account of 'what Heydrich did' have descriptions of his character in colourful adjectives of terror: most evil, most feared, the Blonde Beast, most ruthless henchman, most unpleasant character, etc., and most of them have at least one wrong fact in them. Here is just one example: (we do not have space for them all!)

Heydrich Henchman of Death by Charles Whiting 1999 has an error in the précis on the inside cover which says he was 'mysteriously assassinated in 1943' when in fact it was 1942. Also in the same book Picture 11 has the caption 'Lina Heydrich loved Panenske Brezany' and shows a lovely picture of Karl Frank's Mansion as Secretary of State, not the Mansion that Lina and Heydrich lived in.

Heydrich appears to have carried out his impossible mission with calculated precision and discipline akin to a fencing match. The Czech people were clearly given a choice of behaviours and were told of the likely consequences of their choices. He did not do anything that he had not warned them of beforehand, and he did not do some of the 'demotivating and fear inducing' actions that he threatened. The choices may not have been liked, but considering Germany was a Dictatorship, this appears to be as civilised a process as there possibly could be during a War.

Having achieved his goals quickly and effectively, he then set out as Head of State to make sure 'his people' were as German as possible and benefitted from all the advantages of being so. These actions are scattered across the history books as though separated with a spray gun and I have located as many as I can to list them all together in one place. There may well be more that I have not discovered - and I still search for people with a living memory of such times whose experiences would be valuable.

Here is a list of Heydrich's **'Soup Economics' or 'Suppenwirtschaft'**. The improvements Heydrich made for the Czech people that are mostly missing from the history books:

- 200,000 pairs of shoes were brought from Germany and distributed free to the Czech people.
- Butter (fat) rations were substantially increased for skilled and heavy work labourers and certain classes of workers.
- Tobacco rations were increased substantially for certain classes of workers.
- Three months later in January 1942 Martial Law was lifted in Moravia and Bohemia (Czech Republic and Slovakia).

- April 1942 (just 5 weeks before he died) the German Social Security system was established increasing benefits by around 30% and treating the Czechs the same as native Germans.
- Hotels in the well-to-do resorts of Bohemia were requisitioned as Holiday Homes for Czech workers.
- Important workers who were demotivated were sent on fully paid sessions in the Spas, to bathe in the waters, have free medical checks and care, to restore them to health.
- Sickness insurance was given to workers for the first time in Czech history.
- Albert Speer (Hitler's Architect) was called in to make recommendations on improving the infrastructure of Prague.
- Plans were made to improve the Autobahn system and link them up with the German Autobahns.
- Heydrich reopened the nineteenth century German Concert Hall in Prague that had been used by the Czech Chamber of Deputies.
- He renamed Smetana Square after the composer Mozart.

The working population responded as you might expect. They put on weight, they had money to spend, they had jobs, and they began to cooperate with the Germanisation process. German was to be spoken everywhere, Schools were to conduct lessons in only German, and any dissenters or resistance operators were to be reported to the Gestapo; which they were with enthusiasm. There is a story told by the Czech's today, that the SS were so swamped with reports of dissent, that they put up posters saying, 'Please don't report Czech dissenters to us unless their behaviour is of a very serious nature'. But I can't find any hard evidence of this, so it may be a story that has grown in the telling over 75 years.

Heydrich then went further than any of the other occupied Nations, and demanded that Berlin give German citizenship to any Czech national who wanted to apply. He was quoted as saying that any Czech who builds a tank for Germany should have the honour of doing it for his own country. Surprisingly, this measure was approved of by Berlin (It wouldn't be now; their citizenship Policies are very restricted) and hundreds of Czech's applied and were approved of as German citizens with their Czech names replaced with typical German surnames.

The effect of this unusual package of measures was that Czech workers returned to their factories, were respected as skilled engineers, and the production of 'state of the art' tanks, trucks, weapons and ammunition began to surpass their targets, making huge profits for the factory owners and for the SS. An unheard of result during the War at that point.

Resistance dwindled first from fear and slowly from acceptance, and Czechoslovakia started to merge into Germany. The majority of people in Moravia and Bohemia were pretty much untouched by the ravages of the War that other areas of Europe were suffering, apart from the rationing that affected everyone during that time. There was no bombing in their Cities from the Allies who's Air Force was beyond safe reach. If they complied, they were well protected by their new *Reichsprotector*, with jobs, food, money, and were living with their families as comfortably as was possible in the middle of a World War.

It is easy to understand now why, foolishly, Heydrich drove around in an open topped Staff Car as we now know. At 38 years old, it probably seemed inconceivable to him that every Czechoslovakian wasn't happy and grateful to be a German, or at least protected by the Reich. Perhaps an older and wiser man would have known and understood that patriotism cannot be replaced by force, by fear, or by good fortune and certainly not in the space of just nine months.

There were of course Czech nationals, who remained fervently patriotic to their country and did not accept the Germanisation process, but the new regime rendered them unable to do anything about it. They just held their tongues and waited for their chance.

Chapter Twenty

A Vision of the Future

With industrialised Czechoslovakia now firing on all cylinders, the goods made under the control of the SS were 'sold' to the Reich for the War effort. The SS had to be self-funding and did not receive any money from the State. Its costs were huge and most of the money was in loans from the Banks. When Czech industry started to make a profit, after the Banks were repaid, somewhere had to be found for all the profits to be stashed securely, so that it wasn't swallowed up by the State.

This was not in the remit of Heydrich's role, SS Obergruppenführer Oswald Pohl was the financial controller of the whole of the SS (not just Heydrich's departments) and he was responsible for bringing in enough cash to pay all the SS bills. As the organisation got bigger, so did its financial administration under Pohl.

As luck would have it, after the Great War, the Allies set up a special bank to make sure that Germany repaid its imposed Reparations, and this was situated in Switzerland, in the City of Basle. It was called the Bank of International Settlements and known as the BIS. The Founders of this Bank had incorporated a very useful Charter that the Bank could never be seized, sanctioned or closed - even if another war erupted between the home nations of its member Directors. That clause turned out to be just what the SS needed for a suitable place to stash a lot of its profits.

This Bank was not managed by Germany alone; it was a joint Directorship between the Bank of England, the First National Bank of New York, The Bank of Italy, the Bank of France and the Reichsbank of Berlin. When the Second World War broke out, the Bank of International Settlements continued to operate between the five Banking

Directors. The President of the BIS at that time was Thomas McKittrick of the New York Bank.

Obviously there were officials from both the Allies and Germany working together to manage the Bank who included the Head of the Reichsbank, Emil Puhl and Walter Funk. Comments in the history books state that German big business via the Banks was running the BIS, but how credible does that sound with four other major countries as equal partners and an American President? They may have been pumping more money in than the other countries; but with only one fifth of the power, they had no possibility of being able to 'control the Bank'.

Other accounts also state that Germany was 'hedging its bets' or 'preparing for the worst scenario' (its defeat) by stashing vast amounts of money and again there is no evidence at all of this during 1942. This may well have been the view two and a half years later in 1944-45, but this book only concerns itself with events up to June 4th 1942 and at that point there was no possible reason to imagine that Germany would not end up as the successful ruler of the whole of Europe.

Heydrich himself made reference to the 'New Europe' because at that time the Reich were in control of pretty much all of it, so it was the logical extension of Hitler's aims. His big vision of post war Europe was based on the status quo in early 1942. As it transpires over three quarters of a century after the War, we do have a 'New Europe' but this is certainly not Heydrich's vision of how it would be. Perhaps Heydrich can be credited with the concept of it back in 1942, but certainly not with its eventual administration!

In 1942, the War machine was quite simply feeding all its profits into the Banking systems that were available to it at the time. This was the sole responsibility of Oswald Pohl. Heydrich needed somewhere to put the profits and it was Pohl's job to find it and manage it. As a comparison, if the Head of MI5 in the UK needed somewhere to invest his or her profits, it would be managed by the Governor of the Bank of England – or at least by the Governor's staff. MI5 would not set up its own Banking systems.

It is a difficult concept for both writers of books about the War and for their readers, that knowledge, views, reasons, strategies, and decisions changed as the war progressed. So if writing about a decision made or an incident that happened in 1942, it cannot be explained by a decision made or an incident that happened in 1945. Hindsight is very confusing to any accurate historical record. These decisions and views could be in complete opposition to each other and if you consider an action or decision that was made three years later, with a very different set of circumstances, it will certainly appear to be at odds with what else was happening during 1942.

When carrying out a 'Serious Case Review', the files, notes, documents and evidence from all agencies involved in the case are categorically sealed in a process known as being 'Frozen'. They are taken out of their normal storage system and held under lock and key for the duration of the investigation, which has a Government timescale of six months. That means that nothing can be changed, added or removed until after the investigation and only the information that was known, was available to be known, or should have been known AT THAT TIME is used in the construction of the Report.

It should be appreciated that the prediction of events is not a straightforward matter. There are complex factors and circumstances interacting with each other which make any future decisions or actions very difficult to predict. Equally, the use of hindsight can also convey an impression of clarity and order with regard to retrospective description and analysis, which was not of course available to the protagonists at the time. Therefore any history book should be read bearing in mind this cautionary note.

It is impossible to 'Freeze' all the writing and historical understanding of the prevailing circumstances on 4th of June 1942, without being able to see at the same time everything that happened afterwards. But I seek to disallow any thinking in this book about Heydrich from decisions made or actions taken by others, long after his death. So when considering any account of him I have endeavoured to look only backwards at the journey of the SS to that point, and not forwards to what happened after it.

Responsibility for all decisions made and actions taken after June 4th 1942 must therefore be taken by those who made them and those who carried them out, and not attributed to Heydrich.

The SS was an unbelievably large organisation and it is easy to underestimate this when the History books name only eight or nine members of it. To give you a flavour of the size of it, here is a list of the Officers who held the same Military Rank as Heydrich along with their Role in the SS and, where found, the year they joined. It is very interesting to note that the majority of them had been in service for at least ten years and some of them for as many as fifteen years. The early machinery of the SS had a Policy of taking the most intelligent and brightest Graduates straight from University and making them into Junior Officers. Which is why of course, the German weapons, planes, submarines, tanks, rockets, bombs, guns, battle strategies, codes, and tactics, were so much more advanced than everyone else's.

(I cannot resist a quick comparison with the way Germany won the 2014 Football World Cup. After losing in 2002, they established Academies for young talented players in small town clubs, training them up to professional standards during the next eight to ten years. The

Academies made sure that the best young Footballers were taken into the top Premiership Teams; ready for Germany to select a prospective winning Team from a large pool of excellent international players, which then – unsurprisingly – went on to win.)

Here is the list of everyone with an equal Rank to Heydrich in 1942: (Heydrich appears as number 35 and Pohl as number 60)

Rank: SS Obergruppenführer (Lieutenant General)

1. **Friedrich Alpers**: Staatssekretär / SS -Obergruppenführer /Staatsrat / Generalforstmeister /Major der Reserve (Luftwaffe) Joined March 1931

2. **Max Amann**: Honorary SS Member. Party leader for the Reich of the Department Press

3. **Erich von dem Bach-Zelewski**: Higher SS and Police Leader of Central Russia joined15 February 1931

4. **Herbert Backe**: Minister of Agriculture joined1 October 1933

5. **Gottlob Berger**: Commander of the SS -Hauptamt joined 1936

6. **Werner Best**: Reich Plenipotentiary of Denmark joined 1931

7. **Wilhelm Bittrich**: Waffen-SS combat commander, II SS Panzerkorps joined 1934

8. **Ernst Wilhelm Bohle**: Leader of the National Socialist German Workers' Party Foreign Organization joined September 1933

9. **Martin Bormann**: Personal Secretary to Hitler, Party leader for the Reich in charge of the NSDAP Chancellery joined September 1929

10. **Philipp Bouhler**: Head of the Action T4, Party Leader for the Reich in charge of the Hitler's Chancellery (Kanzlei des Führers) joined April 1933

11. **Franz Breithaupt**: Commanding general of the SS and Police Courts joined December 1932.

12. **Walter Buch**: Party Leader for the Reich as Chairman of the Inquiry and Mediation Board joined July 1933.

13. **Leonardo Conti**: In 1939 Conti was appointed Reich Health Leader, elected to the Reichstag in 1941 and promoted to Lieutenant General in the SS in 1944.

14. **Richard Walther Darré**: First Director of the Race and Settlement Office ('Rasse- und Siedlungshauptamt' or RuSHA), and Minister of the Reich for Food and Agriculture joined July 1930.

15. **Karl-Maria Demelhuber**: Commanded the SS -Standarte Germania, 6. SS -Gebirgs-Division Nord, XII. SS -Armeekorps and XVI. SS -Armeekorps. Joined March 1935.

16. **Otto Dietrich**: Party Leader for the Reich as NSDAP Press Chief, Honorary rank joined 1932.

17. **Karl von Eberstein**: Early member of the Nazi Party, the SA, the SS Reichstag delegate, an HSSPF and SS -Oberabschnitt Führer, head of the Munich Police in World War II joined April 1929.

18. **Joachim Albrecht Eggeling**: Gauleiter of Saxony and Anhalt, High President of Merseburg joined 1935.

19. **Theodor Eicke**: First chief of the Inspektion der Konzentrationslager (Concentration Camps Inspectorate) and commander of the SS Totenkopf Division joined August 1930.

20. **Karl Fiehler**: Lord mayor of Munich/Party Leader of the Reich in charge of the communal policy joined July 1933.

21. **Albert Forster**: Gauleiter of Danzig joined June 1926.

22. **Hans Frank**: Legal adviser to Hitler, promoted to Obergruppenführer in the SS in 1939. Frank oversaw the creation of the ghettoes in Poland for which he would later hang.

23. **Karl Hermann Frank**: Higher SS and Police Leader of Bohemia and Moravia.

24. **August Frank**: SS Administrative Officer of the Special Purpose Troops (SS-Verfügungstruppe) and of the concentration camp guards, the SS Death's Head units (SS -Totenkopfverbände or SS -TV), Chief Supply Officer of the Waffen-SS and SS-TV units under Pohl. Joined April 1932.

25. **Herbert Otto Gille**: Waffen-SS Commander joined December 1931.

26. **Curt von Gottberg**: Also General der Waffen-SS joined September 1932.

27. **Ernst-Robert Grawitz**: Also General of Waffen-SS; Reichsarzt SS and Polizei; Head of German Red Cross; joined November 1931.

28. **Ulrich Greifelt**: Chief of SS German Nationhood Staff from 1941.

29. **Arthur Greiser**: Gauleiter of Reichsgau Wartheland joined 1929.

30. **August Heissmeyer**: Commander of the SS Education Department.

31. **Wolf-Heinrich Graf von Helldorf**: Not member of SS , but

Obergruppenführer in his capacity as Polizeipresident Berlin SA Obergruppenführer.

32. **Rudolf Hess**: Also Deputy-Führer of the NSDAP until 11 May 1941 joined November 1925.

33. **Konrad Henlein**: Gauleiter of the Sudetenland.

34. **Maximilian von Herff**: Commander of the SS Personnel Department joined April 1942.

35. **Reinhard Heydrich: Chief of the RSHA; President of Interpol; Acting Reich-Protector of Bohemia and Moravia joined July 1931.**

36. **Friedrich Hildebrandt**: Reich Governor of Mecklenburg.

37. **Richard Hildebrandt**: Led the SS – Rasse - und Siedlungshauptamt.

38. **Hermann Höfle**: Higher SS and Police Leader in Slovakia.

39. **Friedrich Jeckeln**: Higher SS and Police Leader of Eastern Russia joined January 1930.

40. **Hans Jüttner**: Commander of the SS – Führungshauptamt.

41. **Ernst Kaltenbrunner**: Second Chief of the RSHA after Heydrich's assassination.

42. **Hans Kammler**: Head of V-2 program joined 20 May 1933.

43. **Georg Keppler**: Keppler commanded the 2nd SS-Division Das Reich, 3rd. SS-Division Totenkopf, Ist. SS-Panzerkorps, III.(germanische) SS-Panzerkorps and XVIII. SS-Armee-Korps. Joined October 1935.

44. **Wilhelm Karl Keppler**: Secretary of state in Foreign Office;

founder of the Freundeskreis der Wirtschaft joined August 1932

45. Matthias Kleinheisterkamp: Waffen-SS Divisional and Corps Commander joined January 1934.

46. **Wilhelm Koppe**: Höhere SS und Polizei Führer, HSSP joined January 1932.

47. **Friedrich-Wilhelm Krüger**: Higher SS and Police Leader of Poland joined March 1931.

48. **Walter Krüger**: Commander of 4th SS Polizei Panzer Division, 2nd SS Panzer Division Das Reich, IV SS Panzer Corps, VI SS Panzer Corps.

49. **Hans Lammers**: Minister of the Reich, Head of the Reich Chancellery Honorary rank.

50. **Hartmann Lauterbacher**: Gauleiter und Reichsstatthalter / Oberpräsident / SS-Obergruppenführer /M.d.R. / Preußischen Staatsrat joined November 1940.

51. **Werner Lorenz**: Commander of the Office of Ethnic Germanization (SS-Hauptamt Volkdeutsche Mittelstelle) joined 1931.

52. **Benno Martin**: SS-Obergruppenführer, General of the Waffen-SS and Police and Higher SS Leader (Polizei und Höherer SS) in Nuremberg. Joined April 1934.

53. **Emil Mazuw**: Landeshauptmann (nominal governor) of the Province of Pomerania from 1940 to 1945. General of the Waffen-SS (1944), General of Police (1942) and Ostsee Higher SS and Police leader (1939–1945).joined June 1930.

54. **Wilhelm Murr**: Gauleiter of Württemberg-Hohenzollern. From

1933 held the offices of State President and Reichsstatthalter (Reich Governor) of Württemberg. Made SS-Obergruppenführer.

55. **Konstantin von Neurath**: German Foreign Minister 1932–1938, Reichsprotektor of Moravia and Bohemia joined 1937.

56. **Carl Oberg**: Higher SS and Police Leader of France joined April 1932.

57. **Günther Pancke**: Higher SS and Police Leader of Denmark, Waffen-SS General joined 1931.

58. **Karl Pfeffer-Wildenbruch**: Obergruppenführer, General der Waffen-SS und der Polizei, 4th SS Polizei Division, VI SS Army Corps and IX SS Mountain Corps. Joined March 1939.

59. **Artur Phleps**: Commander 7. SS-Freiwilligen-Gebirgs-Division Prinz Eugen joined June 1941.

60. **Oswald Pohl: Chief of the SS Economics and Administration Office (WVHA) joined 1933.**

61. **Rudolf Querner**: SS and Police Leader (HSSPF) Nordsee in Military district X, based in Hamburg.joined May 1938.

62. **Hanns Albin Rauter**: SS and Police Leader in the Netherlands Joined Austrian Nazi Party.

63. **Wilhelm Rediess**: SS and Police Leader in Norway joined July 1930.

64. **Joachim von Ribbentrop**: Foreign minister 1938–1945 joined February 1938.

65. **Erwin Rösener**: Higher SS and Police Leader SS-Oberabschnitt 'Alpenland' (Wehrkreis XVIII; HQ: Salzburg) joined 1930.

66. **Fritz Sauckel**: Gauleiter of NSDAP Gau of Thuringia.

67. **Paul Scharfe**: Director of the SS Legal Office joined October 1931.

68. **Julius Schaub**: Co-founder of the SS, personal assistant to Hitler joined February 1925.

69. **Arthur Seyss-Inquart**: Leader of NS opposition in Austria prior Anschluss, Deputy governor-general of Poland then Commissaire for the Reich in Netherlands.

70. **Felix Steiner**: Commander of III (Germanic) SS Panzer Corps.

71. **Dr. Wilhelm Stuckart**: Reich Interior State Secretary; author of Nuremberg Race Laws of 1935.

72. **Fritz Wächtler**: honorary rank of SS-Obergruppenführer and Reich Defense Commissar of Bayreuth.

73. **Prince Josias**: Hereditary Prince of Waldeck and Pyrmont Higher SS and Police Leader of the SS-Oberabschnitt Fulda-Werra joined March 1930.

74. **Fritz Weitzel**: Leader of SS in Rheinland and Ruhr. Polizeipräsident in Düsseldorf in 1933, and Höherer SS- und Polizeiführer West in 1938. Joined 1927.

75. **Karl Wolff**: Chief of staff to Heinrich Himmler and Supreme SS and Police Leader of Italy joined October 1931.

76. **Udo von Woyrsch**: Higher SS and Police Leader in the SS-Oberabschnitt Sudost.

77. **Alfred Wünnenberg**: SS-Obergruppenführer und General der Waffen SS and Commander 4th SS Polizei Panzer Grenadier Division joined October 1939.

There may be a few names that you recognise in this list, but amazing to see just how many there were of this Rank who were all managing their own huge departments and interacting with each other on decision making.

For those who like to see hard statistics, here is a breakdown of the above list into the years they joined the SS minus 24 of them that I couldn't track down:

1925 x 2	1926 x 1	1927 x 1	1928 x 0
1929 x 3	1930 x 7	1931 x 11	1932 x 7
1933 x 7	1934 x 3	1935 x 3	1936 x 1
1937 x 1	1938 x 2	1939 x 2	1940 x 1
1942 x 1	Unknown x 24		

Those who have any Military experience will fully understand that with 77 men holding the same rank, neither one of them would be able to issue an order directly to the other. That means that everything they did collectively, must have been the result of orders from above.

Many of the roles had overlaps with other departments, offices or Regiments, and this added to both the difficulty and the unlikelihood of anyone doing something against the Party line or achieving a task off his own bat, which had not been issued to the relevant officers and offices to carry out.

This structure was created purposefully by Himmler so that no Officer could usurp him, and resulted in an ethos of mistrust and competition between his subordinate ranks. They were all far too busy doing their jobs and out manoeuvring each other; to have time to consider outmanoeuvring anyone higher up. After all, these were the sharpest brains in Germany at the time; and if a group of them got together – anything could happen. It worked perfectly.

Chapter Twenty One
𝕳𝖎𝖘𝖙𝖔𝖗𝖞 𝖋𝖔𝖗 𝖘𝖆𝖑𝖊!

During the course of researching for this book, in February 2014, a friend of mine sent me a link to an article in the Daily Mail about a complete Register of the SS that was being auctioned in a specialist sale of Military and Historical Documents.

The story was that a member of the British SOE had stolen this book from the SS Headquarters in Prinz Albrecht Strasse and had then returned to England with it and hidden it in his bedroom for 70 years.

After he died, his family members went through his belongings and found this book. They didn't know whether or not it was important, so they took it to an Auction House specialising in Military documents, who advised them to auction it with a guide price of £1,000.

This book was a priceless record of 28,000 members of the SS and included detailed information and dates of all their ranks, honours, awards, SS registration numbers, Party Member numbers and the dates they were awarded an Honour Ring by Himmler.

Himmler was listed at number 1 in the book and Heydrich had an entry at number 28. Everything I needed to find out was inside this book and I knew that I would need to scratch as much money together as I could, go to the auction, and try to win it.

The day of the auction arrived, and I set out with a close friend who volunteered to drive me to Ludlow Racecourse on Tuesday 18th March 2014 for the 1pm start of the *'Important Sale of Historical Documents, Autographs & Ephemera' by Mullock's Specialist Auctioneers & Valuers.*

I managed to gather £4,000 in cash which was in an envelope ready to go and after a two hour drive through the wilds of Shropshire we arrived at Ludlow Racecourse and parked up with about fifteen other cars at an insignificant looking clubhouse where the sale was to take place.

We arrived before the sale started and in time to view any of the items. I registered at the desk and received my bidding number which I was surprised to see was number 975 although there were only about 20 people in the room and five of them were from Mullock's. The meagre audience all looked like anorak collectors; no one looked like they belonged to any bigger organisation, so there must be a lot of online internet bidders registered and my hopes of winning the book were falling quickly.

I took my bidding number to the side of the hall where boxes of goods were piled up against the wall, with a row of tables in front separating it from the public area. I handed over my bidding number and asked to look at Lot number 136.

It was described in their Catalogue thus:

Lot 136: A Scarce Register of the SS December 1938

WW11-Nazis- the SS

A complete register of the members of the SS dated December 31st 1938. Folio, black cloth covers with embossed title in white lettering. 'Diestaltersliste der Schutstaffel' (Seniority list of the protection staff)

[Diestal actually means 'Service' not seniority, so it is a list of members in service at that time. They were arranged in seniority order, but that was not what the book title said.]

The first two pages list 53 officers of the SS who had died prior to the publication of the list. There is then approx. 425 pp of listings of the living members of the SS at the time of publication. The lists record name, decorations, such as the awards of the Sword of Honour, their rank and division, their Party number, their SS number, date of birth and promotion details.

Himmler heads the list, which also includes some of the most heinous war criminals of all time, such as Adolf Eichman, and Reinhard Heydrich. An alphabetic index is at the rear, together with some statistical information on the areas covered by the SS Divisions.

It is unlikely that many other copies of this book exist. The present copy has an intriguing history: it belonged to a British SOE Agent who was sent to Nazi Germany during the early 1930's in order to infiltrate Nazi High Command. He no doubt obtained this register in order to provide important information on who was in the SS and who he could therefore trust.

Guide Price £1,000 - £2,000

This seemed inconceivable!

SOE activity in the early 1930's?

A 1938 book stolen a whole year before the War?

Two whole years before the SOE was even created?

Something here was very, very wrong. The SOE wasn't established until 1940, so either this 'Specialist Military Auctioneer' doesn't know what he is talking about, or they have completely made up this story to 'sell' the book. Either way it wasn't good. When France surrendered in June 1940, Churchill decided to create a new secret agency to sabotage, subvert and weaken the German Army, so the Special Operations Executive or SOE was set up and they were authorised directly by Churchill at the highest level to use 'virtually any means.'

Was the British Government acting against Germany a year before War broke out and was this irrevocable evidence? Did the family who found the book not give any thought to *why* it had been hidden for 72 years?

Here is another possibility: The British Government gave orders for it to be destroyed after taking the information from it; and the Officer decided to take it home instead. He would then realise that he couldn't take it anywhere, show it to anyone, or sell it, without the British finding out that he had not destroyed it, so that may be why it was hidden under the bed for 72 years.

I realised that this book was far too important for me to be able to win with my meagre £4,000. There would be bigger authorities than me acting over the internet to make sure that this information disappeared from view very quickly. Who would be bidding for it though? The Nazi Hunters? The British Government? The (Ex) Nazi's? The Jews? The Americans? Or the Russians?

I wrote the Lot number on a little piece of card and handed it to a woman on the other side of the tables. She silently took the card and went off to look for the book. In what seemed like an endless amount of time, as the clock was ticking relentlessly towards 1pm, she returned with the piece of treasure in her hands and placed it on the table in front of me. Not wrapped, not covered, there it was as large as life.

I fleetingly wondered if I should grab it and make a run for the door, but my details were registered and I didn't fancy another interview with the Police; this time on the wrong side of the law.

I quickly found the page where Heydrich was listed and asked the woman if I was allowed to take any pictures with my phone. 'Go ahead' she said. I had five minutes and didn't know what to do first. I took pictures of the cover, the title pages and the page listing Heydrich. In the middle of the hall was a raised table where three men in suits sat down ready to begin the Sale. There was a laptop computer in front of them and a microphone in front of the centre man. A dull voice rang out across the hall and the sale had begun. The book was taken from me by the well trained staff, and I sat down with my friend, disconsolately, and waited for 135 Lots to be sold before the book came up, and I was convinced that it would then disappear from me and from the world for ever.

Here are the pictures I took along with two that were in the Newspaper:

This was the picture that appeared in the newspaper

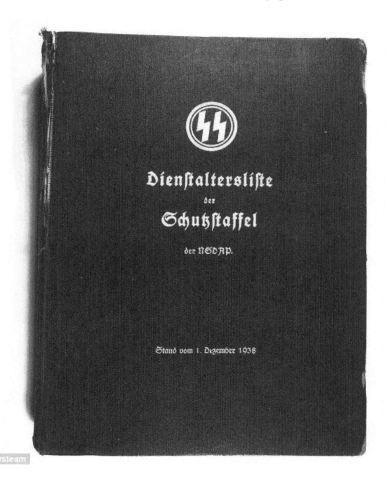

My hasty mobile phone snapshots:

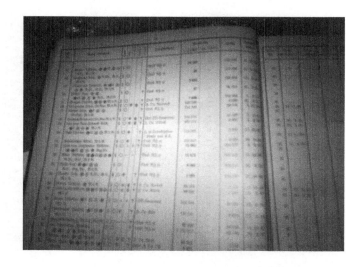

Another Newspaper image:

I was not wrong. The bidding started at £500 and went up in £200's with me bidding against an unknown opponent on the Auctioneers Laptop. When the bids reached £2,000 the Auctioneer jumped up in £500's until I made my final bid based on the packet of money pressed against me in the inside pocket of my coat.

My final bid was topped by another £500, which, plus tax and commission took it well over £5,000.

I knew that evidence as important as this would have an unlimited budget and to this day, I have no idea where it went, but I am confident that no one will see any trace of it ever again.

Thank goodness that I was there and managed to get a few pictures of it or you and I might never have known it existed, or that the British were carrying out secret operations a year before WW2 was declared.

History (and evidence) – Sold to the highest bidder.

Chapter Twenty Two
Pinning the Tail on a Donkey

From the many stories and references about Reinhard Heydrich, you might assume that he had power over many more things than he actually did. By 1942 Germany controlled many large countries, this took a huge administrative staff to manage and decision making and execution was both complex and time consuming, add to that the Party machinery, the Reich Administration, the Wehrmacht Operations and the SS infrastructure that somehow all needed to work together.

To put some perspective on it, think of the UK Government in a time of War. Would the Prime Minister, or deputy Prime Minister instruct the Head of MI5 or Interpol to: manage the Bank of England, make all Military decisions and strategies, decide the policy on Immigration and Emigration, decide on the transport policy – use of trains, boats, planes, manage work and pensions for the workforce, decide prison procedures and working practices, and make key decisions on the future direction and strategy of the overall War? That is just for one country, now carry that line of thinking up a level and apply it to all the countries of the European Union. What were the other 76 Obergruppenführer's, and Hitler's top team of Generals and Chiefs of Staff doing at the time?

The administration and machinery of the Party and the Reich are not pertinent to this 'impartial helicopter view' of Heydrich, so I shall concentrate on the internal workings of the SS, which is the organisation that Heydrich belonged to.

The strategic machinery of the SS was hugely complicated and the Heads of each major administrative office were fiercely protective of their own roles and responsibilities. One simple decision could involve many different departments with an overlap of issues in manpower, supplies, transport, equipment, costs and strategic objectives. Of course there were specific departments and administrative offices deciding each of these things, but they were forced to work alongside other departments to achieve them.

Here is a simplified outline of how the SS was structured during 1942, under the Reichsfuhrer SS Heinrich Himmler. There were eight main Departments (*or Hauptamter*) and each department had a range of operations and responsibilities: Some of them had over a hundred different named 'Offices', so here is just a brief headline along with their major departments:

1. Hauptamt Personlicher Stab RfSS: This was Himmler's personal staff, the chief of which was SS Obergruppenführer Karl Wolff who was Himmler's Adjutant as well as Supreme SS and Military Governor of Italy. Wolff managed 3,000 men whose roles included:
- Heads of each SS Hauptamter (listed below).
- Some Specialist Officials.
- Advisory and Honorary Officers.
- Komandostab RfSS or Field Headquarters, with a Signals section, escort battalion, and flak detachment who accompanied Himmler on all field trips and visits to occupied territories. (NB. The staff of this was doubled after Heydrich's assassination in June 1942).

2. SS Peronalhauptamt (Pers.HA): This was the HR or Personnel office dealing with all records and personal matters of SS Officers only. It was commanded by Obergruppenführer Walter Schmitt and after 1942, by Maximilian von Herff.

3. SS Central Office (SS Hauptamt or known as the SS–HA): Under Gruppenfuhrer Kurt Wittje and Obergruppenführer August

Heissmeyer. From 1942 this office managed the expansion of the Waffen SS and the recruitment of volunteers in Scandinavia, Flanders, Holland, Norway and Denmark to police these countries. Its main responsibilities were:

- Recruitment
- Maintaining records on non-commissioned personnel (NCO's) and all other ranks, except Officers.

4. SS Operational Headquarters (SS Fuhrungshauptamt or SS-FHA): This was the largest department, with a staff of over 40,000, managing the operational needs of the Waffen SS. It was headed up by Obergruppenführer Hans Juttner and Gruppenfuhrer Leo Petri, and responsible for:

- Operational HQ of the whole SS
- Allgemeine SS HQ.
- Operational needs of the Waffen SS.
- Coordinated Training, supplies, mobilisation.
- Payment of Wages.
- Supply of Equipment, Arms, Ammunition and Vehicles.
- Repair of stocks.
- Transport of the SS and the Police.
- SS Mail Censorship.
- Geology.
- War Archives.
- Medical and Dental Services.

5. The Reich Central Security Office (Reichssicherheitshauptamt or the RSHA or RSi-H): This was Heydrich's Department and it looked after the security Police forces of the Party and the State:

- Security Agencies of the Third Reich: SD, Kripo, Gestapo

- Dealing with Intelligence, Espionage and Counter Espionage
- Police Duties of Common Law Crime
- Public Opinion on the Nazi regime

6. The Economic and Administrative Department (Wirtschafts und Verwaltungshauptamt or SS–WVHA): This was headed up by Oswald Pohl and he controlled the supply and demand issues including:

- All SS Finances.
- Administered and managed all the Concentration Camps.
- SS Industrial and Agricultural Affairs.
- Carried out Housing programmes.
- Construction Programmes across the Reich.

7. The Race & Settlement Department (Rasse und Siedlungshauptamt or RuSHA): Commanded by Richard Walther Darre, Richard Heldebrandt, and Gunther Pancke, responsible for implementing the 'Blood and Soil' theories of Darre:

- Racial Purity of SS Members.
- Issued Lineage Certificates.
- Settling ex- SS Servicemen in the conquered Eastern Territories.

8. SS Legal Department (Hauptamt SS – Gericht or HA SS – Gericht) which administered investigations on behalf of Himmler into SS disciplinary offences. It was the supreme authority on all matters of law managing the discipline and liaison between the SS, the State and the Party. In control were Gruppenfuhrer Paul Scharfe and later Franz Breithaupt.

- Discipline of the Code of Laws to which every SS member was subject.
- SS and Police Courts and Judiciary.

- Penal Camps for convicted SS and Police Offenders.

Directly below these centrally run Departments in Berlin, were the SS Regional bases or *Oberabschnitte'* (Oa.) which started at five regions in 1932 and grew to seventeen regions in 1944 with another six established in occupied territories. Each one was commanded by an Obergruppenführer, or the closest rank to it (Gruppenfuhrer or Brigadefuhrer) and they acted as Himmler's representative at military level and also the senior SS and Police Commander over everything that happened in that region.

They answered directly to Himmler as well as to the other seven central offices on matters pertaining to each department. Each region had its own Regional SS Headquarters which was staffed by full time officers along with some additional locally recruited volunteer and part-time officials.

Heydrich's Department - The Security Police

Up until September 1939, the Security Police were in two different groups; The Nazi Party and the German State. The Nazi Party force was called the *'Sicherheitsdienst'* which simply meant 'Security Service' and was known for short as the SD under the wing of the SS.

The State Security Police was called the *'Sicherheitspolizei'* and was known as the 'Sipo' which meant 'Security Police'. This was a general term that referred to both the ordinary 'Criminal Police' called the *'Kriminalpolizei'* and known as the 'Kripo'; along with the newest force created called the *'Geheime-Staatspolizei'*, or 'Political Police', which was shortened to the now infamous 'Gestapo'.

In 1939 all three of these Police groups were amalgamated into a new *'Staatsschutzkorps'* Programme and were made subdivisions of one single brand new SS Department called the *'Reichssicherheitshauptamt'* which meant 'Reich Central Security Office', known as the RSHA.

The Gestapo was originally commanded by Goring, who set it up in 1933. It was merged into the SD and Police Offices in 1939 when Himmler was made overall Commander in place of Goring. The Gestapo alone had more than 600 members and a budget of forty million Reichsmarks. Their Commander was a man called Heinrich Muller who you may have heard referred to as *'Gestapo Muller'*. This Office had only one task; to find and remove any enemies of the Nazi regime.

Heydrich had his own internal personnel team dealing with Security Police and SD which was led by Gruppenfuhrer Dr Werner Best who was also Heydrich's Deputy until 1940, followed by Bruno Streckenbach and Erwin Schultz.

Another Office was Heydrich's administration team which actually ran the RSHA and had three different Heads during the time it was in existence; first was Best, then Rudolf Siegert and finally Josef Spacil.

The SD 'Home Office' was mainly an information collating service looking at data coming in about counter espionage and politics and was managed by Otto Ohlendorf, an SD Officer given the task of managing the 'Spheres of Life' Office. Heydrich tasked him with vetting reports coming in from agents all over the Reich (and there were thousands of them – details further on) known as the *'Meldungen aus dem Reich'* which means 'Reports from the Reich'. These reports were apparently (according to the history books) all sent to Himmler to keep him in touch with what the 'man on the street' was thinking. I can't believe they were all sent to Himmler; he had much more to do than re-read countless reports from a junior officers. Having experience of working within a major Local Government Department, I would assume that Ohlendorf would prepare a summary report that outlined key themes, situations that needed to be watched, and any areas of crisis that would need some kind of more immediate action.

Interestingly, during 1942, while Heydrich was away in Prague, Himmler asked Ohlendorf to stop doing this, and to concentrate on researching how Germany would rule after the War. My assumption from such an instruction is that Himmler was no longer concerned with these insignificant views from the Reich, since Germany seemed almost ready to complete its total domination of Europe and looked undefeatable at that point. Himmler would need to think about administrative processes that could come into force as soon as the War ended, and with access to all the top brains in Germany, recruited straight into the Officer ranks of the SS from University, he could set them the task of working out how to keep order once the war had ended.

Ohlendorf then set up a group called the 'Reichsgruppe-Industrie' with representatives of Germany's top businesses to study exactly how Germany would rule after the war. They set up their own research foundation called the '*Institut fur Industrieforshung'* to plan the post war arrangements. Founder members of this were Switzerland, France, Belgium, Holland, and Luxemburg who eventually turned out to be the founding members of the Common Market. Their research was not completed until the end of 1945 and by then, things looked very different to the origins of the programme started three years prior in 1942. In January 1945 Professor Ludwig Erhard; who ended up as Chancellor for post war Western Germany and Economics Advisor to the US Military Government; announced their final agreed policy which was called The Social Market Economy and eventually resulted in our existing European Union.

The Kripo Office dealt with all common crime and its Commander Gruppenfuhrer Arthur Nebe was hanged in 1945 for his part in the attempt to assassinate Hitler during 1944.

Another separate Office within the RSHA was the SD. An

intelligence-gathering service with staff based in all non-German Countries. This Office was in charge of all organised espionage in enemy territories and was headed by Heinz Jost; then by the more renowned Walter Schellenberg.

The seventh Office in Heydrich's department was for Ideological Research with Prof. Dr Franz Six in charge, to find out about public opinion on various subjects. This office worked alongside the Ministry of Propaganda to monitor the success or weakness of each propaganda campaign.

The RSHA activities were wide ranging and included the James Bond style rescue of Mussolini from his kidnappers by Otto Skorzeny and his team of Commandos with their dangerous crash landing on a mountain top. That action was directly given by Hitler to Himmler, and Skorzeny was summoned to Himmler's personal Office to receive it – nothing whatsoever to do with Heydrich, even though he was Head of the RSHA Services.

The other RSHA operations were mainly anti-terrorism, such as seizing political files from occupied countries. The Gestapo took over the Customs Service, Border Controls and dealt with smuggling. It was a very complex setup and Heydrich's international standing was recognised by his nomination in 1940 to the post of President of Interpol.

Working within the RSHA; and therefore theoretically under Heydrich; were a large number of quite senior ranks which Robin Lumsden quotes in his excellent book: 'A Collectors Guide to the Allgemeine SS' as being:

- 714 Sturmbannfuhrers (24% of the total 3006)
- 240 Obersturmbannfuhrers (20% of the total 1199)
- 95 Standartenfuhrers (15% of the total 623)

- 41 Oberfuhrers (15% of the total 274)
- 31 Brigadefuhrers (11% of the total 270)
- 7 Gruppenfuhrers (7% of the total 94)
- 4 Obergruppenfuhrers (4% of the total 91) by 1945, previous statistic was 77 as at 1942
- 65,000 junior Security Police Officials across Europe and Russia
- 100,000 local informers.

I make that a grand total number of staff working under the RSHA as: 166,132 men in total. That adds up to 1,132 Officers and 165,000 Policemen and Officials. If you divide the number of Officers into the number of men, that gives a very rough average of 145 men per Officer to Command. It certainly wasn't worked out like that though, as the higher ranks would look after a certain number of lower ranks along with their men, but it gives a quick guide to the size of the operation in just this one of the eight SS Departments.

It also reveals how far away Heydrich actually was from the action on the ground, and he would be relying on reports coming in from the commanders of the commanders, of the commanders, of the men. Another thing to consider would be the lack of transportation available for these reports to be brought in with any speed. Trains were all used by the Military and then only under specific permission from Hitler. Trucks had decreasing supplies of fuel for internal use, and the size of the countries involved meant that a report from Latvia to Berlin, would need to travel 2,000km or around 2 to 3 solid days of driving each way in a car that did a maximum of 50 miles an hour, on single track roads, needing to carry their own fuel on board in cans – if they could get hold of any – and then negotiate their way around or through enemy lines, possible bombing by air, snipers, and land mines. Not a reliable and watertight system, which I imagine would irk Heydrich if reports were late or didn't turn up at all.

Was there a functioning postal system? I doubt it, and this would have put confidential information at risk of capture. Telephone lines were mostly cut, Radio signals had to be brief and coded, so if each Officer from each area managed to send a report just once a week, that is a huge amount of reading for one man to do. Again, I would assume that Heads of Staff would summarise them, and submit them to Heydrich as a brief overview. Anything more just couldn't be practical. I wonder if any studies have been completed on how the German Command structure was enabled to send reports back to Berlin. Or how information was passed from occupied territories back to Berlin? And how long it took? And how accurate and detailed they were? I would like to find out more about this process from someone who has a living memory of it. It is easy for us to disregard these important details in our current age of modern technology with Wi-Fi, the internet, and Smartphones; but these are critical pieces of information when considering who made which decision, when and why.

A very small paragraph in Robin Lumsden's book revealed another interesting fact:

During the period 1940-1942 a large number of conscripts were transferred to 30 newly created Independent Police Regiments comprising 100 battalions of 500 men. They were organised and equipped on a Military basis and served as Security troops in all occupied countries. [It was not until] In February 1943 they were officially designated as SS Police Regiments and they subsequently gained a reputation for extreme brutality and fanatical loyalty to Himmler and the Nazi Regime.

In 1942 Himmler was made responsible for all counter guerrilla operations and he appointed SS Obergruppenführer Erich von dem Bach as his Head of Anti-Partisan Units.

An estimated 15,000 Latvians and 13,000 Lithuanians served in 64 other battalions across the Eastern Front from Ostland to Yugoslavia, while the Ukraine alone supplied 70,000 volunteers to staff a further 71 battalions. In Croatia pro-Nazi's set up a regimental sized Einsatzstaffel based on the Allgemeine SS and dressed in quasi SS uniforms that worked to the local Regional Commanders, and ultimately took their orders from Himmler through his HSSPf's.

Interesting news, as many other books cite Heydrich as the instigator of these activities. It is possible that he had no knowledge of these operations at all while he was away and busy managing the situation in Prague. I assume that these 98,000 men were in addition to the previous numbers of German SD (Police, Gestapo and Kripo) staff. All of this shows the complications of the SS Command structure where there were many different Chiefs working with different teams on different agendas, in different ways and under different sets of Orders. Not only that, but it changed from one Commander to another, depending on the date, the activity, and the purpose.

This means that although Heydrich was named as the Head of the RSHA, it is perilous to make any assumption about who was actually in Command of each piece of the puzzle at any one time, and whether a basic instruction to remove any enemies of the State, could have been taken out of all proportion by the untrained Anti-Partisan groups that spoke entirely different languages, thousands of kilometres away.

It reminds me of a party game called 'pinning the tail on the donkey' while wearing a blindfold.

Chapter Twenty Three
𝔗𝔥𝔢 '𝔈𝔵𝔢𝔠𝔲𝔱𝔦𝔳𝔢'

In the last Chapter's snapshot of the SS as an Organisation, we now have a picture of what Heydrich was commanding. The structure of his department, its roles and responsibilities, and the practical difficulties of being able to do this effectively during a fast moving War, over a large geographical spread.

Now let's consider who he commanded. We already know their roles, but what type of people were they and how might this affect the way they perceived Heydrich's personality? How would be best to engage these types of men? What were the difficulties and risks for Heydrich? How might this affect his behaviour to them, and their behaviour to him?

Many of the history books mention that the SD had a membership of intelligent and relatively young Germans, so I looked for evidence of the Education, the average age, and most prevalent family backgrounds of these SS members, and found some interesting facts.

Bernard Rust, Reich Minister for Education set out the clear purpose of Education in Nazi Germany in 1936 in his writing:

The chief purpose of the school is to train human beings in the doctrine that the state is more important than the individual, that individuals must be willing and ready to sacrifice themselves for nation and Fuhrer.

(Engelmann, German Education, p. 79. The excerpt appeared in a new teacher's manual Erziehung und Unterricht in der heren Schule Berlin 1936).

I discovered a Thesis submitted for a Doctorate of Philosophy, in the School of Slavonic and Eastern European Studies at the University of

London in 1976 by Gunnar Charles Boehnert called: A SOCIOGRAPHY OF THE SS OFFICER CORPS, 1925-1939. A little early for my Review based in 1942, but we already noticed in the last Chapter that the majority of SS members in the higher ranks, had been there for an average of eight to ten years, so his findings provided the hard evidence I needed:

This quantitative study of the SS Officer Corps was designed to discover who in German society joined the SS between its inception in 1925 and the outbreak of war in 1939. The study is based on data contained in 5,250 SS officer personnel files which were selected from 61,340 personnel files housed at the Berlin Document Centre.

If a comparison is made between the educational distribution of the sampled SS Fuhrerkorps [or Officer Groups] *with that of German society one must conclude that the educated stratum of society was heavily overrepresented in the officer corps of the Schutzstaffeln* [The full term for the SS] *prior to 1939. According to an official survey conducted in 1962, 82% of the German population had only an elementary school education.* (Institut for Demoskopie, Jahrbuch 1958-1964 Allensbach 1965).

Around the turn of the century 90% of the German population had only an Elementary school education. (Engelmann, German Education, p. 11) *When it comes to the university graduate category, the discrepancy between the percentage of graduates in the SS Officer Korps and the percentage of university graduates found in German society is even more starkly revealed. Whereas 30.1% of the sampled Fuhrerkorps [SS Officers] were university graduates, only 2.5% of German society in 1962 had completed a course of studies at a recognized university.* (Institut für Demoskopie, Jahrbuch, p. 4. See also, Dahrendorf, Gesellschaft, p. 97.) *In the light of these data one has to conclude that the SS during the pre-war years was able to attract a considerable percentage of the educated 'elite' of Germany.*

Across the SS as a total, there was a very high percentage of University Graduates and Doctorates, with the SD having the highest percentage of University Graduates within its ranks.

According to Boehnert: *That the security service of the SS was a collecting point for intellectuals of all sorts has been recognized for some time. Hohne was of the opinion that the SD attracted a group of young National Socialist intellectuals whose object was both '... professional advancement and the improvement of National Socialism.' Thus the SD soon became the refuge for National Socialism's most intelligent men.* (Hohne, The Order, p. 211) *After 1933 the percentage of officers with a university education rises to 44% during 1933 to 1934, and then levels off at about 34% during 1934 to 1939.*

Here are some statistics from his 270 page Thesis that show these incredible numbers separated into the SS Divisions of; Allgemeine, SD and Verfugungstruppe (or 'Waffen' SS, the fighting section of the SS):

- Allgemeine SS: 37.9% were Graduates, with 24.5% holding Doctorates.
- Waffen SS: 2.1% were Graduates, with 1.7% holding Doctorates.
- Sicherheitsdienst (SD): 36.9% were Graduates, with 20.2% holding Doctorates.
- Source: Unpublished Documentary Material - SS Officer Personnel Files - Berlin Document Centre. Records of SS officers for the post-1945 period. Dokummentationszentrum des B. J. V. N., Vienna. Cited as Wiesenthal Archive.

These statistics also evidence the differences in the social makeup of some of the various branches of the SS. The SD attracted an outrageous number of university graduates, and it was Heydrich's happy task to 'manage' them all.

This puts a whole new slant on the history book comments about 'competitiveness' between the Heads of Departments, and between the Officers themselves. I imagine a lot of 'one-upmanship' took place in their zeal to win favour and achieve promotion. They would also be prone to long-winded academic report writing and rambling academic explanations, I imagine that would annoy Heydrich to distraction. This is an opinionated group that would be difficult to keep in check and on-message. Heydrich's management style would need to be: analytical, logical, diagnostic, impersonal, systematic, critical, investigative, organised, disciplined, assertive and so on.

It certainly sounds like an accurate description of Heydrich.

I did some searching on www.*PersonalityPage.com*, *a website about Psychological Type, created by the view from the shoulders of Carl G. Jung, and the work of Isabel Briggs Myers, creator of the Myers-Briggs Type Indicator (MBTI)...* and found an exact match for Heydrich:

ENTJ - The Executive
Assertive and outspoken - they are driven to lead. Excellent ability to understand difficult organizational problems and create solid solutions. Intelligent and well-informed, they usually excel at public speaking. They value knowledge and competence, and usually have little patience with inefficiency or disorganization.

Here is the full description by Myers Briggs of this personality type, and it seems to match Heydrich perfectly. I have highlighted key phrases in bold:

Portrait of an ENTJ - Extraverted iNtuitive Thinking Judging (Extraverted Thinking with Introverted Intuition)

The Executive

As an ENTJ, your **primary mode of living is focused externally, where you deal with things rationally and logically**. Your secondary mode is internal, where you take things in primarily via your intuition.

ENTJs are natural born leaders. They live in a world of possibilities where they see all sorts **challenges to be surmounted, and they want to be the ones responsible for surmounting them**. They have a **drive for leadership**, which is well-served by their **quickness to grasp complexities**, their **ability to absorb a large amount of impersonal information, and their quick and decisive judgments**. They are 'take charge' people.

ENTJs are **very career-focused**, and fit into the corporate world quite naturally. They are **constantly scanning their environment for potential problems** which they can turn into solutions. They generally **see things from a long-range perspective**, and are usually **successful at identifying plans to turn problems around - especially problems of a corporate nature**. ENTJs are usually successful in the business world, because they are so driven to leadership. They're **tireless in their efforts on the job, and driven to visualize where an organization is headed**. For these reasons, they are natural **corporate leaders**.

There is not **much room for error** in the world of the ENTJ. They **dislike to see mistakes repeated, and have no patience with inefficiency**. They may become quite **harsh when their patience is tried** in these respects, because they are **not naturally tuned in to people's feelings, and more than likely don't believe that they should tailor their judgments in consideration for people's feelings**. ENTJs, like many types, have **difficulty seeing things from outside their own perspective**. Unlike other types, ENTJs naturally **have little patience** with people who do not see things the same way as the ENTJ. The ENTJ needs to consciously work on recognizing the value of other people's opinions, as well as the value of being sensitive towards people's feelings. In the absence of this awareness, the ENTJ will be a forceful, intimidating and overbearing individual. This may be a real problem for the ENTJ, who may be deprived of important information and collaboration from others. In their personal world, it can make some ENTJs overbearing as spouses or parents.

The ENTJ has a tremendous amount of personal power and presence which will work for them as a force towards achieving their goals. However, this personal power is also an agent of alienation and self-aggrandizement, which the ENTJ would do well to avoid.

ENTJs are very forceful, decisive individuals. They make decisions quickly, and are quick to verbalize their opinions and decisions to the rest of the world. The An ENTJ who has developed in a generally less than ideal way may become dictatorial and abrasive - intrusively giving orders and direction without a sound reason for doing so, and without consideration for the people involved.

Although ENTJs are not naturally tuned into other people's feelings, these individuals frequently have very strong sentimental streaks. Often these sentiments are very powerful to the ENTJ, although they will likely hide it from general knowledge, believing the feelings to be a weakness. Because the world of feelings and values is not where the ENTJ naturally functions, they may sometimes make value judgments and hold onto submerged emotions which are ill-founded and inappropriate, and will cause them problems - sometimes rather serious problems.

There's nothing more enjoyable and satisfying to the ENTJ than having a lively, challenging conversation. They especially respect people who are able to stand up to the ENTJ, and argue persuasively

for their point of view. There aren't too many people who will do so, however, because the ENTJ **is a very forceful and dynamic presence who has a tremendous amount of self-confidence and excellent verbal communication skills.** Even the most confident individuals may experience moments of self-doubt when debating a point with an ENTJ.

ENTJs **want their home to be** beautiful, well-furnished, and **efficiently run.** They're likely to place much emphasis **on their children being well-educated and structured,** to desire a congenial and devoted relationship with their spouse. At home, the ENTJ needs to be in charge as much as he or she does in their career. Because the ENTJ is **primarily focused on their careers,** some ENTJs **have a problem with being constantly absent from home, physically or mentally.**

The ENTJ has many gifts which make it possible for them to **have a great deal of personal power,** if they don't forget to remain balanced in their lives. They are **assertive, innovative, long-range thinkers with an excellent ability to translate theories and possibilities into solid plans of action.** They are usually **tremendously forceful personalities, and have the tools to accomplish whatever goals they set out for.**

This character profile could easily have been based on Heydrich. Here is a snippet from a letter written by his wife, Lina Heydrich to Jean Vaughan, December 12, 1951, which provides the evidence for the Myers Briggs character, from the only person who knew him intimately, both at work and at home:

TODAY I am going to tell you something about the character of my husband.

The most characteristic trait was that he was a man of few words. He never talked about something or discussed something [just] for the love of talk. Every word had to have a concrete meaning, or purpose, had to hit the point. Therefore he never said even one word more than necessary.

In the morning, while being shaved, he worked at the new reports that had come in during the night (we call that 'Akten,' I don't know whether the correct English expression wants perhaps be 'file'). After breakfast during the 30 minutes ride to the office this reading was continued. He never let his staff had even a minute's rest, it was very hard and strenuous for them.

During lunch... conferences. Lunch was taken in a small dining room in the office. Very often people who had to report on something were ordered to take part in this luncheons. But woe betide him who tried to begin a 'speech'. His own way of expression was the condensed and abbreviated style of telegrams (wires) and in this language he expected the reports, bare of every unnecessary word. If someone did not know that, he was sure to be interrupted after a few minutes by the words, 'der langen Rede kurzer Sinn ist –' i.e., 'that's what you wanted to say, was it not?' (I think the first words of this has been translated into 'the final analysis is...

It could also be translated into: The final solution is...

We all know what that has been turned into the 'acronym' for. But is this where it originally came from?

Chapter Twenty Four
Gathering Intelligence

How did Heydrich manage to keep up with all these academics and stay one step ahead of them? Was he an uneducated and uncultured beast as many describe him? We have already evidenced that he wasn't a cold unfeeling bastard, in his Myers Briggs description; so what was his social background? And how did he compare with the highly educated and sharp thinking men he commanded?

One of the first things he did in Prague was to reopen the German Concert Hall, and rename Smetana Square in honour of Mozart, so music was clearly important to him. They say that being a skilled musician is characteristic of an ability to learn languages and Heydrich was actually an expert in both. He was fluent in English, French, Russian, and obviously German; and spoke a little Czech as we heard from Anna who used to work for him. He played many instruments to String Quartet standard, and was also a fluent music reader. Little is said about either of these skills in the general history books, but you can find a line or two that makes a brief mention of playing the violin or cello among the derisory comments about him being supposedly socially inept, an unfeeling beast, and a Court Martialled Naval Officer.

Heydrich's childhood was in a cultured environment of classical music, with middle-class parents and a Celebrity Father and Grandfather; and it certainly seems a strange journey from the world of Opera and string quartets, to his interview for a job with Himmler.

He was born in the Halle Conservatorium on March 7th 1904; a music school in Halle, where his Father was Headmaster and his Mother, Elizabeth Krantz, was a piano and singing Teacher. He was given the full name of Reinhard Tristan Eugen Heydrich and the middle name Eugen, was named after his maternal Grandfather who was Professor Dr Eugen Krantz, Director of the Royal [Music] Conservatorium at Dresden, which even today, boasts one of the world's finest Symphony Orchestra's.

His Father, Richard Bruno Heydrich, was a popular and well-respected Composer and Musician – what we would today call a 'Celebrity', who named his son Reinhard after the name of the hero in an Opera he wrote and performed nine years previously in Koln during 1895.

Reinhard had a sister, Maria who was three years older and a brother, Heinz, who was born the year after him in 1905. In the photograph below, Heinz, in uniform, is walking in his brother's funeral procession after the ceremony in the Reichskanzlei, en-route to the cemetery alongside senior SS Generals. In the first row behind Himmler is: (left to right) Ley, Karl Frank, Rochus Milch, Joseph (Sepp) Dietrich, Heinz Heydrich, Daluege and Frick. Heinz bears a strong resemblance to his younger brother.

His paternal Grandfather Karl Julius Reinhold Heydrich was also involved in professional music making although not as a performer. He was employed by the famous Pianoforte maker in Braunschweig called Grotrian-Steinweg as an expert cabinet maker and presumably made the wooden bodies for their pianos.

No surprise then that Heydrich was an excellent musician who played woodwind, brass and stringed instruments. I'm sure he was surrounded by them and was put into lessons while his parents were teaching to keep him out of mischief as a small boy. His favourite instrument was the Cello and he proposed to his wife Lina after playing her a piece on the violin. Interestingly, this is the one fact that most history books agree on, that Heydrich was an accomplished musician.

The importance of Classical music in Germany and the status this imparts to those working as professionals within it, whether as musicians, teachers, or composers is an important point to note. The Music Schools known as 'Conservatoria' carried the status of a top class private school, like Eton or Winchester in England, so being the grandson of the Dresden Royal Conservatorium Director and son of the Halle Conservatorium Headmaster would have given Heydrich a very privileged childhood.

Even today, classical music in Germany is still unparalleled worldwide. There is something like 130 professional, publicly financed symphony and chamber orchestras performing in Germany that attract professional musicians from all over the world. There are around 80 Theatre Orchestras playing operas, operettas and musicals in municipal and state theatres, like the opera houses in Berlin, Hamburg, Stuttgart and Munich. Around thirty internationally acclaimed Concert Orchestras performing in concert halls; like the Berlin Philharmonic, the Munich Philharmonic, the Bamberg Symphony Orchestra, the Konzerthausorchester, and the Leipzig Gewandhaus Orchestra. As well as around seven publicly funded Chamber Orchestras, like the Stuttgart Chamber Orchestra, the Württemberg Chamber Orchestra in Heilbronn and the Munich Chamber Orchestra; and about a dozen Radio Orchestras belonging to the 'Consortium of public-law broadcasting corporations of the Federal Republic of Germany', Funded by state or local subsidies and from radio and TV licence fees.

Germany's considerable orchestral history dates back to the 15th century with traditional orchestras, such as the Dresden Staatskapelle, the Weimar Staatskapelle and the Mecklenburg Staatskapelle in Schwerin. This gives you an indication of the historical importance and status of Heydrich's childhood and family background.

Time to bust another myth then....

MYTH BUSTED
Heydrich was an uneducated
and uncultured Beast

Another of the qualities of a talented musician should be noted. If you ask any professional musician what sets them apart from an average musician, they will all give you the same answer, emotion.

It is impossible to play that many instruments to that standard without having any emotion. So here is even more evidence that Heydrich was not without feelings. But don't take my word for this; here are some quotes from some very well-known musicians who give credence to my drawing this conclusion:

- *If a composer could say what he had to say in words he would not bother trying to say it in music.* Gustav Mahler
- *Music is the poetry of the air.* Richter

- *Music is the mediator between the spiritual and the sensual life.* Ludwig van Beethoven
- *I have my own particular sorrows, loves, delights; and you have yours. But sorrow, gladness, yearning, hope, love, belong to all of us, in all times and in all places. Music is the only means whereby we feel these emotions in their universality.* H.A. Overstreet
- *Music expresses that which cannot be said and on which it is impossible to be silent.* Victor Hugo
- *Music expresses feeling and thought, without language; it was below and before speech, and it is above and beyond all words.* Robert G. Ingersoll
- *Music is the literature of the heart; it commences where speech ends.* Alphonse de Lamartine
- *When words leave off, music begins.* Heinrich Heine

I think this final quote sums it up perfectly:
- *Music is the shorthand of emotion.* Leo Tolstoy

Heydrich's accomplishments were not just confined to music and languages. He was also good at sport, and his competitive nature led him to a discipline of practice in swimming, tennis, fencing and horse riding to make sure that he would win at every match, game and competition.

It is very interesting to notice that all the sports he chose, were not team games. They were all single player sports, where winning or losing was entirely his responsibility. They were also sports where mastering technical skills were paramount to being able to 'play' and the ability to win. None of them relied on anyone else's performance, confidence or motivation.

Heydrich did not like losing at all. This is widely known in his

Olympic Gold for Germany in the Fencing Team at the Berlin Olympics during the War. Fencing can only be won with a precise and exacting knowledge of the rules, perfection of movements through disciplined practice, and thinking skills that will out-manoeuvre an opponent. He displayed insight into his competitors, mastery of rules and extreme confidence to implement them. All of these are early traits of his future management style and military strategies.

Heydrich appeared to have a perfect middle-class 'Prep School' style background with his parents directing his schooling towards becoming a Doctor of Music at the University in Bonn. So what happened to change that course?

Heydrich was fourteen years old in 1918 when the First World War ended and Germany fell to pieces with the abdication of the Kaiser. Life must have seemed hopeless with huge inflation and fewer people with the ability to pay for luxuries like music lessons or concerts. He may have felt let down by the adult world, betrayed by the Politicians and disappointed with Germany. As a sixteen year old teenager who was used to winning; watching your whole country loose its morale and self-respect could have been devastating. The world of classical music would seem dull and totally insignificant from then on. He would want to change the world and Germany's fortunes.

A book called *'Reinhard Heydrich Assassination!' by Cowdery and Vodenka* states that at the age of 16 Heydrich joined the Freikorps.

(After 1918, this term was used for the paramilitary organizations that sprang up around Germany as soldiers returned in defeat from World War I. They were the key Weimar paramilitary group active during that time. Many German veterans felt disconnected from civilian life, and joined a Freikorps in search of stability within a military structure. Others, angry at their sudden, apparently inexplicable defeat,

joined up in an effort to put down communist uprisings http://en.wikipedia.org/wiki/Freikorps)

This would have been 1920 and the Freikorps was apparently disbanded in March 1920 after an unsuccessful attempt to overthrow the German Government. Possibly he joined them before 1920, although I can't see a paramilitary organisation allowing a fifteen year old to join. Possibly it was between January and March of 1920, but then two months would not be enough to influence the young Heydrich. Or possibly, the organisation carried on in some form after it was supposed to have been officially disbanded. However this would have been his first lesson in how to apply a forceful military solution to change the fortunes of a downtrodden Germany.

I can't imagine Heydrich's parent's being happy about him being a member, but at 16 he would be testing out his independence and his parents had an important School to run, pupils to teach and may not have had the time to worry too much about it.

There is a historical record of a huge ceremony held thirteen years later on the 9th of November 1933, where the Freikorps leaders symbolically presented their old battle flags to Hitler's SA and SS as a sign of allegiance to their new authority, the Nazi state; so it must have carried on in some form until then. Some of the prominent Nazi's had certainly been members - Himmler, Rohm, Hess, and Erhardt to name four.

In 1921 at the age of seventeen, Heydrich became friends with Reiner Thiess, a Naval Cadet who he met through his then girlfriend's brother and stayed in touch with over the next year until his Graduation in May or June 1922. Within three months of graduating Heydrich was off, on his first adventure, visiting his naval cadet friend in Kiel for 2 months, hoping for a chance of a new and exciting life in the Navy and to see if Thiess could help.

His friend took Heydrich aboard the Naval Cruiser and showed him around. During this tour of the ship, he introduced Heydrich to the man who would then change his life for ever. A man every bit as exciting and adventurous as Heydrich wanted to be. A man who would inspire him, and eventually become his lifelong and only close friend.

A man who was a real-life James Bond, after an 'Odysseus-like' escape from capture by the British near the Falkland Islands in World War 1, his Naval cruiser was captured at Quiriquina Island and he was imprisoned by the British. He escaped by stealing a small boat and managed to row to the mainland without being seen, then stealing a horse and riding for days and days across the Andes to get to Buenos Aires where, using his fluent Spanish, he somehow got himself a new identity in the name of Reed Rosas with a fake Chilean Passport and onto a Dutch ship headed for Rotterdam. Eventually, months later, he arrived back in Germany.

This man was now the Lieutenant Commander aboard the cruiser 'Berlin' and his name was Wilhelm Franz Canaris.

Chapter Twenty Five
A Life on the Ocean Wave

In the space of three weeks, Heydrich was playing in the Sunday evening Chamber Music sessions hosted by Canaris' wife, Erika and accompanying her (singing or playing Piano) on his violin. It turned out that before she had married Canaris, Erika had been a music student of Heydrich's Grandfather, Eugen Krantz at the Royal Conservatorium in Dresden. It was a small world, even in those days.

During the weeks he was staying with Thiess, the young teenage Heydrich, looking for adventure and a solution to Germany's deep depression, would have been heavily influenced by Canaris. Here was an exciting man of action, successful in battle, decorated with medals, enjoying a good income, high status role, good standard of living, and a beautiful and musical wife. It wouldn't take much persuasion from Canaris, (if indeed there was any), to convince him that a career in the Navy could offer much more achievement for him than a life as a Doctor of Music. Especially during the existing financial hardships that Germany was experiencing. As inflation rose more and more people were on the brink of poverty and music lessons were not on everyone's list of essential requirements.

With so much skill and talent as a musician Reinhard' parents objected strongly to his desire for a career in the Navy but, despite their objections, in 1922 at the age of eighteen, he went ahead and signed up as a naval cadet in the Reichsmarine at Kiel Naval Base. He spent the following nine years working fervently and passionately (another example of feelings and emotions) learning three very difficult languages fluently; English, French and Russian; while doing his job so well, that he rocketed up the ladder of promotions at an incredible rate: He was sent to Officer training after only two years as a Midshipman, and promotions followed regularly every two years. It took Heydrich just eight years to reach the status of a Chief Officer, or Lieutenant:

- 1922: Naval Cadet at Kiel Naval Base age 18, then a Midshipman.
- 1924: Senior Midshipman. Officer training at Murwik Naval College. age 20
- 1926: Ensign. Signals Officer on Battleship Schleswig-Holstein, Flagship of the Fleet, age 22
- 1298: Sub-Lieutenant (Oberleutnant zur See) in Naval Intelligence for Admiral Erich Raeder in Kiel, age 24
- 1930 Chief Signals Officer and now fluent in English, French and Russian, age 26.

During 1930 after a fleeting relationship with the daughter of Otto Schlueter, a high powered Company Director of I G Farben, he met Lina von Osten at a Rowing Club Ball, and after a whirlwind romance, they became engaged. Lina was nineteen years old and the daughter of a Schoolmaster from Fehmarn Island, an island in the Baltic Sea off the eastern coast of Schleswig-Holstein, Germany, just eighteen kilometres south of the Danish island of Lolland. It belongs to the district of Ostholstein. A beautiful place that boasts 2,200 hours of sun every year, endless stretches of natural beaches along seventy eight kilometres of coastline, picturesque freshwater lakes and rugged cliffs. Today, Fehmarn is an idyllic water sport holiday destination.

Lina returned there after the War and ran a Guesthouse until the 1950's, one of the only top Nazi wives to be granted a full State Pension until she died. At nineteen years old Lina was a fanatical member of the NSDAP and had just returned from the 1929 Nurnberg Rally, full of praise for Hitler and what he stood for.

In early 1931 everything went wrong for Heydrich which resulted in him leaving the Navy, there are many different stories about what happened. It seems that his previous girlfriend discovered that she was pregnant, and named Heydrich as the father. Her outraged father, Otto Schlueter, demanded that Heydrich marry his daughter. Heydrich was then already engaged to Lina and did not want to break his promise of marriage, so he told Lina what had happened, and asked her if she would prefer to end the engagement. Lina did not. She promised to continue to marry Heydrich, and Heydrich then told Otto Schlueter that he would not break off his engagement, and refused to marry his daughter.

Schlueter was incredulous. As Director of an industrial giant of a company he was not used to being told 'no', and here was a young man standing his ground against him, and refusing his demands, point blank. Schlueter had a lot of powerful friends in both civilian and military circles, and apparently, was causing an amount of gossip about Heydrich and standards in the Navy. It is believed that Schlueter spoke directly to Admiral Raeder and demanded that he force Heydrich to marry his daughter.

The stories then say that Admiral Raeder either *'Court-Martialled'* Heydrich, or took him to a *'Court of Honour'* charged with *'conduct unbecoming to an officer and gentleman'* and then sacked him ungraciously from the Navy.

I don't think that was the case at all, I think this is another myth invented to bolster the 'evil uneducated beast' brigade stories and here are my reasons:

1. No paperwork has ever been brought to light of either of those Court cases and everything in the Navy would have had a prescript set of procedures to be adhered to in either of these instances.

2. No official 'charges' have ever been found in Navy documents, and there would have been strict procedures for needing to 'Charge' a ranked Senior Officer.

3. Heydrich had led an exemplary career thus far, with no possible reasons for the Navy to get rid of him that affected his naval duties. Not drunk on duty, no brawling with other men, no insubordination to senior officers - nothing.

4. Admiral Raeder went on to attain the highest possible naval rank - that of Grossadmiral (Grand Admiral), and by all accounts doesn't seem to be the type of man who could easily be bullied or told what to do with his own men – not least by an overbearing capitalist civilian, who knew nothing of Naval procedure or Military duty.

5. Raeder would not have wanted to lose a good Chief Officer for something that happened outside of the Navy, an insignificant civilian matter.

6. I seriously doubt whether the Navy had any authority at all to Court Martial Heydrich, for a civilian accusation against him by an ex-girlfriends father.

I conclude that what is much more likely to have happened, is a private conversation between Raeder and Heydrich to try and resolve the matter, where Heydrich explained that he could not possibly dishonour the engagement to his Fiancée Lina. I imagine that Admiral Raeder would then sadly but compassionately, ask Heydrich if he wanted to leave of his own accord, for 'Political reasons', to settle the issue, and the Navy would enable this to happen quietly and without dishonour.

This certainly seems to be what happened, as in future years Heydrich always stated that he left the Navy for 'Political reasons'. Here we can see an early example of Heydrich's tenacious obligation to fulfil his duty, even in the face of an influential man, who could cost Heydrich his job and future career. Still he stood firmly by his principles, his duty and his honour.

MYTH BUSTED
Heydrich was Charged with
'Conduct unbecoming to an Officer and gentleman',
Court Martialled and Discharged from the Navy

So in April 1931 at the age of 26, Heydrich was suddenly out of work, out of the Navy, and out of a promising career, all for the sake of his high principles, his sense of duty and his personal honour at all costs. Let us not fail to mention here, his love for Lina.

Lina encouraged him to join the Nazi Party and to look for a role in the ever growing ranks of the NSDAP, and on the 14th of June 1931, he was interviewed for a job by Heinrich Himmler, Reichsfuhrer-SS.

Himmler had decided to establish an internal Police-within-the-Police service; an intelligence service called the *Sicherheitsdienst* eventually known as the SD, and wanted someone with experience in intelligence communication methods to lead it. Heydrich was perfect. Young, highly educated, experienced in communication methods, experience of senior officer status, fluent in three languages, and with a confidence and sporting prowess that Himmler wanted from all his SS Officers. Heydrich was given the rank of Sturmfuhrer-SS equivalent to a Lance Corporal and started work for Himmler on October 1st 1931.

The year of 1931 continued to be momentous for Heydrich, when two months later he married Lina on 26th December, in the Church of a small village called Grossenbrode; a municipality in the district of Ostholstein, in Schleswig-Holstein, Germany. It is situated on the Baltic Sea coast, opposite the Island of Fehmarn, where Lina lived, and was probably the Church for the Island.

Little did Heydrich know then, that within four years, he would be reunited with his old Mentor Canaris, and responsible for getting him a new job, as Commander in Chief of the German Ministry of Defence in Berlin.

Chapter Twenty Six
Canaris... Friend or Foe?

Having evidenced some of the facts about Heydrich's background and accidental journey into the SS, you may begin to wonder whether some of the stories about him are describing a completely different person. In lots of ways, the 'Doctor Evil' type of character may now seem totally incongruent with his family background; social status, education, language skills, sense of duty and principles; although there have been many films made and books written about him for pure entertainment purposes rather than for their accurate historical value. In a similar way, the paraphrased statements about him that appear in every book alongside his name, are an easy way for their writers to 'not rock any boats' by assuming that the writer of the book before had researched and established the validity of his chosen adjectives. Look in any book and you will see them.

Here is one example: *'Canaris and Heydrich, who shared a mutual love of riding and of music, sometimes dined together en-famille. The cold blooded killer Heydrich was also an accomplished violinist and he often played for Canaris' wife.'*

Here is another: ***Heydrich: The Face of Evil by Mario R Dederichs***

Page 139 states: *'Heydrich had probably admitted to himself privately that it was his ambition to become the first man of the German Reich. The Fuhrer would then adopt a ceremonial position.'*

We have already dealt with this Myth a few Chapters back...

Also on page 139: *'whilst her husband made his murderous plans, Lina Heydrich was enjoying, 'the most wonderful time of our marriage'. As wife of the Reichsprotektor, the teachers daughter from the lower nobility lived in style in the Prague Fortress and later in Schloss Jungfern- Breschan (Panenske Brezany) 20 kilometres north of the*

Capital. [Prague] 'I am a Princess and live in a fairy-tale land' she enthused.'

We have already heard a first-hand account from Anna, about the total opposite of this paragraph. Lina behaved as a 'Skinflint', a 'good German woman', who wore dirndl, not pretty dresses, and how she removed the beautiful gardens to plant vegetables, etc. I leave you, the reader to make your own decision as to which account is closer to the truth.

There is one story that has defied the historians and appears to have no hard evidence to back it up, and that is the relationship between Heydrich and Canaris in later years, when they both lived in Berlin and worked in what appears to be opposing agencies.

There are many different stories about Heydrich's relationship with Canaris. Some say that they had a competitive relationship and disliked each other, but it is likely that many of these stories were written after Heydrich's death and were based on the anti-Hitler and anti SS activities of Canaris in later years, 1943 and 1944, long after Heydrich had been assassinated.

Canaris clearly disliked the activities of Hitler and the SS during those years, and this is another instance where looking at the relationship between them can only be done up to the point of June 1942. After that time, the actions taken by Canaris and the staff he recruited appeared to be secretly opposed to the RSHA Security forces of the SS, as their activities became more and more extreme. Had Heydrich still been alive at that point, this could well have affected their relationship, but despite Canaris' secret 'anti Hitler' actions in later years, I cannot discover any definitive evidence that the two men had any antagonism between them prior to Heydrich's death in 1942.

Records suggest that Canaris had been a clear supporter of the Nazi regime, as the only possible way to stop the Soviet Union spreading Communism across Europe. It appears that 1938 was a turning point where he began to change his thinking towards Hitler. This in no way evidences any change in the thoughts and feelings that Canaris had towards Heydrich, whom he had become a mentor and father figure to him over the previous sixteen years, since his entry into the Navy as a young enthusiastic cadet of 18 years old.

Certainly the excerpt from a letter written by Lina Heydrich during the 1950's which I include shortly, will confirm this. Lina had no reason to write anything that was untrue, in fact if there had been bad feeling between them, it would have been much easier to believe than their continued close friendship.

Politicians today are known to switch their allegiance to another Party, causing by-elections in their wake, but this doesn't mean that they didn't agree with their old Party's Policies at the time; it just means that on a specific date in time; they changed their minds. Hitler's policies changed dramatically during the later years of the War which caused many of the Wehrmacht Generals to disagree secretly with what was happening. Disagreeing openly would have meant losing their life and therefore having no opportunities to change it. There are transcriptions of secret recordings made between captured German Wehrmacht Generals, who were held as Prisoners of War held at the exclusive Bletchley Park in England that evidence this mind-set change as the War progressed.

By mid-1943, a whole year after Heydrich's death, the outcome of the War was looking much more uncertain for Germany. This led to a group of Army plotters, secretly enabled by members of the Abwehr; to make an assassination attempt on Hitler in the hope that peace could be negotiated with the Allies before the fruitless invasion of Soviet Russia.

The failed bomb plot by Lieutenant Colonel Claus von Stauffenberg on 20th July 1944 has also been noted as being secretly masterminded by Canaris.

It seems that Himmler had suspected that Canaris was acting against Hitler in other matters and insisted that Hitler dismiss him from the Abwehr in February 1944, five months before the bomb plot. His replacement was Walter Schellenberg from the RSHA which then finally brought the command of the Abwehr directly under the Sicherheitsdienst or SD. Shortly after this, Canaris was placed under house arrest. Following the failed 20 July Plot, Himmler discovered that most of the officers involved in the plot, had been friends with Canaris, so Hitler wanted to keep him alive to find out the names of the other conspirators, but when this failed, Hitler approved an order to court-martial him, and send him to Flossenburg concentration camp where Canaris was executed by hanging on 9 April 1945.

Clearly, Hitler's War machine proved too powerful for it to be stopped.

Let's look at when Heydrich and Canaris met up again, and became neighbours in a suburb of Berlin. How did that come about, and what evidence can be found to support the relationship between them?

Back in full time work again, Heydrich threw himself into his new role with enthusiasm and passion. He spent the next two years recruiting agents and officers into the SD who were from similar backgrounds to himself; from middle class families and with excellent academic qualifications. One of his recruits was his younger brother, Heinz Heydrich – hence the photo of Heinz in Uniform at his funeral.

In 1934 Heydrich moved with his wife Lina, from Munich to Berlin as the ever growing SD needed to establish bigger offices in a central location to rebadge itself as the RSHA, with room to spread out into its different Heads of departments, and different areas of responsibility. Since the new RSHA department reported directly to Himmler, it made sense to locate them both together in the same building in Prinz Albrecht Strasse, this formed the central hub of the SS as well as the SD and made it easier for Himmler to have his finger on the pulse of all their activity.

In early 1935, the German Ministry of Defence known as the Abwehr was looking for a new Chief and Heydrich recommended Admiral Wilhelm Canaris for the job. Its name in title was Foreign Affairs and Defence Office of the Armed Forces High Command and it existed as a German military intelligence agency, set up to gather information and intelligence on behalf of the Army (Wehrmacht), Navy (Reichsmarine and then Kreigsmarine) and Air Force (Luftwaffe) for defensive purposes only. This was a condition placed on it by the Allies following World War 1. The Reichsmarine, was the German Imperial Navy during the Weimar Republic until 1935, when it was renamed the Kriegsmarine by Hitler and made into a branch of the Wehrmacht.

Interestingly, The Reichsmarine intelligence staff was merged with the *Abwehr* in 1928. Probably because the Navy had more experience of dealing with foreign intelligence and had better language skills than the internal Army, with little experience of communications with anyone outside of Germany. This used to be headed up by Heydrich until he left the Navy, so if it wasn't for an aggrandised and aggressive capitalist company Director; it could easily have been Heydrich in charge of the Abwehr, or Ministry of Defence and its outlying Embassy offices.

Canaris as its new Chief, reported directly to the High Command of the Armed Forces which was known as the OKW or Oberkommando der Wehrmacht which translates as Over Command of the War Machine. The OKW sections were the German Army, Navy and Air force (Heer, Kriegsmarine and Luftwaffe) and its headquarters were adjacent to the OKW offices in Berlin. So Canaris and his wife Erika were obliged to move to Berlin.

Below is an excerpt from one of Lina Heydrich's letters to Jean Vaughn that includes the day that Admiral Canaris and his wife Erika moved into a house a few doors along the same road as the Heydrich family. This letter also gives an interesting first-hand account of various other stories about Heydrich already covered in this book. There is no reason to disbelieve Lina's account since she was writing to Ms Vaughn to help her to put together a true story about her husband whom she felt had been much maligned after the War. The letters written by Lina were to be published in a book with half of any Royalties going to Jean Vaughn and half to Lina.

Unfortunately, Jean Vaughn died suddenly and unexpectedly before it was published and the letters along with all her notes were sold at Auction to William Rasmussen, an American, who has since auctioned them on again, and there the trail ends.

A few of the letters can be found on the internet, made available by David Irving who was lucky enough to have permission to view and copy them, while they were owned by Rasmussen. Huge thanks to him for enabling these vital documents to be seen by those who seek them, as the originals have disappeared again completely, from public view and knowledge.

Lina died aged 74 on 14th August 1985 on the Island of Fehmarn where she had lived quietly since the War.

Lina Heydrich, Mar 7, 1951, writes 10 handwritten pages from Burg-Fehmarn, Staakenweg 50 in Schleswig-Holstein, to authoress Jean Vaughan

In June 1934 Himmler was offered the post as head of the police in Prussia (Polizeichef) by Göring. He accepted under the condition that my husband became head of the political police. G. agreed hesitatingly. Diels [Rudolf Diels] was dismissed, my husband was appointed. That happened a few days before June 30th [1934], the day of the Röhm execution.

It is unlikely that my husband knew anything of this affair beforehand, for when he left München on June 28th [1934], he promised to return on June 30th to take me and the child to Berlin. Our furniture was in the van, but he did not come but phoned, that he could not come because 'there was something in the air'. Then the events followed each other unintermittently. The Leopoldstrasse was closed, guards were put before it; a Putsch of the SA was expected.

There were rumours that Röhm wanted [to] seize the Power and proclaim a military government (Militärdictatur) by the aid of a foreign power, rumours [sic] spoke of agreements between him and the French Botschafter (now High Commissioner in Germ[any, i.e., André François-Poncet].) I heard of all this in the Leopoldstrasse where I lived while our furniture was put on the way to Berlin.

Then I went to Berlin too, and moved into our apartment in Südende. I did not see my husband during this time. He lived in Prinz-Heinrich Str. And later on we hardly ever talked about these things. We were too much appalled. It was uncomprehendable for us that somebody wanted to act against Adolf Hitler, the man in whom we saw everything that was good and worth-while living for.

How did we honour, love, and adore this man A.H., though most of us, including me, had as yet not seen him. Even my husband had until then hardly had a glimpse of him. It was Himmler who went to him to report, furnished with the reports by my husband.

A SHORT time after this June 30th, Kapitän z See Schimpf had *committed suicide.* He had been the head of the Abwehr (head of department 'espionage'). My husband and he were well acquainted, they had often dined together in the Skagerak Club, my husband thought a lot of him.*

Now, what had happened? Schimpf, who as a matter of fact was very happy married, kept up a liaison with their secretary. One day he came to know that this girl had been an agent and that all the confidential files had been betrayed. Perhaps Schimpf did not see any other way out. He shot himself. Later on, after 1945, people said that my husband had shot Schimpf. That is absolutely untrue. The successor of Schimpf was [Vice Admiral Wilhelm] Canaris with whom my husband was also acquainted from his time in the Navy.

The subjects of these two offices (SD and Abwehr) had hardly anything to do with each other; therefore we did not pay much attention as to who had become the successor of Schimpf. Therefore we were very much surprised, when one Sunday morning when we returned from a walk with our little son, we met Herr Canaris and his wife in our street.

As a matter of fact our two apartments were separated only by a few houses. Mrs Canaris played the violin and so soon we came to see each other frequently, and this social intercourse which was not to be interrupted until the death of my husband. In the course of time there developed a sharp rivalry between the two men as to their work in their departments, but that did not touch our private and social life. It was an excellent example of two men who were able to [keep] office affairs apart from private life. How many wonderful evenings did we spend with Canaris and Frau Erika [Canaris]; how many tasty dinners did we have there, which Canaris liked to prepare and cook himself. -

In 1934 the Canaris's moved into a [Berlin] suburb, where they had a little house built. A few months later the apartment house where we lived was sold, so we had to move too. We bought a little house in

[Berlin-] Schlachtensee. When we returned from our walk with our two little sons (the second was born in 1934) the first Sunday morning in our new home, we again meet Canaris and his wife, who again lived only a few houses further on. It was like fate itself!

Do you now understand why I think that my husband would never have let Canaris be hanged [in April 1945 at Flossenbürg]? He surely would have influenced to such a degree that everything would have gone all right, if someone should have dared to take steps like the 20th of July [1944] during my husband's lifetime. -

We used to see each other on our birthday parties, the two men went together hunting, no festivities in our houses passed without our reciprocal taking part in them. -- We had a picture of the 'Dresden' [cruiser] in the Battle of the Falkland Isles [in World War I]. It was a present from Canaris; he had painted it himself.

The 'Dresden' was sunk, and he was saved only in the last minute; he had come to Spain then, and there he was sentenced to death. But the evening before the execution he had asked for a priest, a confessor. He succeeded in obtaining this priest's gown, and dressed in his clothes Canaris gained his freedom. Canaris told [us] that, when we received the picture. Canaris and his wife were our last guests in Jungfern-Breschan [in Prague] in the end of 1942. They stayed for several days, and I shall never forget these days.

WITH this talk about Canaris, I told things which happened later. I want to talk about things and an event that happened during the Olympiad [1936].

By the way, I wish you to get this correct now: my husband [Reinhard Heydrich] did not fight duels. He had taken up fencing as sport. He did not approve of duels as a way to settle honour affairs. He was skilled in fencing, if [whether] with Degen, Säbel and Florett (I do not know the adequate expressions in English) in the way they use[d] to fence in Italy and France. Do you know what I mean? [Jan 1952 she adds: 'My husband became German fencing champion in 1940. His trophy, a golden pin, is still in my possession.']

The position of my husband to Hitler is worth-while to be shown. The common idea of it is entirely wrong. My husband has reported personally to Hitler only after he had been appointed in Böhmen [Reichsprotektor in September 1941].

Before that, he wrote reports, of which he did not know whether they were read. Himmler took them to Hitler, and my husband did not know whether he read them to Hitler, or if in which sense he read them. My husband suffered much from the aloofness of Hitler and he criticised sharply his dislike to see things as they really were. But in spite of that my husband held H. in high esteem until his death (perhaps I should rather translate: veneration). The reason for that may have been the fact that my husband had never been able to study Hitler that he had never lived close to him.

During these years the Gestapo, the state institution, and the SD, the institution of the Party, had been fully developed and had become what my husband wanted them to be: a weapon for the good of the state for the good of the people. During this time my husband wrote a booklet, Wandlungen unseres Kampfes (I try to get it somewhere, I don't have it any more myself).

Nothing could happen, the original of which did not become at once known to the Government, and also things that were going on outside the borders of the Reich were well known.

During that time the war began. My husband had just been head of an International Police Committee [Now known as Interpol]. There was to be a great meeting. The heads of the Police of many foreign countries wanted to come with their wives. Preparations had been made for entertainments, social bees (teas?) and so on, interpreters had been engaged; the whole programme was ready, even the tailors were in activity!

Now did my husband not know anything, did he not want us to know, I don't know. At any rate, he kept an absolute silence, and if he knew of what was to happen, he certainly succeeded in keeping it from us.

Miss Vaughan, I want to close for today.

Sincerely,

(Signature) L H

So should we believe Lina's account of the relationship between Heydrich and Canaris, or any of the various other accounts that portray them as rivals or enemies? Let's take an independent view of how their relationship started, how it developed, and the number of years they had known each other as close family friends; celebrating Birthday's together, eating suppers together and living close to each other during the early rise of the SS. My guess is that they remained close friends, and probably had long private conversations about the direction that Hitler was taking Germany.

After sixteen years, Canaris would have been more like a Father figure to Heydrich, especially as his own father died in August 1938.

Heydrich would have known that Canaris would be outside the command structure of the SS and therefore 'unmanageable' by Himmler, so why then did he recommend Canaris for the job as Head of the Abwehr?

Was this Heydrich's only way of attempting to utilise the Wehrmacht (his previous Command allegiance during his Navy years) to control the activity of the SS divisions that were not in his direct power to control?

Was their supposed 'open rivalry' just an outward smokescreen to Himmler and others?

Full and frank 'banter', openly disagreeing with each other, or even openly insulting each other between very old friends in the office, or in a social situation can quite easily be mistaken for rivalry or opposition by strangers who don't know them personally I'm sure that we all have an example of that.

It all raises interesting questions, especially since Heydrich was engaging in secret missions of his own.

Chapter Twenty Seven
𝔉𝔩𝔶𝔦𝔫𝔤 𝔄𝔯𝔬𝔲𝔫𝔡

This Chapter should have been the shortest and easiest of all of them to write; at least that's what I thought before I started. There is a little known story that Heydrich did some flying with the Luftwaffe and this chapter is to find out whether this could add to our understanding of his character. To establish this we first need to find out how and why this opportunity came about, how he managed to train for it, why he wanted to do it, when he did it, who with, who knew and didn't know, and the reasons why he stopped.

This may be informed by some detail about how he got permission, or whether he acted in secret from his seniors – that would certainly be a surprising discovery from the man who appears to be so duty bound to fulfil orders – with no other recorded incident of him ever disobeying an instruction or a command.

It is one thing to always carry out an order given but is quite another to knowingly and purposefully break a rule or command, or to do something that you know has been forbidden. So this was definitely a story to be explored. It could reveal things about his character, his decision making, his level of risk taking and his personal motivation that we can't establish from his normal work ethic. For example; did Heydrich fly with the Luftwaffe for personal achievement, or public glory, or did he just look for a possibility to be able to 'participate' in a front-line situation instead of from behind a desk in Berlin?

This kind of information is completely missing from the history books, and the outcome of some detailed research, was very disappointing, very inadequate and most annoying. The total lack of reliable and accurate historical information about this man is a sad reflection on our historians. Instead of recording actual facts with an independent voice, they have (mostly) all been caught up in the emotive adjective frenzy and failed to provide us (the post-millennium audience of 75 years later) with any official and accurate record that we can be confident in believing.

I found many different accounts of this story, all claiming to be an expert opinion and all claiming to be accurate. The stories varied by many small details, and by many large specifics such as: Yes he did fly one or two missions, six missions, a six week Secondment, a four week programme, his own plane, an SS flying squad, single engine planes only, single and double engines, almost 100 missions, as Gunner, as Pilot, over England, over Poland, shot down over enemy lines, broke his arm, crash landed, ran away in battle, he didn't fly at all for the Luftwaffe, it's all fictitious, no official recorded flights with the Luftwaffe, and he never flew any planes at all.

Historians should be duty bound to record a factual account of what did happen. It is completely irresponsible of them that we are in this situation just 75 years later. All first-hand survivors are now likely to be dead so there is no one to ask. There may be an ex-Luftwaffe member somewhere who may have got a plane ready for Heydrich and may not realise that their first-hand information is vital to us; before it becomes too late. The second generation or children of these historical figures may know more about what happened and could have valuable information for us; but they appear to be too excluded from society to speak out on such matters and tell us what really did happen. There was a huge Daily Mail headline and an indignant outcry of 'evil' adjectives only recently, when one of Heydrich's sons asked the Czech Authorities if he could pay to have the Castle in Brezany restored to its former condition.

All we are left with is an assortment of 'experts' who appear to have completely opposing views, along with some very informative Forum based Websites about the Axis and a lot of re-enactment groups who take pains to remove themselves from any political or ideological beliefs, to concentrate on accurate historical representation. They turn up at shows like the Victory Show and the War & Peace Show, and with perfect uniform and equipment they act out battles with tanks and guns firing very expensive blanks – and of course the Germans always have to lose.

The dedicated enthusiasts who run the Forum based websites have hundreds of conversation streams and discussions with interested people from all over the world who seem to know detailed minutiae of various battles, including names of the protagonists, tank histories, plane numbers, awards and dated accounts of specific incidents. Where this information actually originates is hard to tell, but a large majority of it appears to be reliable. They have huge followings and contain a lot of information that doesn't appear in many of the more general history books. How true and believable it all is, is then up to the reader, but at least the respondents of the Forum are approachable and trying their best to find out and pass on the most recently discovered and accurate knowledge they can.

The fifty year information block of the Official Secrets Act is long past, and I expected many new revelations to follow from their release dates, but getting to see any of these released documents is certainly not available to the man on the street. They are studied by secret experts in secret archives, and in the last twenty five years not much new information has come to light. There have been some new documentary films shown on TV and it seems that many files that were released at their fifty year date were then found to be completely empty. I have heard that Himmler's official file was apparently empty, but how true that is, I may never know.

Some records are so huge that historians are still ploughing through vast collections of documents all in German, and held securely by Government agencies, like the Bletchley Park recording transcripts, where we see an occasional one hour documentary that picks out a few recorded conversations to tell us about. Perhaps 'Gods' like David Irving are allowed to see personal diaries of major figures, to then write a biography about them, but such information is certainly not available to me as an information resource.

These are the reasons that make it very difficult to know which story is the real one about Heydrich's brief and intermittent flights with the Luftwaffe; and annoyingly, this means that I won't be able to look at a pattern of behaviour, or draw any conclusions from it. However, it does serve as a good example of the mess that some areas of history are in right now and acts as a reminder to us that capturing history needs to be done with a voice of independence otherwise it loses its credibility.

So here are just a few snippets of the different accounts about Heydrich Flying for the Luftwaffe; along with my comments about anything that seems incongruent, impossible, or incredible. (As in NOT credible).

The first example is from the place that everyone will head to at the start:

1. Wikipedia

Reinhard Heydrich served as Reserve Hauptmann, then Major in the Luftwaffe. He served in the invasion of Poland as a turret gunner. Then, despite his age, he completed a fighter pilot course in 1940. Heydrich wanted to set an example and show that the SS were not 'asphalt' soldiers behind the front lines, but the elite of the Third Reich. In April 1940 he flew a Bf110 in the Fighter Group II./JG77 'Herz As' in Norway. The planes flown by Heydrich had an ancient Germanic runic character **S for Sieg** – **'victory'** *painted on the side of the fuselage. On May 13, 1940 his plane crashed during take-off and Heydrich was injured. For a short time in May, he flew patrol flights over North Germany and the Netherlands. Then, after another accident, he returned to Berlin. In mid-June 1941, before the German attack on the USSR, he resumed flying, **ignoring Himmler's orders**. He flew his personal Bf109 again with Group II. /JG 77 from Balti, Romania on the southern Eastern Front, which put the wing commander under pressure **due to Heydrich's position and lack of experience.** On 22 July 1941, while on a combat mission, his plane was badly damaged over Yampil by Soviet anti-aircraft fire. Heydrich made an emergency landing in no-man's land, evaded a Soviet patrol and made his way back to German lines. After this, **Hitler forbade him to fly** in combat, as it was realized that his capture as a POW would be a major security breach for Germany. He never flew another operational sortie.*

Heydrich was decorated with the Iron Cross Second (1940) and First (1941) Classes. The number of missions he flew is not known, but he was awarded the Frontflugspange (Front Pilot Badge) in silver, which usually was awarded after 60 combat missions. According to Ballantine Books' Illustrated History of the Violent Century (1973), Heydrich flew 97 missions in a Me110 twin engine fighter.

Comments

- The Sieg Rune is in fact one of the SS runes and not his personal rune. The double Siegrunen were adopted as the symbol of the Schutzstaffel as it represented the S in Schutz (Security) and the S in Staffel (Squadron) as well as meaning Victory - SS.
- Ignoring Himmler's Orders: Really? That would be a monumental incident for Heydrich, not half a line in a virtually unknown story. Where is the evidence for this in other places that Heydrich ever

ignored a direct command from Himmler? Or the evidence of what order he disobeyed, when it was given and why? Not believable.

• How exactly did Heydrich put the Wing Commander under pressure? It implies bad flying, but could just have been the fact that Heydrich was the Head of the RSHA that put him under pressure to do a good job. A totally unjustified implication.

• This complete Wikipedia wording appears in other places as well, although who wrote it and what their credibility or evidence was, we don't know.

2. 'Enigma' by Max Williams, Published by Ulrich of England, page, 25.

Heydrich qualified as a fighter pilot and saw action in a Me-109 during the Norwegian Campaign with Fighter Group JG1.Heydrich's Me109 **displayed his personal runic symbol on the fuselage.**

An Me-110 was also piloted by Heydrich, flying over England and Scotland on reconnaissance missions. During a flight in Norway, he overflew a downed aircraft on landing and crashed breaking an arm. **Both Hitler and Himmler were aware of his sorties** *as an arm in plaster was difficult to conceal, but he was at pains to shown them his duties of Chief of RSHA would not suffer as a result. In doing so he kept from them the actual number of times he was* **engaged in skirmishes with the RAF.** *On one occasion he wrote to Himmler stating... 'I will be back on duty in one week...' Himmler replied in a letter dated 15th May 1940. addressed to –*

SS-Gruf.Heydrich, Chief of RSHA ay present Flight-Captain in the Western Campaign.

My dearest heydrich *, I recieved your card dated 5/5/40. Since then a lot has happened. For the past few days we have been in the headquarters , but the real headquarters is in another place. You know* *what it was like from the Polish campaign. I think about you a lot and hope you are well and wish you again lots of luck and all the best! Let me hear from you every day if possible. Many heartfelt greetings from Wolfschen, Rudi Brandt Haschen , but especially from me Heil Hitler ! Yours faithfully HH.*

Heydrich's next opportunity for aerial combat came during the Russian offensive. He flew numerous times over enemy territory and was engaged in several dogfights behind the lines. It was during one of these flights that he was forced to crashland behind Soviet lines in the vicinity of Berezina. Eventually he was rescued by a German patrol. Lina Heydrich describes this incident as follows... **'Reinhart** *comes home, dirty, unshaven and very upset... He landed behind enemy lines, had hidden for two days and two nights and made his way on foot back to german units'.*

Himmler referred to this mission in his funeral address in 1942 stating that he had been shot down by AA fire. Heydrich was awarded the silver combat bar for combat missions amd the EK 1st class. Hitler noticed the new decorations and was horrified at the thought of his Security Chief being captured by the Russians. From then on, he was strictly forbidden to undertake such dangerous flights again. Luftwaffe reserve major Heydrich was grounded.

Comments

* This again mentions Heydrich's personal rune, rather than just one of the SS runes. Perhaps they did add a symbolic S to his plane, but it was not his personal rune. It was a Sig rune. The huge difference that this makes will become obvious in the following chapter.

* So it seems here that Himmler and Hitler were aware of his Sorties? The Wikipedia account says that they were not, and that Heydrich ignored direct orders not to fly. Therefore one of these is

not correct. Which one?

- Skirmishes with the RAF? Other accounts say his flights over England were reconnaissance missions, not skirmishes.

- A letter from Himmler that opens with 'My dearest heydrich' – if anyone was to call him my dearest, would they not also have used his first name rather than his surname? This is definitely incongruent. It also has a capital letter missing, and I don't think Himmler would have missed it. He was an educated man. Furthermore, the style of writing seems much too informal and 'girlie' for Himmler. Also, in the next Chapter, I will reveal an entirely different method of communication that existed between Himmler and Heydrich that will make this supposed letter totally unbelievable.

- A quotation from Lina Heydrich, his wife, and she has spelled her husband's name wrong. Reinhart instead of Reinhard. That makes it totally not credible or believable for me. Also, she called him Reini, and not Reinhard. Not believable.

3. J D: 24th March 2000 on a popular Forum: (Name withheld for confidentiality)

I am currently reading a book on the history of the SS and it mentions that prior to Reinhard Heydrich becoming Reich Protector for Bohemia and Moravia he had seconded himself to the Luftwaffe as a pilot. This was at the start of the Russian Campaign in June 1941 and lasted for 6weeks. Can anyone tell me in what squadron and planes he served? Thanks for any help in advance.

JD

Reply by Gordon 24th March 2000

That is relatively easy. He flew no combat missions and served in no Luftwaffe squadrons. This urban legend of 'Jagdflieger Heydrich' is some sort of Frankenstein that refuses to die. Luftwaffe Verband, a worldwide organization of researchers and former Luftwaffe personnel, have had a running discussion on the reports of Heydrich's 'service', nearly all of which can be distilled down to a single Luftwaffe pilot's memoirs where he made the claim that Heydrich flew combat missions in the Bf-109. Since no one else in that Staffel in that Gruppe in that Geschwader seems to recall that the #4 man in Hitler's Germany dropped in to fly combat with them, I think the chances are near zero that Heydrich ever flew those missions as claimed.

There are photographs of Heydrich's personal aircraft, but it is not a Bf-109, it is a small transport. Yes, he visited a Bf-109 unit in the East, but serve in that unit as a pilot? (or at all?) No. Given the Nazi's love of propaganda and seeing photos of themselves doing 'manly things', I think it's a little strange that Heydrich's photographs from that visit include none with him in flying gear or in the cockpit of a 109, preparing for a sortie. Draw your own conclusions, John, but decades of research by dedicated Luftwaffe researchers nix the claim that Heydrich was a pilot in the Luftwaffe.

v/r

Gordon

Additional post the following day 25th March 2000 by Gordon:

Heydrich and the Luftwaffe

Please excuse the sniptation, but I am trying to keep this brief. The editor of the Luftwaffe Verband Journal has been kind enough to allow people to copy his material; for the record, I feel the level of discussion within the pages of his magazine is extremely worth reading as it brings neophytes, scholars, and actual Luftwaffe members together to clear the air over unidentified photographs, lost details, and the occasional urban legend.

So far, the discussion has been best summed up by Jean-Louis Roba concerning Heydrich flying with III./JG 52. He writes, 'I am familiar with the 'information' contained in Dichfeld's book. The great problem is that he is not very credible. He lost all of his belongings in the last days of the war and reconstructed everything from memory. After shooting down 130 planes, it is normal for things to get a little mixed up. Could you remember in detail what you did last month? And Dichfeld had to recall five very exciting and hectic years more than 40 years later.' later - I still think that the presence of Heydrich in III./JG 52 for only two war flights is very dubious.

I personally believe that Dichfeld and his comrades (on the Southern front in Russia) heard some anecdotes about Heydrich flying with either II. or III./JG 77 in the same area and later transposed them to his own unit. The story in his book sounds too much like some of the anecdotes (certainly partly false) about Heydrich in JG 77 so I think we must forget that very strange story.

The editor, Barry Rosch, agrees with Jean-Louis about the problems associated with trying to reconstruct memories after four decades or more. That brings us to the next point - apparently Heydrich DID fly at least a mission or two with JG 77. From other conversations among Luftwaffe Verband members, I gather that Heydrich felt himself an accomplished enough civilian pilot to be able to participate in the 'duck hunts' that he expected over the Eastern Front. There is anecdotal evidence that he made at least one combat flight and returned quite shaken by the whole experience and in short order returned to Berlin, never to attempt such an stupid stunt again.

v/r Gordon

USN SAR Aircrew

Comments:

- Quoting what appear to be credible sources for their information and vehemently denying that is any truth in this at all. How does that leave the first two accounts then? And one of them is on a central information source – Wikipedia.

- I wonder how they explain the Pilot's badge photographed on Heydrich's chest in many pictures. Why would he wear it if he had not qualified as a Luftwaffe Pilot?

- The Pilot badge would have been awarded and this would have been recorded on Heydrich's personnel record. If only that SS register hadn't disappeared into oblivion at Auction, I may have been able to check the date when it was awarded.

- Again reference to 'his personal plane with a single S rune' a better description than 'a plane with his personal rune'. But was this plane simply to take him from A to B as Head of the RSHA? Perhaps he piloted it sometimes? Not too difficult to believe.

4. A Website www.asisbiz.com/il2/Bf-109E/JG1-Heydrich.html
Reinhard Heydrich

Units: Stab./JG-77(5/40 Norway), Gruppe Adj I./JG-1 (Summer '40-6/41), Assigned to II./JG-77 July 1941

Awards: Wound Badge, Fighter Operational Clasp in Bronze

Known Aircraft: Bf 109E-3 'Yellow 3' (90% damaged 5/3/40), Bf 109E-7 WNr 3765 (30% dam 7/22/41)

Remarks: Injured in his 'Yellow 3' when he overturned on takeoff from the Sola Norway airfield. Source: SIG Norway. His 109E carried the Adj and SS symbols. A friend of Dr. Erich Mix, he was known to have flown a few missions with JG-1. On 22 July, 1941, in Wk# 3765, he volunteered, along with pilots of II/JG-77, to fly a couple of combat missions against Soviet pilots. He was promptly shot down by flak and force-landed in Moldavia. Following this experience, he made a quick return to his headquarters in Germany. He was most likely the victim of fighters of the 55th Fighter Aviation Regt., who attacked the Beltsy AF the day before. Hitler personally forbade his making any more such flights.

Since there was only a small unit of a 'SS-Flying unit' the so called SS-Fliegerkorps (a small branch of the NS-Fliegerkorps), wich actually never saw combat operations because these Fliegerkorps where never intended for combat than civil or training issues, mostly due to lack of serviceabilty, combat ready aircrafts and experienced members. So this one and only SS-Flying unit was nothing more than a representative unit for Hobby-pilots. Amongst others Heydrich (as a member of the SS) was in service with regular Luftwaffe units, he served some Time around 1940-1941 in Stavanger-Sola Norway-Campaign, Wangerooge (defending Germany's coastline) and Balti (Romania Eastern Front) with JG1 and JG77.

The below is from a message written by Michael Miller a while ago:

'SS-Obergruppenführer Reinhard Heydrich, a talented civilian pilot prior to the war, flew combat missions with the Luftwaffe. His first mission was as a gunner in Kampfgeschwader (Bomber Wing) 55 on 12. Sep. 1939. He then passed an examination as a Bf 109E pilot, serving as an Oberleutnant der Reserve and Adjutant of Jagdgeschwader 77 during the invasion of Norway in Apr. 1940. He then flew reconnaissance flights over England and Scotland in a Bf-110 outitted for aerial photograph. He rose to the rank of Major der Reserve, flying further missions as a reconnaissance pilot in the Russian Campaign. In the process, he received the Iron Cross First Class and the Operational

Flying Clasp

(Reconnaissance) in Silber (Frontflug-Spange für Aufklärer in Silber). (Most of the info. on Heydrich's Luftwaffe service is from Günther Deschner's Reinhard Heydrich)'

There are some details in Ch. Bergström's Barbarossa: the Air Battle. Seems that Heydrich was shot down either by St. Lt. Aleksandr Pokryshkin or Ml.Lt. Leonid Dyiachenko from 55 IAP who both claimed a Bf 109 in the combat. Pokryshkin and Diyachenko were flying as escort to some Su 2s whose mission was to bomb Dniestr Bridges at Yampol when a pair of Bf 109 attacked the bombers. Only one Messerschmitt was lost though and it was the one piloted by Heydrich who came down in a no man's land and was later rescued as described by one of the posts above.

Diyachenko was to be killed just three days later, probably in combat with Uffz. Franz Schulte from II./JG 77 (his claim no.2) while Heydrich was assassinated by members of Czechoslovak exile army in May 1942. Pokryshkin went on to claim 59 aerial victories throughout WW2 and become one of the most notorious Soviet aces and 3 x HSU.

Comments:

- This website is full of references that should be easy enough to verify by Luftwaffe records. Have they been? I don't have access to them. During a Serious Case Review, if I come across an instance such as this, the agency concerned is asked to provide its own files that either prove or disprove the facts in question. This appears not to have been done by anyone and I don't have access to them.

- I have cleaned up some of the spelling and grammar to make it legible, the original text could be because the writer is not a native English speaker, and nothing to do with the credibility of the message.

5. Another Forum based website that quotes Max Williams page 25, appears to be a completely different text to the first one.

Heydrich did indeed pilot on several reconnaissance missions during the war (source 'Reinhard Heydrich - The Biography Vol.II/Enigma' by Max Williams, page 25) - some excerpts from this publication: Quote:

As soon as war had broken out, Heydrich was impatient to see active service. He obtained permission to fly as a Luftwaffe Reserve Officer with Bomber Group KG55 and first saw action on 12th September 1939 as a gunner.

An ME 110 was also piloted by Heydrich, flying over England and Scotland on reconnaissance missions. During a mission in Norway, he over-flew a shot-up aircraft on landing and crashed, breaking his arm. Both Hitler and Himmler were aware of his sorties as an arm in plaster was difficult to conceal, but he was at pains to show them his duties as Chief of RSHA would not suffer as a result. In doing so, he kept from them the actual number of times he was engaged in skirmishes with the RAF. On Heydrich's return to SS duty, he was proudly sporting a newly awarded bronze combat mission bar on his left uniform breast.

Heydrich's next opportunity for aerial combat came during the Russian offensive. He flew numerous times over enemy territory and was engaged in several dogfights behind the lines. It was during one of these flights that he was forced to crash-land behind the Soviet lines, in the vicinity of Berezina. Eventually he was rescued by a German combat patrol. Lina Heydrich describes this incident as follows: '...Reinhard comes home, dirty, unshaven and very upset...He landed behind enemy lines, had hidden for two days and two nights and made his way on foot back to German units'.

Heydrich was awarded the silver bar for combat missions and the

Iron Cross First Class. Hitler noticed the new decorations and was horrified at the thought of his Security Chief being captured by the Russians. From then on, he was strictly forbidden to undertake such dangerous flights again. Luftwaffe Reserve Major Heydrich was grounded.

Comments:

- A totally different quote from the same page of the same book?
- This time without the 'supposed' letter from Himmler.
- This time Lina's quotation at least spells her husband's name correctly.
- Plenty of references to awards made to Heydrich, and we have pictures of him wearing them, so how can the reasons for them being awarded have not been recorded in any official capacity?

6. Post Number:#9 by Larry D. on 24 Oct 2004, 01:04 Another Forum contains this post:

For whatever it's worth: Reinhard Heydrich the Flier

Heydrich, in the uniform of a Luftwaffe Hauptmann, joined 6. Staffel/JG 77 at Kristiansand-Kjevik in South Norway in mid-April 1940 for a month's stay after completing fighter training at Jagdfliegerschule 1 Werneuchen. Those who flew with him say he was a highly motivated, aggressive pilot and a very friendly and jovial personality off duty. Heydrich wrecked his Bf 109E-1 while taking off from Stavanger-Sola on 13 May. He was not injured. For his month of service in Norway, where he saw little or no action, Heydrich received the EK II and the silberne Frontflugspange.

(Source: Prien, Jochen; Geschichte des Jagdgeschwaders 77, 4 Bände (Teile 1 – 4) (Eutin, c. 1992-93). See Band 1 pages 209, 220, 221 and 223. Account based on statements of two 6. Staffel [Squadron]

pilots who flew nearly every mission with Heydrich: Frank-Werner Rott, 28 April 1990 and Berthold Jung, 4 November 1989. There are also several photos of Heydrich with his plane.)

In mid-July 1941, Heydrich once again donned his Luftwaffe uniform, but now as a 'Major', and rejoined II./JG 77, now based at Balti-East in Moldavia. Heydrich arrived with his 'own' Bf 109, which he claimed had been given to him personally by Generaloberst Ernst Udet for favors rendered. He flew for several days, but did not score. On 22 July he was shot down between the lines by Russian AA fire, belly landing his Bf 109E-7 (Werknummer 3765) near the village of Olshanka. He was rescued unscathed within a few hours by a patrol from a nearby German infantry division and returned to Berlin the next day. Heydrich received the EK I for his brief, week-long stay with II. Gruppe.

(Source: Prien – op cit, Band 2 pages 704, 709, 710, 711, 729 and 873. Account based on JG 77 Kriegstagebuch (war diary) and the January 1990 statement of Georg Schirmböck, who flew with Heydrich during his week at the front).

Regarding Heydrich's alleged missions as a gunner with KG 55, I can only say that there is no mention of him in the KG 55 unit history (Wolfgang Dierich, Kampfgeschwader 55 'Greif': Eine Chronik aus Dokumenten und Berichten 1937-1945 (Stuttgart, 1975).

Nor is there any mention in any of the reputable aviation history books of Heydrich flying Bf 110s over England. He was only licensed to fly single-engine fighters and he was never with any Luftwaffe unit that was equipped with twin-engine Bf 110s.

The account of Heydrich coming down 'behind enemy lines' in the vicinity of Berezina and hiding out for several days is pure, unadulterated fiction. The village of Ol'shanka is located 223 km ENE of Balti, which is exactly the sector of the front over which II./JG 77 was operating at the time. There are four villages named 'Berezina' in Ukraine, and none is within the mission radius of a Bf 109 operating out of Balti-East.

Finally, Dr. Jochen Prien is internationally recognized as Germany's finest World War II aviation historian. His 4 volume history of JG 77 (2,507 pages) is meticulously researched with 2 to 6 footnotes on every page, nearly all from primary documentation. He has also published full histories of most of the other Bf 109-equipped Jagdgeschwader. As a bilingual researcher and historian of the Luftwaffe for nearly 40 years, I trust in Prien's account.

Comment:
- The Flier? Shouldn't it be The Pilot?
- This one says he had a one month secondment and the other accounts mention a six week secondment. It also mentions a further one week exercise, so five weeks altogether?
- Another reference to Prien, the Luftwaffe Historian, who claims it all to be untrue but then doesn't explain the Pilot badge or wound badge worn by Heydrich.
- *a very friendly and jovial personality off duty?* Does this sound like Heydrich? Nowhere has he ever been referred to as friendly or jovial. Totally unbelievable

7. Post Number:#15 by Max Williams on 25 Oct 2004, 23:17 A direct quote from Max Williams himself, on another Forum:

Heydrich's first combat mission as a gunner with KG55 on 12 September 1939. Source: Der Spiegel 9 Feb 1950 and Deschner p114.

Himmler remained in contact with Heydrich via Feldpost and telex messages from KG55. Source: BDC Heydrich personal files and

Deschner p114.

Emergency landing east of Berezina. Source: Himmler's memorial speech, 'Reinhard Heydrich, Ein Leben der Tat' Prague 1944 and Deschner p114.

Heydrich flew Me110 on reconnaissance flights over England and Scotland in an aircraft fitted for aerial photography. Source: Deschner's interview with Lina Heydrich. It is also a well-known fact that Heydrich personally piloted larger aircraft than single engine planes between Berlin and Prague.

Max.

Flight Historians Christer Bergstrom *reveals the truth about Heydrich background.*

Time in Norway:

In mid-April 1940 the German hunting flotilla II. / JG 77 in Norway received two fresh hunt pilots from fighter school in Werneuchen. One was the 36-year-old head of the Nazi security service RSHA, Reinhard Heydrich, who bears the rank of captain (Hauptmann). The other was his fighter trainers from Werneuchen, Second Lieutenant (Leutnant) Frank Werner Rott, who had the task of protecting Heydrich during combat flights.

Heydrich served in II. / JG 77 in about four weeks. He participated in many combat missions with the dressing over Norway at this time. It is likely that his first dogfight took place on 16 April 1940, when Ensign Rott shot down a British Lockheed Hudson. This was a twin-engine bomber and coastal reconnaissance aircraft, a relatively easy target for the Germans who flew Messerschmitt 109 fighters. At this time met with II. / JG 77 mainly small formations of relatively antiquated British bombers over Norway, and the unit's own losses were very small. In fact, between mid-April and mid May 1940 and joined II. / JG 77 only two combat losses.

However Heydrich jammed one of the unit's aircraft. It was May 13, 1940 that he failed at a start from the base at Stavanger Sola and crashed his Messerschmitt 109 E-1. Heydrich survived the crash but was himself injured and chose to return to Germany.

Tuesday, July 22, 1941 - just a few days after Heydrich arrived at the eastern front - he started on a combat mission of the Romanian - Soviet front. Heydrich flew with Lieutenant Joachim Deicke. Was about two o'clock in the afternoon and over the radio was informed by the two German hunting airmen that a formation Soviet bombers attacked the German bridges over the river Dniester at Jampol. There were nine single-engine Su-2s from the Soviet bombing squadron 210 BBAP. Deicke and Heydrich put full speed to the specified area. Pretty soon they caught sight of Su-2s. These were protected by two I-16 fighter jet.

Pokrysjkins attack came so suddenly that Heydrich never had time to determine the direction of the firing came. Afterward, he reported that he must have been hit by anti-aircraft! In any event, he luck in the misfortune to succeed crash land their battered Messerschmitt 109 E-7 (Werknummer 3765) in the no man's land.

When the Germans had realized that no less than Gruppenführer Heydrich had been shot down, organized a force that went to the place where Messerschmitten gone down. They found a shaken Heydrich and brought him quickly back to safety.

The last battle:

It seems that Heydrich confidence hunting aviator never picked up again after the meeting with the Soviet ace Pokrysjkin. Heydrich did II. / JG 77 and went to a different hunting units on the eastern front, III. / JG 52nd But even where he was particularly prolonged.

Heydrich was placed as wingman to Lieutenant Adolf ****feld, one *of the best pilots of III. / JG 52nd Apparently, Heydrich flew only one mission with III. / JG 52nd ****feld tells how he worried supplied SS Gruppenführer with some important advice for their first combat flight:*

- I gave Heydrich a clear description of what he might expect if it came to battle, and stressed how important it was that he kept beside me all the time. I told him that if it would come to a situation where it was about life or death, it was better to flee than to embark on adventures with Ivan, as they certainly were better than a Gruppenführer.

Heydrich seems to have taken ****felds words a little too literally. The two got into battle with twelve Soviet aircraft. As a wingman, it was Heydrich to protect ****feld from attack from behind, and when the battle began, ****feld called:

White 4, stay close, but do not shoot yet!

The next moment, Heydrich Messerschmitt was disappeared. ****feld had to fight the battle with the twelve Soviet aircraft on your own. He survived thanks to his great skill (****feld attributed to far more than 100 air victories during the war and still alive today), but was somewhat surprised when he later landed at the airbase and discovered that Heydrich was standing on the ground to receive him.- Where did you go, asked ****feld.

With a shamefaced expression Heydrich said:- Everything went too fast for me and I did not want to disturb you, so I flew back home!

Shortly afterwards got ****feld a sharp reprimand by his commanding officer for having 'abandoned such an important person Heydrich'!

The next morning, says ****feld,the He 111 as Heydrich arrived with, disappeared at the direction of Germany, with a Gruppenführer board. I never saw him again. A few weeks later was appointed Heydrich to riksprotektor in Bohemia-Moravia.

Comment:

• This appears to be taken from the book written by Dichfeld 40 years after the War, which has been slated as nonsense by previous posts above. I included it here for a full picture of the information available.

• Is it any wonder that apart from the Luftwaffe badge worn by Heydrich in 'photo's, it is almost impossible to dig out the fact from the fiction.

• Heydrich was a world class Fencing Champion, with lightning speed reactions and the proven ability to out-think his opponents – also world class – so this account insinuating that Heydrich is slow witted, is totally incongruent.

• Shamefaced? Not a word you would expect to be associated with anything that Heydrich did, and not a character trait that has ever been used to describe him anywhere else. Not believable I'm afraid.

• Heydrich was fearless and confident in everything he did. He rode through Prague in an open topped car. Why would his character suddenly change in one incident? Not a believable behaviour based on everything else we know about him.

The final example is strangely titled: Aircrew Luftfaffe SS etc... Why?

8. Aircrew Luftwaffe SS Obergruppenfuhrer Reinhard Heydrich grave 01

The GRAVE OF REINHARD HEYDRICH

by Ray & Josephine Cowdery © Copyright 2002

We would like to thank all MI readers for their wonderful response to our series of four articles on the assassination of SS-General and Acting Reichsprotektor of Bohemia and Moravia, Reinhard Eugen Tristan Heydrich. In response to many inquires and requests for a photo of Heydrich's grave, we are pleased to provide the very rare image as seen at the left.

Heydrich was buried beneath a simple wooden soldier's grave marker in the shape of a 1939 Iron Cross in Berlin's Invaliden Cemetery on 9 June 1942. Invaliden Cemetery is the final resting place of many famous German statesmen and soldiers and is located just north of the huge Friedrichstrasse railway station in central Berlin. Reinhard Heydrich's grave was only a few feet away from those of Prussian General Gerhard von Scharnhorst and Reichsautobahn builder Fritz Todt, and a few steps away from the graves of renowned German flying aces Werner Mölders, Ernst Udet and Baron von Richthofen.

The Heydrich grave disappeared in the spring of 1945 before the Russians ever entered Berlin. There is little doubt that it was relocated by loyal SS comrades. If any reader has information on the current whereabouts of Heydrich's grave, please write us in care of MI Magazine.

Ray & Josephine Cowdery

Comments

This article about Heydrich's grave states that he was Luftwaffe Aircrew I wonder why?

I have used this chapter to demonstrate the huge differences of opinion that exist about Heydrich, making the need to establish some kind of reality even more necessary.

Heydrich had total discipline in anything he chose to do and that would include learning to fly. My guess is that he did learn to fly and that he practised until he was fully confident. He was flown from place to place in the course of his work as Head of the RSHA, and being able to pilot the plane himself would be an excellent safety measure for him. I would also assume that Himmler would have given permission to him gladly, because if his Pilot was hit, Heydrich would be able to safely take the controls. That would be very sensible and very believable. Who better to train him than the Luftwaffe? I certainly think he was sent to them for perhaps four weeks to train as a Pilot. That does not make Heydrich a member of the Luftwaffe – just trained by them. I also guess that, understanding Heydrich's character a little, he would have asked to fly out on a few missions, to test his new skills in a real situation. That also doesn't make him a member of the Luftwaffe – but it does explain the recorded missions.

Heydrich held a firm belief in acting with honour – indeed this was such a large part of the SS that it was made a part of their slogan – My honour is loyalty. So I cannot believe that he would wear any badge that he had not earned. Surely that would be picked up by his superiors? Himmler was a very clever observer of detail and would notice immediately if Heydrich wore an underserved award. Indeed it is almost certain that Himmler would have awarded Heydrich with his Pilot's badge, so would of course have known about it, and approved of it. Withdrawing permission for him to fly later on as War became more difficult would also be a perfectly sensible decision by any commanding officer.

We currently have the first and second in line to the Throne of England serving in the Armed Forces. But should their safety ever appear in danger, I'm sure that senior officers would move them to less front-line tasks.

Perhaps the Luftwaffe military establishment do not wish to recognise that a senior member of the SS was 'within their ranks' for a time, for their own political reasons. This could be very believable.

It is time to take a much closer look at the relationship between Heydrich and Himmler and the significance of the silver bell.

Chapter Twenty Eight
In Search of the Devil

It was impossible to bust any myths in the last chapter without conclusive information from military sources; so instead, I will bust a myth about Himmler as we take a look at the probable relationship he had with Heydrich over the course of eleven years from Heydrich's start with the SS in October 1931, to his death in June 1942. This will lead us into the reason for the beautiful Silver Bell and the evidence for its purpose. But before this can make any sense, we need to look at something that Himmler is often accused of in books and newspaper articles, and that is his supposed penchant for 'DEVIL WORSHIP'.

There are many strange stories about the SS taking part in midnight marches by torchlight around the grounds of Wewelsburg Castle and this is often cited as an example of Himmler's secret occultism and devil worship.

My findings suggest that this actually couldn't be further from the truth and again shows a total lack of factual or accurate historical recording and the need to always shock and repel readers about anything connected with Nazi Germany and particularly Himmler.

Himmler was in fact interested in ancient Viking Germanic culture, medieval history and Germanic legend, which all started with his collection of medieval artefacts as a small boy and evolved into his membership of a Germanic and Pagan society created by German nationalists in 1912 called the Thule Society, the symbol of which was a sun wheel swastika.

Himmler certainly seemed to like secret codes and symbols, and added hidden meanings to every part of the culture and symbolism of the embryonic SS organisation. He particularly liked the ancient Germanic and Viking Runes, and he re-used 14 of them as meaningful symbols that represented something within the SS.

The SS runes themselves were taken from the original Viking symbol that means 'good fortune', or success; and was also in the Elder Futhark (Viking alphabet) representing the letter S. This explains why two of them were used to represent the SS. Walter Heck the graphic designer for a badge company in Bonn, 'invented' it as a symbol, and was paid two and a half Reichsmarks for his design.

The Hakenkreuz or Swastika has been used by many civilisations not just the Third Reich; including Tibetan, Native American, Japanese, Greek and Indian cultures. Mostly it has represented the sun although in the Viking tradition it was used as a sign sacred to the God Thor. This was chosen by Hitler as the new symbol of the Nazi Party, and as an accomplished artist, set it onto a white circle within a red background. Have you ever noticed that some swastikas are shown flat and square, while some are shown on a diagonal, resting on one point? This was to represent 'forward movement' whether through battle, or achievement, and during the War years, they mostly appear on the diagonal.

The Sonnenrad is the sunwheel swastika and was originally the ancient Norse symbol for the Sun. This was re-used by two of the Waffen SS Divisions, in Scandinavia.

I won't list all fourteen runes and their uses in the Nazi Party, but the original Viking qualities they represented were things such as: communal spirit, self-sacrifice, zeal, enthusiasm, life, death, leadership in battle, success, good fortune, unshakable faith, kinship, family, and blood bonds. They were all allocated to a very specific SS Division, or used in some kind of award by Himmler, based on their original Viking attributes.

Five of these runes are used on the SS Honour ring to symbolise; communal spirit, nationalism, success, good fortune and unshakable faith, and these were reinforced by the Citation that was written by

Himmler and presented to the future owner of each Honour Ring. We have already noted the wording of this in an earlier chapter. We can now begin to see that it wasn't a random occurrence, but all had a significant meaning that was grounded in ancient Viking legend and Germanic folklore.

Himmler's ultimate aim was to establish a cultural framework that would completely replace Christianity, and he used ancient Germanic heritage as a basis for the development of alternative rites and rituals for the SS.

It is a well-known fact that the concept of the Devil is only a construct of the Christian religion which represents the total opposite of Christ, so where Christ represents all that is good; the Devil represents all that is bad. Taking that to its natural conclusion, if you believe in Christ, you must also believe in a persona called The Devil, but if you don't believe in Christ, then the Devil is totally meaningless.

If Himmler had been a Satanist worth his salt, he would have used iconography that included; quotes from the book of Revelations, inverted Pentagrams, the head of Bathamet (the goat of Mendez), Biblical passages about 'The Beast', mentions of 'The Antichrist', and of course the infamous '666' the number of the Beast. None of these symbols have ever been attributed to the Third Reich. (Except in entertaining films)

Himmler was besotted with the romantic Arthurian Legend. The story of King Arthur or 'Le Mort d'Arthur' was written by Sir Geoffrey of Monmouth, a famous Monk of the 12th Century. Arthur was represented as a King who united all the Britons and fought against the evil Sorceress Morgana and her illegitimate and incestuous offspring son, Mordred. It is a story purely about good conquering evil, and nothing to do with devil worship. The romantic story of Arthur doesn't have an Antichrist although the closest character in the story would be the evil Mordred, but then Himmler did not align himself with Mordred, he aligned himself very definitely with King Arthur.

We are all aware of Arthur's 12 Knights of the Round Table, and this is what Himmler created at Wewelsburg Castle, the cultural centre of the SS; with the 12 Tutonic Knights of the SS. He even installed a round table in the great Hall, and in the Crypt was a casket of Honour Rings that contained every ring from all the SS Officers who had owned one and then lost their lives. This was surrounded by 12 plinths that were supposed to have had statues of the 12 Teutonic Knights of the SS. (which was based on an ancient order of German chivalrous Knights who incidentally, had a golden eagle as their central symbol that looked very much like the Art Deco eagle of the Third Reich) Wewelsburg Castle is often referred to as 'Himmler's Camelot' and he had great plans that the Castle should be the centre of the Thousand Year Reich. On my recent trip to see the Castle for myself, I saw printed plan drawings of the expansion of the village around it by a 2 kilometre circle that would contain everything needed to be a cultural and spiritual training and holiday centre for SS Officers and their families. A sort of early holiday camp idea, and indeed families did stay at the Castle for holidays and the elite Officers received training in the School rooms there. The village extension though, was never completed.

There is some recent historical evidence that Arthur was most likely a Romano Celtic Briton Chieftain – rather than a true King – who led the ordinary people with his warriors against the migratory invading Anglo-Saxons. Himmler may not have known about this version at that time, and would have probably have grown up with the Geoffrey of Monmouth story.

Perhaps the image of members of the SS wearing black has led to being misunderstood as Devil worshippers. But the crusading Knights Hospitallers wore black robes with a white symbol on the front (the

Cross) and the SS uniform may have been influenced by this; although they could just as easily have been a mixture of fashion and practicality. Interestingly, the modern day high ranking Police uniforms in the UK are not dissimilar to the SS black uniform, they even have silver piping but the insignia is different and they are certainly not accused of devil worship.

The SS performed torchlight processions at the Winter Solstice on the 21st December, a direct replica of the ancient Viking torchlight processions and some of the Celtic pagan fire festivals – which incidentally still happen in England from October onwards in places such as Hastings and are even funded by Hastings Borough Council, so nothing to do with devil worship. Here is a link to pictures of Hastings people processing through the dark streets carrying torches and lanterns, usually complete with marching drummers as well: www.hbbs.info/

The SS soldiers were all given a special lantern called a Julleuchter which was made of earthenware and 2 places for candles to be lit in it; one outside and on the top, and one inside it, at the bottom. It was to be used during the festival of Yule. Wikipedia states: *In 1936 Nazi-era Germanic mysticism, Heinrich Himmler set forth a list of approved holidays, in part supposedly based on 'pagan' traditions, including a 'Julfest' [Yule Festival] intended to replace Christian rites. The Julleuchter and other symbols were also meant to serve as a consolation to women who, by having married into the SS, had to renounce the spiritual shelter and service of their church. The SS soldier was instructed to set up a shrine that included a 'Julleuchter' in the corner of one room of his household.*

So we find a grudging agreement that it was based on Germanic Pagan tradition, and of Himmler's intention to replace the Church festivals with it.

The winter solstice and Yule are two completely different festivals 2 days apart, and Yule starts at midnight on the 20th December and lasts for 12 days. It is a Germanic Pagan ceremony and involves many articles of symbolism, that SS soldiers were expected to decorate their family homes with. Most of these have since been 'kidnapped' by the Christian faith for their Christmas festivities. Symbols such as:

- The Christmas Tree: custom according to the Encyclopaedia Britannica, 'The use of evergreen trees, wreaths, and garlands to symbolize eternal life was a custom of the ancient Egyptians, Chinese, and Hebrews. Tree worship was common among the pagan Europeans and survived their conversion to Christianity in the Scandinavian customs of decorating the house and barn with evergreens at the New Year to scare away the devil and of setting up a tree for the birds during Christmastime.'[[Scaring away the Devil – not worshipping him?]

- Mistletoe: from the story about Baldur, grandson of the Norse god Thor woke up one morning certain that each and every plant and animal on earth wanted to kill him. His mother consoled him. His wife consoled him, but all to no avail. His mother and wife decided to ask every living thing to leave their poor Baldur in peace. They begged the kindness of the oak tree, the pig, the cow, the crow, the ant and even the worm. Each agreed. Then, as Baldur paused to celebrate his release from torment, he felt a pain in his chest. He had been stabbed and killed by an arrow made from the wood of a mistletoe plant. Mistletoe was the one species on earth his wife and mother had failed to notice. Baldur died, but a lesson was learned: Never forget about the mistletoe. Mistletoe would come to hang over our doors as a reminder to never forget.

- And of course Saint Nicholas who needs no explanation.

I wonder if any Christians actually know that by putting up these items at Christmas, they are actually performing an ancient Germanic Pagan ritual.

Himmler was fascinated with the search for the Holy Grail, but this was more to do with the fact that it was supposed to have unknown power, everyone else wanted to own it, and it was believed to have been protected by the Knights Templar. Perhaps the iconic films 'Hell Boy' and 'Raiders of the Lost Ark' have had a lot to do with his image as a devil worshipper.

The word 'Occult' often appears in headlines and book titles about Himmler and is a word which the true meaning has become distorted and changed in the public arena over time. Its meaning is: late 15th century (as a verb): from Latin *occultare* 'secrete', frequentative of *occulere* 'conceal', based on *celare* 'to hide'; the adjective and noun from *occult-* 'covered over', from the verb *occulere*. It is used in medical terms where the symptoms are hidden or cannot be easily seen. So again, it is nothing to do with the devil.

Another word with a similar transposed meaning is the word 'incredible' which popular culture takes to mean 'Brilliant and fantastic', but which actually means 'without credibility' – pretty much the total opposite.

All religions including Viking legends and Germanic paganism recognise that there are forces for good and forces for evil, but only Christianity embodies this into a character which they call the Devil, and Himmler was most certainly not a Christian. In fact he did not connect himself with anything to do with the Christian faith; none of their festivals or special days, none of their symbols or traditions, and none of the standard Satanist symbols were ever used in his SS iconography, therefore based on this evidence, it could be viewed as being virtually impossible for him to have ever been a 'devil worshipper'.

MYTH BUSTED
Himmler Was a Devil Worshipper

Again, as in a previous Chapter, I challenge all Historians, Journalists and Authors who have used Devil worship in their descriptions of Himmler, to retract, research, and re-write them more accurately.

So what was his Pagan Order all about?

Ancient Germanic legends are full of stories about knightly chivalry that do battle against the forces of evil. In one famous tale, there is an enchanted ring and a magic sword that bestow unlimited powers of invincibility upon the bearer.

Now it all begins to make some sense, as the two most coveted items that belonged to prestigious members of the SS were the Honour Ring, and the Dagger, complete with their very particular inscriptions. We have noted the inscriptions in the rings in earlier chapters, but the dagger carried the SS runes, the German eagle and the Swastika on its hilt, and an inscription along every blade that said:

Meine Ehre Heist Treue
Or, My Honour is Loyalty

Himmler established special days of celebration based on the Pagan solstice days, and there were some spectacular events held by torchlight. One of these was in the Berlin Olympic Stadium on 21st June 1939, where over 120,000 Germans watched the impressive celebration of the Summer Solstice by torchlight. The two solstice celebrations of summer and winter were designed to completely replace any Christian Festivals. The Summer solstice was always held alongside sporting activities and the winter solstice was to celebrate and honour their ancestors. The

211

dates of these are of vital importance to this story: The Winter Solstice is always on Dec 21st and the Summer Solstice is always on June 21st

June 21st is one of the dates that Himmler presented the Honour Rings, the other dates are 30th January – the NSDAP anniversary date, the 20th April – Fuhrertag - the Fuhrer's Birthday and 9th November – Munich Putsch anniversary .

So we have a connection with the Honour Rings and the Summer Solstice, so how does this have any bearing on the winter solstice?

The winter solstice is always held on the shortest day, December 21st, which is during the 12 day festival of Yule and 24th of December, the traditional day for Germans to give presents to their friends and family. This happened long before Christmas was ever introduced by the Christians, which then took over the present giving with Christmas trees and Father Christmas, on the 25th December. Many Germans still exchange presents on 24th December to this day.

The 24th of December is the date engraved on the silver bell which was presented to Heydrich so we now have insurmountable evidence that to Himmler, this date was very significant, and would have been the date that he would follow Germanic tradition and give presents.

Hooray! Evidence that the date inscribed on my bell is a date that Himmler would have given it as a present to Heydrich.

Evidenced also by the book about Honour Rings, that gives an incomplete list of other rings given as presents on that very same day. The same book states that the rings were 'probably' given as part of a present from Himmler to his closest friends and most meaningful allies.

I am definitely getting closer to the great secrets held by this significant and beautiful item, but first need to establish the relationship between Himmler and Heydrich in more detail.

Chapter Twenty Nine
Secret Messages

There are many references to the relationship between Heydrich and Himmler in books, films and Newspaper articles, but how true are they? The reason for looking at this is two-fold: firstly, they worked together for eleven years therefore they must have had at least a fairly good relationship, otherwise my reasoning tells me that either Himmler would have found a way to move him somewhere else, or Heydrich would have requested or applied for some other role under one of the other key figures of the Third Reich; and this did not happen. Heydrich's secondment to Prague was simply that, to achieve a goal, but at the same time to carry on with his 'day job'.

Secondly, if I am to succeed in evidencing that the silver bell was a Yule present from Himmler, then it must also follow that the relationship between them warranted it otherwise Himmler would have been likely to just award Heydrich with his Honour Ring and citation, and nothing more.

The engraving on the bell itself tells us that it is the latter. It clearly says 'I present you with this ring' and the only person who could have done that was Himmler. So either the comments in the books are wrong, or I have a 'made-up' article that is not genuine or original, but why would anyone think to invent a silver bell? And why would they add an inscription giving the date that Heydrich received his Honour ring, when the two specialist book writers on Honour rings don't even know when this took place? It's all very puzzling.

Let's look at some of the remarks about their relationship that appear in our history books. If you Google this phrase, you will find 52,300 results! It is clearly a subject that many people have an interest in.

This is a quote found in many places, and even as a book title –

although the book is mostly an imagined fictional account of the conversations the characters 'might have had' leading up to the assassination attempt of Heydrich. '*HHHH, Himmler's Hirn heißt Heydrich which translated means: Himmler's brain is called Heydrich*'. This implies in a rather derogatory way that Himmler was less than intelligent and no one who had established such a complicated and efficient structure as the SS could ever be labelled as unintelligent. I have read parts of speeches made by Himmler that have been translated online, and none of them seem unintelligent to me.

There is no definitive owner of this phrase, some accounts say that it was said by Goering, some say it was Goebels, and some say it was said by Bormann. Some accounts of this statement say that the phrase was said by most of the SS. We have already heard a first-hand account from Anna who worked for the Heydrich family, that none of the SS, either soldiers or officers ever dared to call Heydrich any name at all, for fear of their lives, so I would imagine this fear would be even greater about Himmler. If Himmler summoned you to his office, I imagine you would be very fearful of why. So perhaps it was Goering or Goebbels then? My view is that it is unlikely to have been Goering, since he was busy running the Luftwaffe and wouldn't have had day to day dealings with Himmler. Goebbels was a renowned orator, a master of propaganda and its techniques. Why on earth would he wish to spread any kind of 'anti-Nazi' stories about a high status commander? Both seem totally incongruent.

So perhaps it was Bormann? It was Bormann who was closest to Hitler. Bormann and Himmler were probably the only two men who would have had open access to Hitler; and everything Hitler did or didn't do, would have been via one of these two men. So why might the two men closest to Hitler take a dislike to each other?

Was it jealousy perhaps? Was it an internal competition to be the most valuable follower of Hitler? Himmler was a very clever man and wielded a lot of military power. Bormann on the other hand, was not a military leader, but seems to have assumed control over many military matters in the guise of his responsibility to handle the domestic policies of Germany. Bormann had de facto control over all domestic matters, and his new appointment as both personal secretary to the Fuhrer and Minister of the Interior seemingly gave him the power to act in an official capacity in any matter.

Perhaps this was the reason for possible animosity between the two men? Or was it an unspoken (to Hitler) clash of the Titans! I wonder if either of them kept a Diary. It would answer a lot of questions, and certainly explain the odd insult thrown between them. Insults are thrown around between Ministers and Politicians in the UK Government every day in the House of Commons and it has developed into a kind of Gentlemen's sport; the trick is to be as damming as possible while at the same time delivering it as politely as possible. 'Yesterday in Parliament' on BBC Radio 4 is sometimes more entertaining than their 'Afternoon Theatre!'

If Himmler was leading the SS and Bormann was making decisions and signing orders instructing them to take particular actions, was this usurping Himmler's Command structure? I suspect that might be a valid reason for Himmler to take a professional dislike or irritation to Bormann, so perhaps if Bormann invented this statement, it may have been just to 'rattle Himmler's cage'.

Here are some of the disturbing examples of Bormann's decision making that have had enormous repercussions for both Heydrich and Himmler:

Bormann advocated the use of extremely harsh and radical measures when it came to the treatment of Jews, prisoners of war and all conquered proletariat peoples, and it was Bormann who signed the decree of 31 May 1941 extending the 1935 Nuremberg Laws to the annexed territories of the East. It was Bormann who signed the decree of 9 October 1942 setting out the permanent and 'final solution' stating that emigration was no longer an option and evoking the use of 'ruthless force in the Eastern Camps', or extermination by an alternative label. On 1st July 1943, Bormann bestowed absolute powers over all Jews to Adolf Eichmann, who was then operating under the offices of the RSHA with exclusive jurisdiction over the Gestapo. This was over a year after Heydrich's death and yet another example of the confusing hierarchy of power that makes it very unwise to 'pin' any decision made about 'front-line' action under any of the SS formal offices, onto the direct chain of administration that was theoretically in command of it.

I have read that Himmler was afraid of Heydrich, hated him, was jealous of him, scared of his power and secret files, and even that Hitler and Himmler secretly killed him by sending their Doctors to him to make sure he didn't recover from his wounds.

I found statements about Himmler and Bormann playing Heydrich off against each other. Bormann was Hitler's personal secretary who must have had a great influence over who was seen or not seen by Hitler, something like a Government PPS or Private Personal Secretary to one of our Ministers today. There are also statements about Heydrich seeking to overthrow Himmler, that he wore his ring on the wrong hand to annoy Himmler, that they were friends, were not friends, were secret enemies, it just goes on.

The only option open to us to try to establish which story is the real one, is to look at other aspects of their relationship to see if it reveals any probability of the truth. This is a standard process in a Serious Case Review, which is performed following a murder, where the question is not 'did it happen', but whether it could have been predicted by any of the agencies involved with the perpetrator, or whether it could have been prevented by any different action or actions taken by them. Since we are not looking at any of the things that Heydrich did or didn't do – they have been covered ad infinitum by many other writers – I am only looking at things which have not been recorded accurately or not recorded at all, and his relationship with Himmler is definitely one of them.

It is clear that Himmler enjoyed using ancient runes to represent parts of the SS organisation, and it is rumoured that he also had special runes designed for some key people and one of these was Heydrich. A rune that is made up from a number of single runes and all put together onto one 'stalk' is called a 'Bindrune' and I discovered this information on a blog from an expert in Runeology:

This emblem is the personal runebinding for SS Obergruppenführer Reinhard Heydrich.

The binding is based upon the Hagal rune as the central rune.
All the runes - H (Hagal) T (Tyr) E (Eh) R (Rit) –
(his initials) can be found in the binding.

Here is where I found it:
www.volkisch-runes.blogspot.co.uk/2014/07/heydrich-tristan-eugen-reinhard-this.html

This is the reason that I took pains to clarify the Rune on the side of Heydrich's plane in the previous chapter. Heydrich did have a personal Rune but this was not on the side of his plane (whether he was a briefly seconded member of the Luftwaffe, or not). Heydrich did have 'his own plane' because he needed to get from place to place quickly and safely (which he may or may not have piloted now and again). The rune on Heydrich's plane was *just* a Sig Rune, or one of the SS flashes.

✓ Personal plane with rune
X Plane with personal rune

I have never seen any other account of this strange rune, so assuming it is true, this is a definite clue that Himmler's relationship with Heydrich was signified as a special one. I think the idea of it was so that Himmler could send letters to Heydrich without the use of any names or other official identifying marks, so we might call them 'secret messages', or at the very least, personal messages. Would Himmler bother with this for someone that he didn't care much for? It is not very likely. Himmler doesn't strike me as a man who would waste his time on people he didn't like or respect. So we have clue number one.

One of the Collectors I came to know from the Arms Fairs and Militaria Shows, recently found himself at an 'invitation only' sale of a large collection of Third Reich items, which included original oil paintings, books, uniforms, and personal items. Among the vast collection was an old book about Heydrich's life, which is long since out of print, and some papers – all in German- with Heydrich's name on them. Knowing that I had an interest in Heydrich, he took a few photocopies for me of a few of the papers that had Heydrich's name on them, and photocopied a couple of pages of the book; before it all disappeared with their new owners after the sale.

One of those rough photocopies was a letter from Heydrich to Himmler which began: 'Reichsfuhrer!'

And at the top left of the page there was a feint mark on the photocopy that I recognised immediately.

Chapter Thirty
An Unbelievable Discovery

It was a very feint mark of an embossed character in the original paper, and I screwed my eyes up to make out what it was. I am certain that it is the personal Rune of Heydrich, as designed for him by Himmler and as shown in the previous Chapter!

So it really did exist, and was used for unofficial communication between them both. The date of it is 1942 and was written from Prague, so whatever relationship they were rumoured to have in those later years, they were still clearly on very good terms. I include it here for you to see.

The condition of the original was not great. It had been hole-punched and shoved into a file with other papers and the embossed mark is certainly faint, but look at the detailed picture of it, then look carefully at this photocopy and you will definitely be able to see it.

The salutation is interesting. It doesn't say 'Heinrich', so doesn't give us first name terms; but it certainly isn't 'official' either. It looks like a tongue in cheek name as it has an exclamation mark after it. Now what could be the meaning behind that?

If a colleague of mine was the President of the USA, I might write to him as 'Mr President!' instead of Dear John, to indicate that I was familiar with him, but at the same time treating him with the respect that goes with his title. The Official salutation would be: 'Heinrich Himmler Reichsfuhrer- SS' but this just says: 'Reichsfuhrer!'

A scribbled note, in his own hand – not dictated to his Adjutant – another sign of informality and no sign of hostility between them. An example of this kind of relationship might be a School, where the Teachers and Head Teacher call each other by formal surnames (Miss Smith or Mr Brown) even though they may have worked at the same School for over ten years, and know each other very well as a work colleague, but not at all socially. This might be a similar relationship if the Teacher wanted to write a personal note to the Head-Teacher; and might well address it as 'Headmaster!' It denotes familiarity in a work environment, but not socially. It would be very odd for the Teacher to address the note as Dear Fred, or as Dear Head-Teacher.

Clue number two is the fact Himmler wrote a six page eulogy and read it out at Heydrich's official funeral in Berlin. Would he do this for anyone he didn't like? Again, I don't think so. My guess is that Himmler would have done his duty and appeared at the event, but would not have credited him with the status of having Himmler himself write the eulogy or read it.

It takes a long time to write six pages. This was no perfunctory duty for Himmler; this was something he spent valuable time doing for a colleague that he had worked with for eleven long and very traumatic years. Heydrich was someone he could trust, who would carry out his instructions to the letter. We have already seen evidence of competition between Bormann and Himmler, so if Himmler didn't have a subordinate he could rely on, his own position could be vulnerable. I would surmise that Himmler relied totally on Heydrich, and part of that relationship being successful, would be Heydrich's sense of duty to never; absolutely never; treat Himmler as anything less than his Commanding Officer.

Also at the Funeral, Himmler personally took charge of both of Heydrich's two young sons, Klaus and Heider. This is something that you would expect a close relative or close friend to do, not an enemy. Himmler had a daughter whom he was very close to, and so would have been very sympathetic towards Heydrich's sons.

Clue number three is that Himmler was Godfather to Heydrich's eldest son Klaus, and had been since July 1933, one month after he was born. Considering Himmler's anti-Christian beliefs, this was not an insignificant task for him to agree to take on. It is not something that an enemy would be asked to do and not something that a superior officer would normally agree to do. Most people today will ask their closest friends to take on this responsibility, and not their employer or Commanding Officer.

Unfortunately Klaus was killed in a cycling accident at the Castle in Prague when he was ten years old, and this has been explained by the first-hand account of Anna, in a previous Chapter.

The two men may well have had their differences over the years, I can't imagine their relationship didn't have any differences of opinion, but their two skill sets were very different and Himmler was clever enough to know that his own traditional folkloric and esoteric views would be either reinforced or refuted by Heydrich's analytical and logical calculations. This appears to be a good way of two opposites working together. Without commenting on what they did, the way they worked together was very effective. Himmler had the vision and Heydrich found practical ways to achieve it. In business, this would actually be the perfect CEO and MD partnership.

In general terms, and not accounting for the odd difference of opinion; Heydrich appears to have had a good relationship with Himmler. It is a fact of history that only the differences of opinion are recorded; the newsworthy arguments, or moments of conflict; giving the impression that their relationship was very confrontational.

I would assume that Heydrich had little concern for the ethereal concepts of Pagan ritual and ancient Germanic tradition and was probably a little bemused by Himmler's obsession with it, but nevertheless, their relationship withstood eleven years, marriage, children, changes in job roles, and a world war.

Time to bust another myth:

MYTH BUSTED
Heydrich and Himmler Hated Each Other

In the collection of white photocopies I had, there was one other sheet that caught my eye. Officially typed in German and signed by Himmler, I recognised it immediately.

I couldn't read a single word of the German text, but I knew what it was, what it said and what it signified.

At last the search was over.

Chapter Thirty One
The Revelation

The document was typed in the well-known German font. It was headed *Der Reichsfuhrer SS and dated: 24th December 1933.*

It began: *Herrn. SS Brigadefuhrer H e y d r i c h*

It was the Citation from Himmler for the Totenkopf Ring

I rushed to my copy of the book by Craig Gottlieb: THE TOTENKOPF RING: 'An Illustrated History from Munich to Nuremberg' by Schiffer Military History Books, to see if it was the same as the early citations from 1933.

Page 42 showed me a copy of an official document that was written by SS Sturmbannfuhrer Ulrich Graf to the Personnel Office in Berlin to update the Dienstaltersliste (Service Record) with the date his Totenkopf Ring was awarded and it was dated 24th December 1933.

I could hardly breathe, but managed to turn to page 65 where the Chapter was called AWARD DOCUMENTS. It took me ages to be able to turn the page.

Page 67 shows a replica of the earliest known document for a Totenkopf Ring. The document shown in the book is one of ONLY TWO 1933 dated documents known to be in existence. It was presented to: Herrn. SS Oberfuhrer v.d.Bach – Zelewski. The salutation differs from subsequent documents in that the salutation reads: *Ich Schenke Ihnen* which translates as *I present to you.*

Gottleib goes on to explain this in his book. [This is a direct quote from the book and it does have a grammar error in the first line]

Type 1. This type has only been observed was used exclusively for 1933 rings, and unique with respect to the introductory wording used, which was Ich Schenke Ihnen, which translates 'I present to you'. This makes sense, as the early 1933 rings were not awards per-se, but were given by Himmler as gifts.

All observed examples of these extremely rare documents were presented from Munich (Munchen) and bear SS in gothic script, instead of Sig-runen. All type 1 documents I have observed do not contain the awardee's unit in the typewritten area at the top of the document – only the name and rank are included.

Of interest is that all observed documents of this type use the prefix HERRN before the name.

On page 69 is a replica of the only other Type 1 document ever seen. This one was presented to: Herrn. SS Gruppenfuhrer D a r r e

I studied my photocopy. It was exactly the same!

I studied the rest of the replica document. It was exactly the same!

Even the way the surname for Darre had been typed with a space in between each letter was the same as the way H e y d r i c h had been typed on my copy.

Done it, done it, and done it!

This is the evidence I had been looking for of when Heydrich was awarded, or rather, presented, with his Totenkopf Ring. It was almost certain now that this really was part of a 'Christmas' (actually a Yule present, as we have previously deduced) and the same date as the other rings given as presents by Himmler. The date engraved on the silver bell is 24th December, and the same day of present giving in Germany as previously explained.

So the Silver Bell appears to be the only surviving evidence of the way Himmler presented it to his special 'Corps d' Elite' in December 1933. I now have both the bell and the citation that match (admittedly it is just a photocopy, but I'm sure Messrs Gottlieb and Boyle will be very keen to see it – and I will be happy to show them.

Here it is for you:

Der Reichsführer ⚡⚡   Herrn   München, den 24.Dezember 1933.

SS-Brigadeführer H e y d r i c h

Ich schenke Ihnen den Totenkopfring der SS.

Er soll sein:

Ein Zeichen unserer Treue zum Führer, unseres unwandelbaren Gehorsams gegen unsere Vorgesetzten und unserer unerschütterlichen Zusammengehörigkeit und Kameradschaft.

Der Totenkopf ist die Mahnung, jederzeit bereit zu sein, das Leben unseres Ichs einzusetzen für das Leben der Gesamtheit.

Die Runen dem Totenkopf gegenüber sind Heilszeichen unserer Vergangenheit, mit der wir durch die Weltanschauung des Nationalsozialismus erneut verbunden sind.

Die beiden Sig-Runen versinnbilden den Namen unserer Schutzstaffel.

Hakenkreuz und Hagall-Rune sollen uns den nicht zu erschütternden Glauben an den Sieg unserer Weltanschauung vor Augen halten.

Umkränzt ist der Ring von Eichenlaub, den Blättern des alten deutschen Baumes.

Dieser Ring ist käuflich nicht erwerbbar und darf nie in fremde Hände kommen.

Mit Ihrem Ausscheiden aus der SS oder aus dem Leben geht dieser Ring zurück an den Reichsführer SS.

Abbildungen und Nachahmungen sind strafbar und Sie haben dieselben zu verhüten.

Tragen Sie den Ring in Ehren!

H. Himmler

What a journey it has been. The first thing I did was to phone the Dealer (sorry – collector!) who sold it to me, and told him what I thought it was. I imagined that as an avid collector, he would be pleased to know the real history and purpose of the strange little item. How wrong I was.

His attitude became distinctly cold as he suddenly realised the true significance of the Silver Bell, and that it wasn't just a dinner bell, as he had described it. In fact I still have the original ticket that was tied to it which says 'Dinner Bell'. He has barely spoken to me since then.

As far as collecting similar items goes, I wouldn't like anyone reading this to think that they will be able to find rare and valuable treasures from the Third Reich by visiting the Arms Fairs and Militaria Shows. Quite honestly, everything you see in these shows has been studied by experts many times, sold back and forth between themselves, long before any of it reaches the grubby tables where it is then made available to the public.

There is a huge trade in fakes, which started in the late sixties and seventies. Unfortunately though, the fakes look very genuine, as they are now forty to fifty years old themselves, so be warned. Candelabras, Salt and Pepper Pots and Ink Wells, are particularly popular fakes, and as some of these are fifty years old, they can look very authentic.

Award Badges and Iron Crosses are a real minefield, as these are easy to create and 'age' to make them look real. Even the old style backs can be replicated, so it is probably best to just stick with one of the reliable replica suppliers such as; Soldier of Fortune, Epic Militaria, and Militaria.net; where you will pay a sensible price for something that looks pretty much like an original.

A friend of mine bought a supposedly genuine brass Inkwell that was engraved with SS runes, an Officers name and his award dates. He was charged £3,000 for this item, and has now discovered it to be a worthless fake. Firstly, bare brass or any gold coloured metal was not a usual finish for any genuine SS object. It would usually be finished with plating that was made from silver, nickel, or chrome. All the SS Dress Uniforms displayed silver insignia; which included: piping, buttons, collar patches, pips and silver wire embroidery. Furthermore, we have already noted the influence of Viking and Germanic tradition to the SS; and this reliably informs us that silver and iron had more significance to them than gold. The inkwell was also embossed with roses, and this was a huge warning sign, as roses were not used in the SS iconography at all.

Another perilous area to watch out for is any item which has been engraved with SS runes to make it more desirable, expensive; and collectable; but really isn't anything to do with the SS at all. A good example of this was an old wooden sundial that I came across recently, which was surrounded by the twelve signs of the Zodiac. This is clearly something related to astrology and should therefore not be misrepresented as having anything to do with the SS, or implying any connotations of Devil Worship, Paganism, or the Occult. It featured a central brass pointer that had SS runes engraved onto it, which quite frankly could have been done by anyone. By the look of it, this really wasn't a lost occult treasure of the SS worth £2,000; but just a tatty old sundial probably worth less than £20, that you might easily pick up from any car boot sale.

To be honest, anyone could buy an old silver item and engrave a high ranking German Officers name onto it. When my friend had his brass inkwell verified as a fake by an expert at Sotheby's; he was told that they are asked to evaluate a different pepper pot, supposedly belonging to Herman Goering every week. These items appear to be churned out in places such as Latvia or Poland and then sold in secret auctions and Militaria sales. So do be careful; especially if the price tag is over

£2,000, and you are told that they have allegedly been stored in someone's lock–up for the last fifty years. Just ask yourself, why on earth would they have done that, and then brought them out to be sold to you today? If it seems too good to be true, then it probably is.

Matthew Bell, a reporter for The Independent published an article on Sunday 11 March 2012 that was headed: 'In Search of the Nazi Memorabilia Collectors':

The article stated: *The trade in artefacts linked to Hitler is booming in Britain. Matthew Bell uncovers an astonishing auction, where a tray listed at £600 sells for £28,000.*

There is no legislation in Britain against the trade of Nazi memorabilia, and no plans to ban it, but in France, Germany, Austria and Hungary it is illegal. In 2001, the online auction house eBay imposed a ban on 'items that promote or glorify hatred, violence, racial, sexual, or religious intolerance', singling out Nazi memorabilia and books such as Mein Kampf. Sotheby's and Christie's do not trade in Third Reich material, and in 2010, Bonhams changed its policy to stop accepting it.

The Imperial War Museum in London has a large collection of Nazi and Holocaust artefacts, some of which it buys at public auction. Richard Westwood-Brookes, a historical documents specialist at Mullocks, believes it is important that Third Reich documentation is preserved.

In November, a single bedsheet 'believed' to have belonged to Hitler sold for £2,000. In 2010, the historian David Irving sold Hitler's walking stick to a New York collector for more than £7,000.

I can't help but comment to Richard Westwood-Brookes from the Historical Auction House at Mullock's, that he didn't appear to be quite so concerned with preserving Third Reich documentation, when he put the complete Register of SS members under the hammer not so long ago!

So please be careful. I wasn't looking for a unique and irreplaceable piece of history when I found the bell. I bought it because its true purpose intrigued me, as I didn't believe it to be just a dinner bell. It has taken me two years of investigation, an expensive collection of books and many trips to Germany to find out what it really was.

Now I know more about it, I feel duty bound to make this information available to those who have any historical interest, in the hope that it will add to our collective knowledge and also a more accurate recording of history.

Who knows, perhaps one day, Wewelsburg Castle might be allowed to display it with one of their Totenkopf rings carefully positioned on the stem. This would portray exactly how Himmler would have most likely presented the original ring to Reinhard Heydrich on the 24th of December 1933.

Lightning Source UK Ltd.
Milton Keynes UK
UKOW07f0656050115

243994UK00003B/11/P

reasons I was drawn to the hobby. Our woodland community was a conscious attempt to be a part of a loose movement called "New Monasticism" (an attempt, usually by lay people, to emulate the communalism of monastic life, to recreate its rhythm of prayer, manual labour, and hospitality).

Monasteries have often produced expert beekeepers, and understandably so: there's both a peacefulness and a courage about beekeeping which seems to mirror monastic life. So having our own hives seemed a good way to cement the connection between us and the monks and friars of traditional orders.

Of course, none of it worked out like that. The first colony I got – a swarm that Dad and I collected from a cottage in Charlton Horethorne – was safely placed in a new hive with a lovely gable roof. The next day we went up to see them and it looked suspiciously quiet. I took off the crown board and the hive was completely empty. It was like that eerie feeling you get when you push the open door of a friend's house and no-one's in. "Bees, eh?" Doctor Bob quipped. "They've never read the text books."

We got another swarm a few weeks later, and everything seemed to be going well. I used to enjoy watching the brown dots alighting on the landing board with bright orange pollen on their legs like a skateboarder's kneepads. Bringing in pollen meant that the queen was laying and there would be brood inside. When I opened up the hive I pulled out a few frames and saw the sealed creatures there like loads of liver spots. The fear of those first few explorations was acute: the ferocity of the whine they make when you open up their home is far worse that the bark of a dog. But there was a beautiful geometry to the frames: the perfect hexagons, slowly drawn out by the wax from the worker bees' thorax; the 7.5mm of "bee space", which they'll fill up if the place is too gappy.

By then we had been running our woodland community for a year, and had discovered – D'oh! – that communal living is often chaotic and noisy. As the notional "father" of a refuge for troubled, wounded characters, I was always in demand. But down there, by the hives, no one dared disturb me. It was the one place I could finally find a bit of solitude and admire a very different community which really knew about order, duty and sacrifice (when a bee stings to defend its own, it dies). But then those bees swarmed too. It was when my wife was in hospital having our third child. I was supposed to be looking after our other two, aged four and two but, fool that I was, I was damned if I was going to let a couple of toddlers get in the way of me recapturing the swarm. I could see the furry tear-drop of bees at the very top of the quarry rock-face, hanging off a horizontal branch of hawthorn. Bees tend to swarm on sweltering summer days, and this one was a scorcher. I put on my veil, bee-suit and boots and enclosed the kids within the chicken fence. I then went rock-climbing with my skep (a wicker basket to catch the blighters), sweating like I was in a sauna. The idea is that you thwack the

15

branch and the blob just drops into your basket; as long as the queen is there, the others will slowly follow.

But my veil got scratched by the thorns and the bees got in. Within a minute I was being stung all over my face. A sting is a bit like a papercut – so quick and cold you barely notice it at first. But then the poison starts to pump in and your mug begins to look like you've done a dozen rounds with Joe Frazier. The children a hundred feet below were beginning to get scared as the chooks pecked at their toes. I slid down the rock face like a cartoon character, his head surrounded by a blur of furious bees. Later, as we nursed our wounds indoors, I felt a very bad beekeeper – a bee-loser more like – and an even worse father.

There were so many other mishaps. One time I was feeling blasé and inspected the hive in my sandals. I had often seen experienced beekeepers picking up the frames in their bare hands, and I liked the idea of being close to the critters. They didn't, to say the least, return the compliment. Within seconds of lifting off the queen excluder, they were going for my ankles. I had none of my father's calm assurance and ran to the pond, diving in as the only way to get rid of them. The children attending our forest school looked on, bemused by the sight of a wailing adult diving into the green water.

By then we were organising all sorts of workshops and classes for our guests: we had sessions on psychodrama, non-violent communication, the Enneagram, anger-management, self-compassion, anxiety and so on. One of the weekly things we laid on was art therapy with an elegant woman who quickly got the nickname "Perfect Petra". One of our guests – a cheerful risk-taker and reformed coke-fiend – was called Macca. As part of the art-therapy session, and for reasons best known to himself, Macca decided to make a seat by the hive as a gift to one of our other guests. Both he and Petra ended up getting stung, Perfect Petra right next to the eye. It was beginning to seem like our bees were a source of pain and nothing else.

But paradoxically, the threat and menace of the bees occasionally helped our guests. It was our philosophy here that we always worked alongside each other, chopping logs or weeding the poly tunnel or whatever, because it was invariably during manual labour that the deep conversations somehow happened. One morning I had to look at the bees, but one of our guests was having a serious panic attack. Graham was scratching at his face, saying "going to die" over and over again. As usual when these things happen, I just took him along with me so we could work together, forgetting that I was about to open up a hive. He stood there, bees flying around his curly hair in the midst of his panic attack and he actually calmed down. I saw him at one point with his arms outstretched, grinning at the energy of the beasts circling around him. "It was", he told me later, "like the real but minor threat replaced a vague, terrifying one." Because there was a concrete scare, he had paradoxically found some serenity.

16

The years went by and we never got any honey. But in a way, taking honey wasn't the point of keeping bees. It was about pollination for our little orchard, it was a chance to spend time with my father, an opportunity – in a chaotic community – to go somewhere people couldn't follow. There were other by-products, too: from the wax we made candles for our shelters and polish for our carpentry projects.

And I slowly remembered, or was reminded, that actually it had taken decades for my father to learn his craft. I remembered that when we were growing up he would often have swollen, itchy forearms where the blighters had stung him. He jokingly reminded me all the mistakes he had made over the years, such as the time he tried to mark the precious queen (putting a dot of paint on her thorax) but had actually pressed the queen cage too hard and killed her. There had been plenty of mishaps in his beekeeping career: I still remember the first time I saw him vulnerable, with his head in his hands in the changing rooms of a swimming pool after a swarm had got inside his veil and repeatedly stung him. He too had had his battles with bees.

I was gradually becoming more competent. I began to acquire, I think, that cool curiosity about the bees' unpredictable behaviour, going through the hives not on edge, but simply fascinated. What are they doing now, and why? It was almost as if my softer approach had made them more compliant, and somehow more cooperative. When I looked through the hives now, the bees seemed more gentle because, perhaps, I was too. Near their hives I sowed all sorts of plants I knew they liked – broad beans, borage and so on.

And then, finally, last summer the brood chamber was chocker with bees and brood. I put on the queen excluder and a super (the shallower chamber where they put their stores of honey). By mid-June, when I lifted off the super to inspect below, it was as heavy as a bucket of water: all those tiny hexagons had been filled with honey, and capped with wax. I put on another super and that, too, slowly filled through June and July. At the end of the summer I took them round to my parents' place, the same house where I grew up.

We took the uncapping fork and scraped off those wax cappings, and then placed the frames inside a stainless steel extractor about the size of an oil drum. We then turned a handle which spun the frames around, flinging honey against the side of the extractor. It sounded like hundreds of fingernails tapping a window as the tiny splats of honey hit the inside wall. We let it settle in the "ripener", for the bubbles to disappear, and then opened the tap at the bottom and honey glugged into the jars like some sort of translucent snake.

Seeing those 40-odd jars stacked safely under the stairs was a bit like seeing stores full of logs. They exuded a sense of hard-won abundance. They seemed to suggest that we would be safe for another year; and that, for all my doubts, I was up to the immense challenge of looking after our experimental community.

More than that, they seemed to say that I wasn't just a keeper at last, but also somehow kept: that I was being looked after too.

Honey had never tasted so good!

Tobias Jones's book about his woodland community, 'A Place of Refuge', has recently been published by Quercus and is available in print or digital format. It will be reviewed in the November issue of The Beekeepers Quarterly. The above article was previously published in the Guardian.

SUSTAINABLE BEEKEEPING WITHIN A PRISON

Heidi Herrmann
Patron,
The Natural Beekeeping Trust

●

Places of 'violence, squalor and idleness' where one prison officer 'wouldn't keep a dog': Prisons are in their 'worst state for 10 years".
- HM Chief Inspector of Prisons for England and Wales, Nick Hardwick
https://www.psychologytoday.com/blog/socially-relevant/201508/the-rise-green-prison-programs

Telling the Bees
When you have bees in your life you tend to talk to them, tell them what's happening, consult them. In that vein, we told our bees some time in Lent that they had to move. The pleasure of their company was wanted in a prison.

Years ago, the Trust had received a message from Dave Bloomfield, Substance Misuse Services, HMP Rye Hill, to inquire about teaching convicts to take care of bees and make hives. "Your approach to bee husbandry would suit us here; we'd like our people to learn to give rather than take. We envisage gardens with sun hives". Could it be true?

The British penal service is, regrettably, the shame of Europe. While other countries succeed in reducing prisoner numbers dramatically without descending to lawless anarchy, in Britain they are at a record high. According to Nick Hardwick, Her Majesty's Chief Inspector of Prisons for England and Wales, prisons are in their worst state for ten years. The report observes: 'It is hard to imagine anything less likely to rehabilitate prisoners than days spent mostly lying on their bunks in squalid cells watching daytime TV. For too many prisoners, this is the reality.' Nick Hardwick's latest and last Annual Report 2014-15 reveals that by almost every measure, adult male prisons in England and Wales have been deteriorating. Psycho-active drugs, so-called legal highs such as Spice and Black Mamba which sell for far more inside than outside jail, have become a cause of violence and debt. The prisons are less safe than five years ago, with more prisoners murdered, killing themselves, self-harming or being attacked. They are overcrowded and undermanned. Assaults on prison staff are up, and so forth.

But at Rye Hill Prison, soon, so it seemed, there would be meadows, and a garden! Offenders would learn to sow, cultivate and reap, make beehives, become beekeepers. 'A bee-loud glade' and a hive for the honeybee, in a prison! We were delighted to get on board.

A prison with gardens and sun hives - what an exciting opportunity to make the lives of prisoners more meaningful and humane . . . . (Photo: Amit Lennon)

It was our first encounter with committee culture - nothing much happened for months on end, not counting an avalanche of correspondence, followed by silence. Had the plan been shelved? A year later a greenish light: the project is before the management! Approval is imminent. Could we reserve a date for a hive-making workshop please? Making sun hives away from home base is a big hassle, involving lorry loads of specialist equipment, straw, two instructors etc. Dates had been offered, accepted, then cancelled. In some exasperation, but hopeful still, we offered another. Next came an official request from the governing committee: where was the evidence that caring for bees was of therapeutic value. Could we provide it? Time to throw down the gauntlet, we reckoned. We regret to inform you that the submission of evidence about the therapeutic value of caring for something, especially a creature vital to mankind, is beyond the remit of our charity; abundant literature testifying to the benefits of vital and wholesome pursuits on the human soul is extant. You may wish to peruse it. Perhaps they did. Perhaps the bees invaded their dreams, who knows - the date pro-offered was accepted. A workshop took place in which seven prisoners and

members of staff patiently wove six impressive hives for their future bees.

The inmates took part in a workshop to make hives from organic rye straw.

Making a home for bees mysteriously connects the maker to the bees. In the days of steadily weaving a hive with loving hands, inner pictures arise, tender bonds are woven with the future bees. Sun hives are designed for the heights where bees want to live. They need special stands and covers. When the prototype appeared from the prison's carpentry workshop, Peter Brown approved. An impressive stand had been designed for the new hives. And there was even talk of the prisoners' new skills leading to a novel cottage industry: making skeps from biodynamically grown rye straw for the beekeeping world outside.

An ingeniously designed stand was manufactured in the prison workshop. It allows the sun hive to be easily lowered for inspection.

Bees for Sun Hives
With six perfect hives now awaiting, the prison asked us to procure bees. We scoured the bee market for colonies naturally reproduced from swarms, untreated, raised on organic/biodynamic land. Such bees don't exist outside our apiaries, and those of a few like-minded souls. Bees are local creatures, adapted to the flora and fauna of their origins; moving them is not ideal. Gareth did not relish the prospect of parting with any of his bees, but procuring bees from chemically treated stock was not an option, and a journey from Sussex too hard on the bees. One, not six, would go, we decided. When you've settled, dear bees, and if you like the place, go forth and multiply. Six perfect hives awaiting. Sun hives!

The hive embodies an ideal. Guenther Mancke, the German sculptor and bee father, says: "… the impetus for the hive's development came from the need to free the bees from a principle at once earthbound and cuboid, one

that goes against every law of form - we are dealing here with laws that are a particular expressions of a creature's life." There are many reasons for bees' present-day afflictions. We can be sure, however, that one of these is the fact that the creature, as a physical and ethereal entity, can no longer live its life as it is meant to.

Gareth John, one of the trustees of the NBKT, and thanks to 40 years of living with bees, one of our most experienced beekeepers, describes his first foray into one of Her Majesty's penal institutions. together with a hive full of bees: *'At about mid morning, we arrived at the prison with a hive full of bees, and - on my part at least - mixed feelings. We introduced ourselves. Peter Brown had been before and knew the ropes, or rather the walls. Photos were taken, and fingerprints too. The whole prison was aware of the arrival of the bees. We were given a list of the items that cannot be taken inside. Neither bees nor hives featured, so we waited our turn to go through the entrance gates with the land rover and its cargo. Just as our turn arrived, a medical emergency was declared: no vehicles in or out until the ambulance had come, collected the patient and departed. Nothing happened for a very long time. I mean, nothing! My bees stuck in the back of the car. Not a great start. I started fretting for my bees lest they overheat. Locked up, taken on a few hours' car journey, staying locked-up. A poignant picture, given the circumstances. Thankfully it was cool, and a slight breeze would reach them. Finally, more than three hours after arriving, we were ushered into the vehicle search compound. We were patted down. The vehicle was searched, but not the hive. The inner gates opened and we were inside. When we arrived at the garden area with our precious cargo the prisoners gathered round in keen anticipation: "Are you the beekeeper? Is this our hive? Where are you going to put it?" Prisoners are allowed budgerigars and, now, bees. That leaves a whole alphabet to play with. Before the hive entrance was opened, crowding prisoners had to be shooed back to a safe distance. After a hive has been closed up all day, the bees often rush out in a state of some excitement. This can lead to awkward introductions. As it was, only a few bees came out to explore their new quarters. Thankfully, leaving the prison was far easier than getting in; which left me something to ponder on the drive home.'*

Convicts and Bees

Now it was time for the bee course, to tell the prisoners about the bees, how they live and what they need. Getting lost in the triste environs of the prison on my way there, my heart sank. Where would our bees find food in these monotonous wastelands of chemical farming? Bees go far for forage, it is true, but there wasn't much to be seen.

By the time Gareth and I had declared our intent, stowed away our bags in lockers, had fingerprints and photographs taken, waited, got searched

and walked on command through screens and armoured doors to emerge in the first wire-fenced compound, all I could think of was Dostoyevsky. The degree of civilisation in a society is revealed by entering its prisons. This was bleakness taken to a whole new level of menace. Gates, treble locks, red-lettered warnings of huge fines for security breaches. Razor-wire coils stretching into infinity. The prison is run by security services giant G4S. **'Securing your world'** is the company's maxim. Outsourcing of penal services is a growing trend in Britain, following in the footsteps of the US.

Gareth's white-painted Warre hive.

We arrived in the project area. There stood a little white hive. Gareth's bees! Content looking bees, returning with pollen loads. Exceedingly comforting to see. The garden - the manifestation of the "horticultural intervention" was buzzing with life. Casually dressed men tending to weeds, planting, watering. Lettuces, broccoli, herbs, sweet williams, wallflowers in a pristine bed of rich dark earth. Winding paths lead to poly tunnels, sheds and a pond: a very pleasing layout devoid of hard lines. We learnt that the prisoners, involved from scratch, had pleaded for meanders and curves. Straight lines dominated their lives here. We spotted a little stand of rye swaying in the wind - the prisoners had saved the seeds left over from the sun hive workshop detritus and planted them! Then we saw the hives, woven in prison, from rye straw grown at two biodynamic farms, Tablehurst and Hungary Lane.

The gardens full of bee-loving flowers were beautifully laid out - and, as the prisoners requested, with no straight lines.

The men who had made them would now attend the bee course. Except for one who was barred because of a violent incident. Violence is rife in the hell of incarceration. A prison is like a gigantic quarantine facility. Terrifying, demeaning, ugly. Staff shortages spell extended lock-up periods for inmates. Self-harm, suicides, depression are pervasive.

In a hive, every single bee always knows what to do and when to do it. And does it, we explained, after our students had introduced themselves - all men, most on life sentences, all ages. Every single bee relates to the other, and works for the well-being of the hive. All that is brought into the hive - nectar, pollen, propolis, water - is shared for the good of all. The queen, that heavenly creature, is the mother of all. We showed those on the course pictures - told them that:

- the young nurse bees must visit their charges thousands of times before the cradle is closed with wax;

- that it is always warm inside the hive - the bees making sure of this by thousands fanning with their wings; the bee babies must never get chilled, they need the same warmth that we do;

- and the bee is perfectly fitted to the world into which it emerges.

The men began to engage. Questions galore. Good questions. The sessions were short. Lock-up times are tightly prescribed. After lunch, one of the group was missing. Bad news from home had upset him, so he stayed locked-up.

Attention was being paid to every last detail. We learnt that many of the men had already taken to standing near the hive in quiet moments, watching the bees come and go. How quickly will the hive swarm so that we can have bees in our sun hives? Engagement indeed! Steve Hammond, one of the instructors here, told us about the huge changes he'd seen over time in the men working in the garden. It's not like this, normally. You should see them on the wings. Tense, closed, unpredictable. They are different people when they work in the garden.

Next, swarming was the theme. What happens in the hive before the bees take-off for the wild abandon of swarming. Will our bees do it? How do we tell? When? They were keen on the detail, on imagining the swarm that might issue and hopefully set up home in one of their hives. What if the scout bees find a better place over the wall? Will we lose our bees? We suggested that the bees might well choose to stay with them. They were animated now, keen to rush out and get their sun hives up so that the scout bees, the house hunters could find them. There was plenty of time. It was mid-Easter. The men were relating to their bees now. Tomorrow, weather permitting, we'll have a look inside the hive, was how we left them. Remember to prepare for it.

Meeting the Bees

Inner calm. A quiet attitude. No anger, no fear. Would these troubled individuals be mindful of what we had impressed on them? Had they remembered to think about meeting the bees last thing at night? Bees are highly sensitive to people's emotions and react in kind. Watch yourself, they say. Bearing in mind that all of the prisoners were here because of acts of violence, it was a tall order. But Gareth, bent over the busy hive in shirtsleeves, trusted that they would be mindful and the bees forgiving. We assembled around the hive. Things can go wrong quickly if you're not on your best behaviour. The bees remained calm. The men pointed out the pollen-bearers to each other. Then, silence, save the music of thousands of wings as the bees were leaving and arriving at the hive. Were they aware of us, aware that something extraordinary was unfolding for the men watching them?

Gareth gently loosened the boxes. Two men slowly lifted the top, others took turns to draw closer to gaze at the mass of bees in full view now. Indrawn breaths. What were the men feeling? Nobody spoke. Hundreds of bees were circling and spiralling above our heads, chanting softly. Of course the bees were aware of us. The circlers above are the watchers. They keep an eye on things, on behalf of the hive. Ready to deploy their defences should danger arise.

A face appeared at one of the barred windows behind. "That's A., the one who made the sun hive ever so well," Steve explained quietly. A reminder of where we were. When the bees draw you into their world, all else fades into oblivion, for a time. Bee time. The hum of the bees became louder now. A certain pitch expresses a higher state of alert. It's best to take notice. We closed the hive and thanked the bees.

The prisoners' first encounter with the Bee had gone exceedingly well. But we had noted that one of the men was constantly bothered by a single bee that buzzed around his veil insistently. He resisted swatting it. He moved away and came back, the bee with him. When a bee lands on you, say hello. Do nothing. He hadn't forgotten. Self-control is essential in the presence of bees. Sitting quietly on a bench in the garden a little later, he confided to Gareth that he had been feeling very angry. "Couldn't shift it. When I am feeling better, I'll go and stand by the hive and say sorry " he said, " It wasn't fair on them". The bees were already showing that they have gifts to bestow more precious than honey.

The Rye Hill Garden project is bearing fruit. Prisoners are keen to be involved. The work is voluntary, there is no pay. "I am proud to be working here, with these guys, I am proud of what they achieve." Steve Hammond told us; he took early retirement to follow this vocation. Robin Baxter is employed by Garden Organic. For both, working here is full of rewards. The prisoners can feel that. Robin and Steve are treated with the greatest of respect.

The project's impact was evaluated by Coventry University. *"Participants related well to the activity of gardening and were aware that in undertaking the programme they had a common bond; this is important as prison is almost always a very individual experience. In addition, the staff working directly with participants on the Master Gardener programme were accepted by participants to be part of the community, and viewed themselves similarly too. A community spirit was created so that all felt part of something greater than their own role".*

The food grown in the garden is for the inmates to keep. To eat or share around on the wing. Steve tells me that some of the men had never tasted a salad leaf, or fresh vegetable. But they have come to love what they grow, their lettuces, herbs and fruit. Consider this against the dispiriting scenario described by the Howard Trust: Prisons are so unhealthy that people are considered to be old at 50 years of age. The poor diet, lack of exercise, lack of sunshine and daylight make for poor physical health. Many people going into prison have already lead unhealthy lives and the prison regime compounds that. The budget for food per prisoner is less than £2 per day. Cuts in staff numbers means that prisoners often get no outside exercise, etc.

The evaluation report describes how prisoners were seen to be supporting each other in countless ways, with gardening tasks, making each other beverages, supporting each other with literacy and numeracy skills, even recognising when someone was having a difficult day and offering help and solace. The warmth and kindness shown them by Robin and Steve, who guide the garden work, and Paul Evans, who manages the project, were noted by all the prisoners whose diaries formed part of the evaluation. It is great to be part of a team, it makes you proud to see what we have done together. We have achieved quite a lot.

Convicted criminals bring to prison issues that evolve directly from poverty, social inequality, broken homes, schools and communities, illness, alcoholism and addiction and estrangement. Every day prison reality is grim, brutal, demeaning. In a piece entitled *'Britain's prisons reek of a desperately backward nation'* Sir Simon Jenkins, journalist and editor, says: *"Not only does Britain imprison far more of its citizens than any other country in Europe, it imprisons for more offences and for longer terms, and is obsessed with incarcerating women and children. The British are prison addicts. We scour the country for reasons to imprison."*

Seen in this light, or darkness, growing flowers for bees in prison gardens might offer new perspectives for 'securing our world'.

Birth of A Bee Colony

The swarm so keenly awaited by the prisoners duly happened. Thousands of bees poured from the hive to rise heavenwards and join together in a wild dance, circling in the heights with joyful abandon, each bee perfectly

attuned to all others. Imagine the sheer delight of a swarm within those walls! Please stay, dear bees, don't fly over the fence, will have been on the mind of all who stood watching the formation wavering to and fro, coming breathtakingly close to the razor-wired wall - hovering - moving back again towards the garden. The bees finally settled on the canopy of the newly installed sun hive. Who chooses to end the dance, who decides where to land? That which guides the wisdom-filled rhythms of the hive eludes us, is not accessible to what can be gleaned by our ordinary senses.

The bees now had to be coaxed from the canopy of the hive into the hive proper. Steve and two prisoners stepped into the breech, all hopes upon them. Security had to relent and put back the two prisoners' lock-up time. They had been on the bee course, and now nothing could go forward without them. After four exhausting hours atop a high ladder, and a series of trial and error manipulations to get the great cluster to move inside the hive, the bees were in the sun hive at sunset. A truly fantastic achievement for Steve and his men. Their exhilaration was boundless. The first swarm is a happening never to be forgotten.

The project's open day celebration was a great success. "Our bee conservation project is truly rewarding", says project manager Paul Evans. "The bees received massive attention, they were out in force. We were watching them closely. We think they feel at home now. So we now have our very own Rye Hill bees in our Rye Hill-made sun hive, in a garden we created together." Steve wrote, "Do I sound proud or what?" We all share Steve's sense of pride, as well as his sadness upon learning that Rye Hill prison which already houses nearly 700 inmates, is destined to become a mega-prison. A large area earmarked for flowering meadows has been withdrawn to make space for more cell blocks.

The bees responded with unequalled fecundity as if to assert themselves and blazon their message in this strange world where prisons grow faster than flowers. They are knowing, the bees. Thanks to social media we now get instant news about them:

Stephen Hammond @steve9491 May 17 So excited, no sleep yet. First swarm collected & only one sting. Not bad.
Stephen Hammond @steveh9491 May 26 Bees swarm again at HMP Rye Hill, witnessed incredible scenes and still had the luck to collect and add to 2nd sunhive with inmates help.
Stephen Hammond @steveh9491 May 27 Quite amazing 3 swarms from 1 hive in 11 days, have some great photos for you. Great work from the prisoners at HMP Rye Hill.
Stephen Hammond @steveh9491 May 27 Bees must love it at HMP Rye Hill, 3 swarms in 11 days, from 1 to 4 hives in the blink of an eye. Plus 4 baby wagtails in raised beds.

Whitsuntide at Rye Hill Prison 2015.

Three sun hives alive with bees. Many thousands of bees have swarmed into the prisoners' lives from the mother hive. Three new bee colonies born within those walls. When I returned recently with Peter Brown to inspect the new colonies, we were delighted to find that the bees had already caused much wonder and excitement. The sun hives, mounted high, make for a strong presence in the prison yard. Where previously the eye travelled inexorably to the razor wire on top of the wall, one cannot but look up to the bees now. A gracious change indeed. The swarms, we found, had been well looked after, they had been fed and the bees' every movement observed with interest. Prisoners were keen to learn to 'read the combs', to become familiar with the ways the life of a growing colony manifests, to get accustomed to standing within a great cloud of bees. We had an inkling that these would be the most avidly observed bees in the whole of England. Subsequent teaching visits have confirmed this.

Update September 2015
(Gareth John)
When one has formed a relationship with a hive and those bees subsequently come under the care of another it is normal to worry about their welfare. Will they be well looked after? Will they prosper in their new location? Will they perform in the manner expected of them? All of these questions arose in my mind with respect to the hive of bees that I transferred at the end of March from my apiary to a high security prison some 50 miles away.

The first visit to the prison subsequent to delivering the hive was a fortnight later, to teach beekeeping. At that stage the hive was much as it was when I last saw it. The main question from the prisoners was 'will the bees swarm?'. I had this hive down as one that was likely to swarm, and part of the reason for placing the hive in the prison was to supply swarms for the sun hives that had been so carefully made by the prisoners. But, of course, I could not be sure. One never can be.

Some time later, we received news that a swarm had indeed left the hive, and had been placed by the prisoners and staff in a sun hive. Hooray! The bees had performed as hoped. By the time the swarming season was over, this hive had swarmed 5 times; each swarm had been taken and hived. Two swarms had left for other quarters, leaving 4 hives in the care of the prisoners and staff.

It has been a difficult year for bees in my home apiary; the main honey flow failed completely. Would the prison hives be in good shape? We had advised feeding, but those in charge of the bees were all complete beginners. Although other members of the NBKT had visited in the interim and had given glowing reports, it was with some trepidation that I returned to the prison in late August.

A swarm taken by the beekeepers and added to a sun hive.

The first thing I noticed inside the high and forbidding walls was the plethora of flowers. Every path was skirted with flowers in full bloom. The garden project, of which the bees are part, was clearly having a significant impact. Then, rounding a corner, I caught my first glimpse of the sun hives, made by the prisoners, on tall stands, also made and designed by prisoners. What an impact! The whole ambience was different. Standing tall in the midst of straight wire fences and harsh brick walls were rounded, wooden structures, and from the sun hive baskets held aloft by these stands flew bees; bees that had swarmed from the hive I took in March; swarms that had been collected and hived by the prisoners and staff. It is always a joy to see prospering a swarm that has issued from one's own hives, but here were 3 such swarms, in circumstances that are, to put it mildly, unusual, maybe even unique.

On entering the bee garden area, I immediately went to the Warré hive in its corner. How would it be after throwing 5 swarms? Had it managed to keep a queen for itself and get that queen mated? The wind was blustery, but bees were flying at the entrance and through the observation window activity could be seen. We decided to take a look inside the hive by rotating the top box to be sure that all was as well as it appeared. And indeed it was! Plenty of sealed brood was evident and, although not overly heavy with stores, the hive was not as light as some of my own after the poor season. Maybe the season here had been better: this hive had thrown 5 swarms and was in good

condition. The quick inspection felt like being reunited with an old and dear friend; one who had been through considerable adventures since we parted. The bees were as quiet as I remembered them, a joy to behold; hadn't they done well!

Despite throwing out five swarms, the bees in the Warré hive were in excellent shape.

The prisoners then joined us for an inspection of the sun hives. We first approached the one known to be the weakest, having been started by the smallest swarm. One of the prisoners and a staff member went through a smooth and obviously much practiced routine of pulling out the pins securing the hive and lowering it from on high to its inspection position. We had agreed to check the condition of the hive in terms of having a laying queen (or not – not all swarms manage this) and to check its level of stores. We also wanted to demonstrate what to look for on future inspections. Carefully the top basket was removed and we began to peel back the cover cloth. As is my practice, I explained to the bees what we were doing and addressed them in affectionate terms. I find this helps enormously in having calm bees, especially, as is also my practice, I was not wearing any protection.

Inside the hive were beautiful arches of comb and I was able to point out the various things that were key to understanding the state of the hive. I congratulated the bees and told them how beautiful they were. The staff member standing opposite me joked that I should perhaps not look him in the eye when saying 'you are beautiful'. One of the prisoners, in his protective garb, commented that I had courage to handle bees without protection, placing my hands deep in the hive. I replied that it was not courage but trust, me of the bees and the bees of me.

All three sun hives were in excellent condition bearing in mind the season we have had. The feeding regime that we had recommended had clearly been assiduously followed. We had a full debrief in a meeting room and answered many perceptive questions about the bees, their behaviour and welfare. It was clear that there had been occasions when the bees had not been as quiet as they were today and the reasons for this were discussed. It was evident that the prisoners had developed an excellent understand of bees and their ways and had learned that a calm and caring demeanour is a pre-requisite to having calm bees.

Few beginners would cope as well with so many swarms in their first season. Few beginners would be as acutely observant of their bees and their ways. Here were men who had committed serious crimes of one sort or another (that's why they are in prison) and yet they still have within them the ability to observe and care deeply for another creature. As I left, I felt humbled, impressed and deeply moved. I felt that the bees in that place know they are in a special relationship, beyond the norm. The prisoners know it too.

Afterword
Thanks to Northern Bee Books as well as John Wiley and Sons Limited, the prison library has now been enriched with beekeeping books. "**The Bee-friendly Beekeeper**" and "**Natural Beekeeping with the Warré Hive: A Manual**" - both by Dr David Heaf, will no doubt be studied on "Bee Wing".

Those of us privileged to bring to Rye Hill Prison sun hive-making skills, beekeeping instruction, as well as bees and their wondrous ways, we share a deep sense of gratitude for the kindness we have met, for the hope embodied in the growing gardens, and for all the people who have opened their hearts to the bees in this prison. The bees are doing good work here, they are loved and most keenly observed. Now the prisoners will learn how to take care of them through the seasons of the year. They will grow flowers for the bees. They will be bee guardians. Bees are in their lives now. May it help them and offer much solace and understanding.

Bees always foster change in the lives that they touch. They are good at that, it's what they do best!

(All photos unless indicated were taken by Stephen Hammond)
(Part of this article was published in the July issue of "Star and Furrow" - the journal of The Biodynamic Association).

THE BEE, ITS KEEPER AND PRODUCE, IN IRISH AND OTHER FOLK TRADITIONS

Eimear Chaomhánach
Department of Irish Folklore

Introduction

In this essay, I hope to present a synopsis of the most important features of my M. Litt. research. Most of my work, to date, has been carried out in the Irish Folklore Commission Archive, situated within the Irish Folklore Department, UCD [i]. This archive includes two manuscript series — the Main Manuscripts which contain over 2000 bound volumes and the Schools' collection which amounts to over 500,000 pages. The manuscripts contain material from all over the country, from both children and adults. This material derives from responses to various questionnaires sent by the IFC to households around the country, and also transcripts from recorded sessions with various informants from around Ireland. The manuscripts are in both the Irish and English languages.

My particular interest in the folklore of the bee and its keeper evolved due to my constant involvement with the bee-keeping calendar from an early age — my father being a bee-keeper for over thirty years. In my final year as an undergraduate, I undertook a primary study of the bee within the area of Folklore. I soon learned that there was potential for a broader, more detailed study, and continuing the research has introduced me to an abundance of

previously undiscovered material.

This essay will concentrate on some of the myths, legends and beliefs which are attached to the Bee itself within Irish Folk Tradition.

Shakespeare

"...So work the honey bees,
Creatures that by a rule in nature teach
The art of order to a peopled kingdom;
They have a king and officer of sorts;
Where some like magistrates, remain at home,
Others like merchants venture trade abroad;
Others like soldiers armed in their stings,
Make boot upon the summer's velvet buds;
Which pillage they with merry march bring home
To the royal tent of their emperor:
Who, busied in his majesty, surveys
The singing masons building roofs of gold,
The civil citizens kneading up the honey,
The poor mechanic porters crowding in
Their heavy burdens at this narrow gate,
The sad-eyed justice, with his surly hum,
Delivering o'er to executor pale
The lazy yawning drones" [ii]

It is important, before embarking on the study of lore and legends surrounding the bee, to have some understanding as to how this creature and its family operate and survive. This is eloquently related in verse by Shakespeare, where he manages to encompass all the elements which feature within a hive. Shakespeare commends the bee's artistry and order, and asserts that humankind can learn from this. In addition, the poet describes the ruling body of the King (Queen), whose presence assures life in the hive; the drones (magistrates), who lazily inhabit the hive and await the return of the workers (soldiers), off whom they steal the fruits of their labour. Finally, the brutal massacre of the drone is described, whereby the workers kill their brothers, and banish them from the security of the hive.

Egyptian Inscriptions

Such documentation of bees in literature and in art has allowed the approximate date of domestication of the bee to be estimated. In fact, the earliest reference documenting bee-keeping appears on the walls of the Egyptian sun temple of Ni-user-re at Abusir which dates from around 2400 B.C. [iii] These inscriptions appear in the form of hieroglyphs, giving reference to the use of beehives. This early interest in bee-keeping in Egypt most

probably evolved due to the popular belief that the bee originated there, from the sun god, Ra. [iv]

Imentet and the Sun God Ra - from the tomb of Nefertari (c.1298-1235 BCE).

Telling the Bees

Within our own tradition, bees are said to have been brought to Ireland from Wales in the 5th century, by a saint named Modomnóc. This date of arrival is substantiated by linguistic evidence of native Irish words existing at this time (the 5th and 6th centuries); such as beach (bee), mil (honey), and miodh (mead, i.e., fermented honey served as an alcoholic beverage). [v] St Modomnóc, possibly to be identified with St Molaga (or Molaige), is said to be a native of Fermoy in Cork, having a field, Páirc Molaga, named after him. [vi]

The legend which concerns St Modomnóc's introduction of bees to Ireland begins in Wales, where he is appointed caretaker or keeper of the bees in a Welsh monastery. When ordered to return to his kin in Ireland, Modomnóc was followed to the port by his loyal bees. The saint brought the swarm with him to Wexford, where they settled and spread throughout the rest of the country. After Modomnóc's swarm fled their native home in the monastery in search of their master, it was said that bees were never again encountered in this area. [vii] In some variations of this legend, the bees are said to have followed Modomnóc three times before being accepted by their keeper. [viii] Both of these features pertaining to the bees — that of following their master with a sense of affection and loyalty and that of devotedly abandoning their home after the loss of their keeper — are recurring motifs which can be witnessed in many folktales and legends concerning the bee.

St Modomnóc

One such story, contained in an early Ireland's Own magazine, describes a real life experience of how bees can possess a certain bond with their keeper, as seen between St Modomnóc and his swarm. [ix] The story describes the death of a small scale farmer from Missouri, USA, named Charles D. Hitt. As Charles specialised in water-melon production,

he decided to take up bee-keeping, knowing that both trades would profitably complement each other. Regrettably, on a cold day in February 1959, Charles D. Hitt met his death after a severe heart attack. After the body had been removed from the funeral parlour, the mourners assembled in a nearby farm house. At this time, a distinctive buzzing sound was heard resounding above the mourners' heads, despite the highly unlikely appearance of bees in mid-winter months. When it was time for the body to leave the church, and the mourners also made preparations to leave, bees were seen to be 'flying around in the strangest manner'. Could they possibly know that their friend and master was dead?' An hour or more later, family and friends congregated around the grave of Charles Hitt. As they neared the grave, one of them exclaimed:

'The bees are coming!' The funeral director, the sexton and others watched as the bees swarmed. A great black cloud of them flew from the farm across the valley, covering every blossom on the flower-bedecked grave. They settled harmlessly on the faces, arms and hands of those around...'

In incredible excitement, the bee-keeper's son observed similar movements at home: 'Dad's bees are leaving the hives by their hundreds. I don't think they will come back...'. The bees never returned.

In folklore tradition, bees are seen to have a sense and understanding of death. They appear to realise the connotations of death and its absolute nature. They react accordingly, by giving respect by what means they can. The reason for the fleeing of Charles Hitt's bees may be related to the fact that they were not notified of their master's death. The old custom of 'Telling the Bees' ensures that the bees will remain with the family following a death, and that they will feel involved. It will also guard against any feeling of offence the bees may experience due to exclusion from family affairs. An IFC informant from Glenariffe, Rosie Emerson, relates the importance of sharing such information with the bees:

'...They said that if you didn't tell the bees of a wedding a birth or a death they're that Gentle, they would take offence and leave...Who was it beside Jimmy Bann that didn't bother telling the bees and they said not a bee stayed with him after...'. (x)

Mrs Emerson continues to describe the procedures undergone by one of her neighbours when relating the news of death to the bees:

'Old Stewart...Jimmy Bann's above in Carnahaugh, he surely told the bees everything. He wouldn't miss it. When his mother died he put on his best suit, washed and   shaved himself...this is all gospel remember, you ask Quinn, too...washed and shaved and in his best polished Sunday boot: the same as if he was going to Mass. He went out to the scaps (old straw bee-hive) and told them (the bees)that their mistress was dead, and not a one of them left...'. (xi)

There are further procedures undertaken when relating the news of death

36

to a hive of bees. Hilda Ransome describes one woman preparing some spice cake and sugar in a dish, placing the sweets before the hive, then rattling a bunch of keys, and repeating:

'Honey bees, honey bees, hear what I say. Your master, J. A., has passed away.

But his wife now begs you will freely stay. And gather honey for many a day.

Bonny bees, Bonny bees, hear what I say.' (xii)

The death of one's bees is the penalty for failing to inform them of important news. However, this show of neglect has been blamed for other, more serious mishaps. We are told of a woman whose husband — a bee-keeper — died at the time she was expecting their second child. She believes that her failure to tell the bees of their keeper's death is responsible for the loss of her child in labour. (xiii) It appears to be a prevailing consensus, that by doing 'harm' or offending the bees, one could be open to punishment. Such was the reality for an individual in Cork, who smothered and killed a hive in order to steal the honey produce from the workers' labour:

'It was considered very unlucky to interfere or do any injury to bees. I heard my mother saying there was a person smothered a hive o' bees on 'em wan [one] time, to stale [steal] the honey. They never knew who done it, but they suspected the people, for they hadn't a bit o' [of] luck after...'. (xiv)

Another custom carried out immediately following a death, is the positioning of a black crepe upon the hive. This serves to safe-guard the health of the bees. Informants from Cork and Limerick verify the practice of this custom in their counties:

'If there are bees in a place and anybody dies in the house, unless they put a piece of crepe on top of the beehive, all the bees will die'. (xv)

Telling the Bees -
detail from a painting by Charles Napier Hernier,
1841-1917 (Wolverhampton Arts and Museums Service)

John Whittier (1807-1892) successfully coalesces all above beliefs and customs in his poem, aptly entitled Telling the Bees:

"Just the same as a month before, —
The house and the trees,

The barn's brown gable, the vine by the door, —
Nothing chanced but the hives of bees.

Before them, under the garden wall,
Forward and back,
Went drearily singing the chore-girl small,
Draping each hive with a shred of black.

Trembling, I listened: the summer sun
Had the chill of snow;
For I knew she was telling the bees of one
Gone on the journey we all must go!

And the song she was singing ever since
In my ear sounds on:-
'Stay at home, pretty bees, fly not hence!
Mistress Mary is dead and gone!' " [xvi]

Swarms - bringers of Good or Bad Luck

It is not all darkness and death which surrounds the bee in folk tradition. The positive energies of fortune and luck can also be attributed to the insect. A common belief amongst many communities considers the arrival of a swarm of bees to be a lucky omen. [xvii] The arrival of a single bee is equally capable of endowing a home with good luck. [xviii] Walter Gojmerac however, relates that this luck is dependent on the behaviour of the bee whilst in the house. If the bee flies in and out of the house, good luck is rendered. However, if the bee dies within the house, this abode receives bad luck. Gojmerac also contradicts the belief that the arrival of a swarm produces good luck. He relates: *'It is bad luck for a swarm to come to you, even in a dream. To dream of bees in a swarm is an omen of death, and dream of a sting means a friend will betray you.'* [xix] This view of bees bringing bad luck is echoed by another informant from Co. Roscommon, Mrs. Anne Hanley. She relates how a swarm of bees came to her property just before her husband died: *'I was glad to do away with them then, for I considered that they brought bad luck about the house...'* [xx]

Elsewhere, however, attitudes to bees are more positive. In Germany, for example, if bees swarm on a branch, this branch when used to direct cattle to the market, will ensure that the animals sell at a good price. [xxi] If a bee alights on someone's hand, it connotes that money is close to hand, and if a single bee lands on someone's head, this person will experience great success in life. [xxii] The presence of bees is said to promote productivity, as demonstrated by the story of the Reaper, who always kept a bee close to his scythe:

Once upon a time there was man cutting oats with two other men and he was able to show two swarths [piles of grass] to their one, and he went over the ditch and the other men went to look at his scythe and there was a little box at the bottom and was a trap door on it and they opened it and a brown backed bee flew out and when he came back he could not row [cut] at all and went off home. (xxiii)

Swarms might be portents of good or bad news.

Similarly, the reward of the worker's labour, honey, is also endowed with good luck and fortune. In Germany, the custom of anointing a baby's lips with honey guarded against any death in family. In fact, in early Christian days, honey was often used at Baptisms along with holy water. In other parts of Europe, it was customary to use honey in matrimonial ceremonies, again, by placing honey on the lips of the bride. Moreover, the sign of the cross, made with honey, was often put on the door of the new house to bring luck and banish demons. It is also a custom for the bridegroom's mother to await the newly-wed couple in their new home, bearing the gift of a jar of honey. (xxiv) It is possible that this custom was the seed from which the 'honeymoon' was born, or perhaps it evolved from the belief which regards honey as a powerful aphrodisiac! (xxv)

Bees and Lovers
Other associations between bees, honey and lovers, demonstrate people's trust in a bee's ability to distinguish true love from a mockery of love. One tradition from Central Europe describes how women used to lead their lovers past beehives, believing that if their partners were unfaithful, the bees would detect this, and sting them. (xxvi) The hurtful implications of a sting in such a situation is also adopted by Truman Capote in his story House of Flowers. Here, the confused character of Ottilie resorts to the God of Houngan to discover how one is to know when one has experienced true love. Houngan gives sound advice: *'You must catch a wild bee, he said, and hold it in your closed hand [...] if the bee does not sting, then you will know you have found love...'.* (xxvii)

The connection between bees and the gods is an integral part of the lore and legends surrounding this creature. With Christian folk tradition, bees are said to derive directly from God, through the tears of Christ and also the wounded skin of Job. (xxviii) A Welsh legend describes how bees derived from Paradise. In Paradise, bees were white in colour, and it was only after Adam and Eve indulged in the fruits of the garden, that they turned brown. (xxix) This

belief reappears in the form of a simile in a poem by Dafydd ap Gwilym, a contemporary of Chaucer. Gwilym likens snowflakes to bees from heaven:
Gwenyn o Nef Gwynion ynt.
[Bees from Heaven white are they.] (xxx)

Saints and Beekeeping
It can be seen, therefore, that the bees are largely associated with what is sacred. After being brought to Ireland by St Modomnóc, the bees' connection and relationship with various other saints flourished. Thus, bees have been assigned their own patron saint — Gobnait, from Ballyvourney, Co. Cork. Counties Kerry, Waterford, and Tipperary also lay claim to this saint who is also known as Gobnata and Gobnet. This has led to uncertainty as to the rightful place of birth of Gobnait. One theory gives Dún Caoin as her place of birth, where her name still adorns the village and church of Cill Gobnait. (xxxi) Similarly, there is a parish named Cill Gobnait in Co. Waterford, explaining why St Gobnait is held as the patron saint of this area. Another source renders her a native of Co. Clare, from which she ventured to the Aran Islands. Regardless of her genuine place of birth, it can be seen through folk narrative that St Gobnait is a much admired and highly reverenced saint in Ireland.

St Gobnait.

St Gobnait seems to be best known for her courage in protecting her people by miraculous aid. As with many Irish saints, St Gobnait reveals her wondrous influence over animals and nature itself. Thus, she is seen to combat a team of enemies single-handedly, with the use of her bees alone:

'Tháinig na saighdúirí Gallda agus tógadar mórán stuic i mBaile Mhuirne, ach ar an slige dhóibh ag imeacht an bóthar soir do scaoil Naomh Gobnait na beacha as an mbeachaire. Tosnuigeadar ar nasaighdúirí a chealg chun nar fágadar súil ná srón ionnta agus b'éigin dóibh an stuic fhágaint 'na ndiadh'.

[The English soldiers came and took a lot of stock in Ballyvourney, but on their way out the east road, Saint Gobnait released the bees from the bee-hive. They started to sting the soldiers until they were left without an eye or a nose and they were forced to leave the stuff behind them.] (xxxii)

Another story relates how a powerful chief prayed to Gobnait for assistance, recognising his troops to be incapable of victory. Gobnait granted his request by transforming a hive of bees into military men. (xxxiii)

40

Another rendition tracing the steps of Gobnait describes the saint fleeing her native land of Clare in order to escape a family feud. From here, she travelled to the Aran Islands, were she erected a church which still retains her name. Gobnait was spurred to move again following a visit from angels. The angels told her she must seek her place of resurrection, a place were nine white deer grazed. She moved to Waterford, where she founded a church at 'Kilgobnet', and it was here that she encountered the nine white deer as predicted by the angels. (xxxiv) The IFC manuscript echoes the legend of St Gobnait's association with white deer, and suggests that the saint was indeed resurrected in the guise of one of the aforesaid animals: *'I heard the enemy was hunting Saint Gobnait and they met seven white deer in the forest and they passed on, but what was it, but St Gobnait and her six sisters...'.* (xxxv)

Bee-keepers have also been awarded their own patron saint, the early Christian St Ambrose, born in the year 340 in Lyon. Ambrose displayed his affection for bees at avery young age. Whilst in his cradle, a swarm of bees settled on him and he showed no distress when they ran over his face and even in and out of his mouth. After some time, it is recorded that the swarm flew very high and disappeared into the heavens. On 7th December 375, he was consecrated Bishop of Milan, having been elected by popular acclaim, against his own will and despite his strong objections. In office he worked for the poor, gave justice with compassion, resisted imperial tyranny and was loved by the people. (xxxvi)

St Ambrose, Bishop of Milan and the Patron Saint of Beekeepers.

Another saint, Bega, otherwise known as St Bees, is best remembered for her work and care for the poor. Bees was the daughter of an Irish king and was said to be the most beautiful woman in the country. Similar to St Gobnait, Bees experienced a sacred encounter with an angel at an early age. Following this meeting, Bees vowed herself to the Spouse of virgins, and received a bracelet marked with the sign of the cross from the angel, which served as a seal of her celestial betrothal. The day before her arranged marriage with the son of the king of Norway, Bees fled and sought to follow the religious life. She soon received a nun's veil from St Aidan of Lindisfarne, and continued the work of founding monasteries around the country. She was epitomised by her eagerness to work and serve the people, and was affectionately remembered as one *'hastening from place to place like a bee laden with honey.'* (xxxvii)

41

St Bega of St Bees. (Doug Sim)

Ostensibly, this sacred association of the bee is not widely experienced in today's society. However, a Harvest Festival is still celebrated in Stoneleigh in Britain once a year, to commemorate the reaping of honey from one working year. Also known as the 'Bee-keeper's Service', this festival has been a vibrant feature of the bee-keeping calendar since the 12th century. The service consists of a gathering of bee-keepers from different parts of the country who surround a hive holding brass candlesticks. The hive — like an altar — is adorned with gifts of honey, which are later distributed by the vicar to local almshouses and old folks' homes. (xxxviii)

The Mystery of Bees
Honey, after all, is the bees' gift to the world and reward for their labour. Moreover, this ability to produce honey remains a gift unique to bees alone, a concept which taunted the Greek Philosopher, Aristotle. There were only three phenomena which remained a mystery to Aristotle:

(1) Intinn Mná [Woman's mind]
(2) Líonadh agus trághadh na taoide [The coming and going of the tide]
(3) Saothar na mbeach [The work of the Bees]. (xxxix)

In his endeavour to understand the work of the bee, Aristotle erected a glass box, in which he placed a working hive. The bees instantly denied the philosopher such access to their activity, as their first task on entering the glass box was to cover its walls with wax.

Aristotle, the great Greek philosopher, was mystified by the mind of women, the tides and the work of honeybees.

The main manuscripts of the IFC offer many renditions of this folktale. One informant from Tipperary, assigns the name of 'Harry Stackle' to the 'clever man' involved. (xl) Similarly, 'Harry Stattle' appears as the confused philosopher in an account from Cork, the name of whom was most probably altered by oral transmission. In the following account, we witness how the philosopher's curiosity results in his blindness:

There was a clever man there long 'go and his name was Harry Stattle. He was supposed to be the cleverest man that ever lived and no one could be good enough for him. He was the best huntsman of his time and he had

42

fourteen dogs and their names were — Fifo, Fiddler, Juno, Jiggles, Fido, Fanny, Farmer, Spanker, Spoken, Tannin, Joker, Dido, Miller, Ranger... But as clever as he was, there was one thing that went beyond him all his life and that was how did the bees make the   honey. He tried every plan and couldn't find out. So to look, he made a glass hive and put the bees into it. Now', says he, 'I'll find out how they make the honey'. But when he came to the hive the next day to watch 'em making it, 'tis how they had it plastered all over with wax inside and he couldn't see a bit. He was so vexed that he hit it a kick and broke it and all the bees flew out and stung him and blinded him... He went away travelling then and he blind, and no one having any meas [respect] on him   because he was blind and he had no meas on himself because he couldn't find out how the bees made the honey... [xli]

It is no wonder that someone would seek the recipe of honey-making as it has been, and remains today, one of the most versatile of all food-stuffs and medical aids. The earliest inhabitants must have availed of the sweet tasting honey from wild bees' nests. Fermented honey, in the form of mead, was one of the few beverages available in mediaeval times, its prominence being preserved in the name of the Great Banqueting Hall at Tara, Tech Mid Chuarda (Mead Circling House).[xlii] In 'Celtic Paradise', as described by Hilda Ransome, there were rivers of mead, as in the home of Oisín and Niamh in Tír na nÓg, where:

*Abundant there are honey and wine
Death and decay thou wilt not see.* [xliii]

Medicinal Use of Honey

Apart from this mystical aura which radiates from honey, there are also the medical properties which are attributed to it. The cold and 'flu are ailments commonly treated by honey. Similarly, sore throats, asthma and lung trouble all find in honey a natural cure. [xliv] Less obvious are illnesses such as backache, psoriasis, arthritis, chicken-pox, whooping cough, ulcers, boils, gangrene, hay-fever — and many more — which have all owed their cure to honey's antiseptic nature. Apitherapy (medicine from bees) is also said to assist problems of sleeplessness, bed-wetting, hyperactivity and stress. Less conventional is the idea suggested by Albert the Great, teacher and theologian of the Middle Ages, who offered a special contraceptive formula, that of spitting thrice in the mouth of a frog or eating bees. [xlv] This prescription is later contradicted, however, by Ó Catháin, who cites a recommendation to swallow a bee to ensure pregnancy, as it is said that women who keep bees are unable to bear children due to their profession! [xlvi]

Beeswax and its Uses

Wax, in the form of honey-comb, is the bees' primary produce, in which the honey is stored. Wax is likewise regarded with mystical and medical value.

In Wales, a tenth- century king named Hywel the Good was responsible for drawing up a series of codes, which included many laws from earlier periods. One such law documents a familiar theory as to the origin of the bee:

'The origin of Bees is from Paradise, and on account of the sin of man they came hence, and God conferred his blessing upon them, therefore the mass cannot be said without the wax...' (xlvii)

As previously ascertained, we witness the bee being presented as a somewhat mystical and sacred creature, thereby making its produce — beeswax — the only substance deemed worthy enough to use for making candles for the sacred mass.

Medically, wax has been a popular traditional cure for various ailments throughout the ages. Melted wax from a blessed candle, placed onto brown paper and positioned on the chest, is said to cure a cold on the chest. (xlviii) Wake candles — candles which are used in the wake ceremony itself — broken up and tied with a cloth around one's head are deemed a cure for headaches. (xlix) Wax has also been used to remove thorns, cure burns, warts, blisters, ring-worm and even the common cold. (l)

The wax candle, in its own right, is the subject of much lore and legend in folk tradition. The way in which a candle burns can indicate whether luck or misfortune is bound for a household. If a candle is not seen to burn evenly when lighted on Christmas Eve or All Souls, it is said to be a sign of death. (li) By contrast, on Hallowe'en, two lighted candles should be set over a fireplace, and if they are seen to burn clear, this is indicative of good luck for the future. However, if they smoke or splutter, bad luck will reign. (lii)

Beewax candles were not only important for lighting churches, but were symbols of purity, reverence and remembrance.

Indeed, the bee, its honey and comb of wax are all credited with the ability, in folk tradition, of predicting the arrival of good and bad luck. The endowment of such a gift derives from their near sacred image which has thrived since early times. Bees are seen to share much of the magical ability possessed by the Saints who acted as their patrons. They are seen to protect and remain loyal to their master. Their ability to predict the arrival of luck or misfortune is indicative of the sacredness which adorns them. An underlying bond between bees and the mystical world is encapsulated in the many legends which describe their origin being from Paradise, from the tears of Jesus and the wounds of Job. The custom of 'Telling the Bees' of an important event originates from the

possibility that there is an ingrained connection between the bees and the souls of the dead. [liii] This belief derives from ancient Egypt, where bees are seen to take the form of the soul. Ransome reminds us that bees were in contact with the gods when supplying the sacred mead, and suggests that 'It may be that the bee was not regarded so much as a live messenger between man and the gods, but as a form of the soul itself...'. [liv]

The Awesomeness of Bees

The ability of the bee to construct a perfect hexagonal-shaped comb, as a foundation to breed, to work and produce, and to survive, is the only verification needed to proclaim this species as one of hyper-intelligence. Within their own community, they can communicate by dance, giving information of distances, locations and abundance of nearby food stores. Their intelligence is reflected in humankind's confidence and trust in their wisdom. Thus, we witness people relating to the bees proposed projects to be undertaken, and acting according to the behavioural pattern displayed by the bee. The reaction of the bee would indicate whether or not it was wise to continue with the plan. [lv] More fantastically, we witness the bees outwitting the intelligence of Aristotle, leaving him in awe of their superb architecture and impressive honey production.

The absolute admiration, awe and respect held by bee-keepers for their bees, explains why this relationship has become embedded in folklore tradition in Ireland and elsewhere. Regardless of the unprecedented fecundity of this insect, the emotions bees have spurred surpass all. The following final anecdote, from 1854, encapsulates the beautiful relationship which can be achieved between a bee and its assistant:

A gentleman was staying at a friend's house and in the garden was a large beehive on the model of a house. One day his friend's niece (a child of nine years) was standing by him watching the busy throng in the hive; at last she said to him, 'What are these?' He answered her with some surprise, 'Bees'. 'No', she replied, 'we only call them so, they are fairies, or rather they are souls. If you had watched them as I have, you would not say that they were mere insects...' [lvi]

JOURNALS
An Beachaire
British Bee Journal Ireland's Own
The New Zealand Beekeeper

PRIMARY SOURCES
Irish Folklore Commission Archive (IFC)

SECONDARY SOURCES
Ó Catháin, S. (1995), The Festival of Brigit, Dublin, DBA Publications Ltd. Charles-Edwards, T. & Kelly, F. (1983), Bechbretha. Dublin, Dublin Institute for Advanced Studies
Gojmerac, W. T. (1983), Bees, Bee-Keeping, Honey and Pollination, Connecticut, AVI Publishing Company

Maeterlinck, Maurice (1954) (1901), La Vie des Abeilles, English translation, The Life of the Bee, by Alfred Sutre, with an Introduction by Edwin Way Teale, New York, Mentor

Mahon, Bríd (1991), The Land of Milk and Honey, Dublin, Poolbeg Press Ltd.

Ransome, Hilda (1986), The Sacred bee in ancient times and folklore, London, Burrowbridge

Watson, J. K. (1981), Bee-Keeping in Ireland, Dublin, Mount Salus Press

REFERENCES

(i)   The Commission, founded in 1935, is hereafter abbreviated to IFC.
(ii)   Shakespeare, W., King Henry the Fifth, I, ii, lines 187-204.
(iii)   Charles-Edwards, T. & Kelly, F., Bechbretha, Dublin, 1983, p. 39; Anon., The New Zealand Beekeeper, Vol. 5, March 1998, p. 25.
(iv)   Gojmerac, W. L., Bees, Bee-keeping , Honey and Pollination, Connecticut, 1983, p. 10.
(v)   Charles-Edwards, T. & Kelly, F., op cit., p. 40.
(vi)   IFC 947:109 (Cork, 1943).
(vii)   Mahon, Bríd, Land of Milk and Honey, Dublin, 1991, p. 82.
(viii) Ibid., p. 81; Watson, J. K., Bee-Keeping in Ireland, Dublin, Mount Salus Press, 1981, p. 2.
(ix)   Anon., Ireland's Own, 19 May 1978, p. 5.
(x)   IFC 1386:102 (Cork, 1954).
(xi)   bid.
(xii)   Herbert Valley, 'Telling the Bees', British Bee Journal (BBJ) 4233:309, 26 December 1970.
(xiii) Extract taken from: Ransome, Hilda, The Sacred Bee in ancient times and folklore, London, 1986. BBJ 4259:301, 25 December 1971.
(xiv)   IFC 1174:431 (Cork, 1949).
(xv)   IFC 42:148 (Cork,1928), 2105:124 (Limerick, 1978), 789:311 (Cork, 1941).
(xvi)   Quoted in BBJ 4233:309, 26 December 1970
(xvii) IFC 591:492 (Limerick, 1939), 782:253 (Kerry, 1941(, 1386:102 (Cork, 1054).
(xviii) IFC 1386:102 (Antrim, 1954).
(xix)   Gojmerac, W., op. cit., p. 11.
(xx)   IFC 1550:342 (Roscommon, 1959).
(xxi)   Ó Catháin, S., The Festival of Brigit, Dublin, 1995, p. 60.
(xxii) Jilly Pickup, 'The Honey bee in Lore and Legend', Ireland's Own, 9 October 1988, p. 11.
(xxiii) IFC 265:399 (Mayo, 1935).
(xxiv) C.R. Middleton, 'Bees and Honey: Some Rites and Superstitions', BBJ 4263:42, 19 February, 1972
(xxv)   Cecil Tonsley, Editorial, BBJ 4217:109, 16 May 1970.
(xxvi) Maeterlinck, Maurice, La Vie des Abeilles, 1901, English translation by Alfred Sutre, The Life of the Bee, with Introduction by Edwin Way Teale, New York, Mentor, The New American Library, 1954,. p.9.
(xxvii) Capote. T., 'House of Flowers', in Breakfast at Tiffany's, 1958, paperback edition, Harmondsworth, Penguin, 1977, p. 106.
(xxviii) Ó Catháin, loc. cit.
(xxix) Ireland's Own, op. cit.
(xxx)   Ransome, Hilda, op. cit., p. 197.
(xxxi) IFC 947:54 (Kerry, 1943).
(xxxii) IFC 1139:270 (Cork, 1940).
(xxxiii) Ransome, Hilda. op. cit. p. 213.
(xxxiv) Ransome, Hilda. op. cit. p. 213.
(xxxv) IFC 789:312 (Cork, 1941).
(xxxvi) M.C. Keniry, 'Cribbago', An Beachaire, May, 1976, p. 98.
(xxxvii) Tadhg Gavin, 'Saint Bees, Friend of the Poor', Ireland's Own, 26 August 1977, p. 7..
(xxxviii) Anon., 'Honey Harvest Festival', BBJ 4175:223, 5 October 1968, p. 233
(xxxix) IFC 204:55 (Kerry, 1932).

(xl)   IFC 1234:447 (Tipperary, 1952).
(xli)   IFC 306:482-6 (Cork, 1036).
(xlii) Watson, J. K., op. cit., p. 9.
(xliii) Ransome, H., op. cit., p. 190.
(xliv) Extracted from a study carried out in Wicklow, completed by a student in the Irish Folklore Department, entitled 'Folk Medicine' (IFC Archive, Box 5).
(xlv)   Reader's contribution, BBJ, 4236:31, 6 February 1971, p. 31.
(xlvi) Ó Catháin, op. cit., p. 60.
(xlvii) Ransome, H., op.cit., p. 196.
(xlviii) IFC 1879:146 (Ballinacor, 1933).
(xlix) Irish Press, Roddy the Rover 'Traditional Cures Competition', 1933 (IFC Archive, Box 63).
(l)   Ibid.
(li)   IFC 42:147 (Cork, 1928).
(lii)   S.C. (IFC School's Collection) 15:176 (Roscommon, 1938).
(liii) Ransome, H. op. cit., p. 218.
(liv)   Ibid., p. 219.
(lv)   Information collected by Seán Ó Súilleabháin, a full-time collector of the IFC.
(lvi)   Notes and Queries, 10, 1854, p. 500. The writer signs himself 'Eirionnach'. Reprinted in BBJ 4162:77 (6 April 1968).

48

BOOKS: BAITS, BEES AND BUTTERFLIES

John Kinross

●

The time has come again to have a look at the new books on bees - including bumblebees. My colleagues Ina Strainer and Professor Dripitoff have both retired - Ina has gone to live with a cousin who is a keen bird watcher on Fair Island. She has managed to get her Morris Traveller over there where it has been turned into a chicken shed. It is too windy for bees. The professor, who took over Ina's bees, has retired to the Scottish Borders so that if he gets pestered by the Scottish Bee Inspectors, he makes sure his bees are all in England and vice-versa. He also plans to resurrect his Harley bike as the roads are nice and straight there.

First on my list this year is **"Beekeeping No 1, by Ron Brown, from the archives of The Beekeepers Quarterly for a new generation of beekeepers"** (NBB £9.95) edited by John Phipps, 2014. Here are some articles by Ron which appeared in early editions of the Quarterly - I especially found the the varroa article of interest with the diagram rather like a sideways view of the Tower of London, showing the knock down using

Bayvarol strips. Note that his "Ex-Africa" book has a chapter on African bees. His RAF memoirs "All Round the Compass" is a best seller in the English bookshop in Gibraltar. Beware those of you who use the Rock's cash dispensers before travelling home - all the notes are Gibraltar pounds and not valid in the UK. One slight criticism - Ron's handwriting does not reproduce clearly and the words on diagrams on pages 21, 24 and 25 would be better typed out to help aged readers like myself. We look forward to Volume 2 - let us hope it will match the size of Volume 1.

From Ireland comes Ben Harden's book **"Some Alternative Pathways for the Hesitant Queen Rearer"** (NBB £9.90). This is a very thin book with some excellent colour illustrations. I like the one of the Chinese grafting tool with its plunger which reminds me of my aunt's Victorian WC. Plungers move upwards and not downwards but we didn't always remember this, with drastic consequences. Ben manages to get all the essential points here and this should help novice queen rearers. The last photograph shows his man-sized finger hole scissors - I must get a pair of those - and a sensible sized matchbox with 'Up" written on it so that if you put the queen in it you know she is not Australian and doesn't want to be put upside down.

An American book that has come my way and seems popular is **M Taylor's "Swarm Traps and Bait Hives"** published by the author (£13.75) which has excellent colour plates and just enough information to get by. "Catching free bees is an easy biologically-driven process - nothing fancy, nothing expensive, nothing dangerous. In fact it is downright fun" is how the author describes his hobby. So it should be!

A change of subject, but a book that I should have mentioned in 2011 when it was published. I have been re-reading **Carol Ann Duffy's "The Bees"** (Picador, £14.99). It starts with a short poem:

*"Here are my bees,
brazen, blurs on paper,
besotted; buzzwords, dancing
their flawless, airy maps.*

*Been deep, my poet bees,
in the parts of flowers,
in daffodils, thistle, rose, even
the golden lotus; so glide,*

gilded, glad, golden, thus -

wise - and know of us:
how your scent pervades
my shadowed, busy heart,
and honey is art."

There are two or three other bee poems but more with some page-size hand-drawn slogans such as: "Bees are the batteries of orchards, gardens, guard them". A book every beekeeper should obtain and guard for special days.

I recommend **"Field Guide to the Bumblebees of Great Britain & Ireland"** by Jenner and Edwards (Ocelli £12.99) with colour plates which cover the identification of most of our bumblebees. The book goes well with **Jeremy Thomas and Richard Lewington's "Pocket Guide to Butterflies of Great Britain and Ireland"** (British Wildlife Publishing - or Bumble Bee Books £9.95). I also much enjoyed **Patrick Barkham's "The Butterfly Isles"** (Granta £20) in which Patrick sets out to find every one of the 59 species of butterfly in the UK. Read the book and you will find out if he succeeds.

I am still the editor of the Nutshell series, a joint series of A4 booklets on important bee subjects. The most recent of these are No 111 **Karl Showler's "Significant Women Beekeepers"** and No 112 **"A Question on Drones"** by P Whyte of S Ireland. To come is No 113 on the **Bee Farmers Association, by M Ginman and M Ballard**. If one of the Annual readers wants to try writing a Nutshell, please contact me c/o The Annual.

BARRYTOWN, AUGUST, 1888.

A Puzzler ?

Editor Bee-Keepers' Magazine :

Can any of your readers solve the following puzzle : Two bee-keepers drove to the market ; each one had thirty jars of honey. They made the agreement to share the amount equally between themselves. The first one sold his honey at two jars for one dollar, which entitled him to fifteen dollars ; the second sold his at three jars for a dollar, for which he was to receive ten dollars. This together would amount to *twenty-five* dollars. But the dealer when he was told to pay each man an equal sum of twelve and a half dollars, said : "See here! As you two had sixty jars together, and one sold me two and the other three jars for one dollar, it follows that I have to pay you two dollars for five jars. As twelve times five is sixty, I owe you twelve times two, or *twenty-four* dollars." Now the dealer was perfectly right in his way, but how can the difference of one dollar be explained ? Yours,

A. HEINZ.

Syracuse, N. Y.

WORD SEARCH

The grid below contains the names of fifty authors of books and beekeeping - all of which have been published in the last few decades. Their names may be found by searching the grid horizontally, vertically and diagonally, both backwards and forwards.

```
E J O I M I C H E N E R I S E N O J W F
N H O O P E R J L I S P C N W O R B I B
A R O B S O N B S L A Q K W A H S S N C
L N O S N I K T A T U S T O R E Y K S O
P H A W K E R R T P C B D L E E V S T N
A N T Z U W E E M A W S N K R N R A O N
L M Y M I B R A R O J I H R B K I U N E
E A U L A S R R W E H V C I U D N G A R
D W S T O C E Z X B E A R K C T I Y E M
Q O J N T C P F N M L D O G K Y T E N R
N F R T K O O J M O O P T F N G U V C W
Q A A A H X L I A C O H S G A R Z B O P
S E K S T W O F N I T I G O L E A E F D
T H I R A A P S G D O P Y U L G L N S A
N B O R I R M D U D R P E L P O N J T H
B P I W E T R M M I S S L S N R O A E S
T N N S L O S L A W M D E O R Y T M V K
G G T H F E V K X S I L E N O T S I E I
G O I L U F R H Y K S P S S H V A N N M
N N A E W O R H N A M T H G I E W W S A
```

ANSWERS ON PAGE 200

53

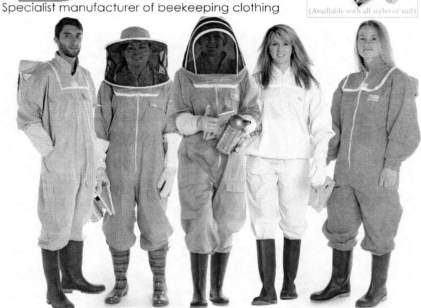

DIARY & CALENDAR

- PART II -

*SR (SUNRISE) SS (SUNSET) FOR LONDON UK.

A swarm that was unable to find a home before the weather changed for the worse.
In the warmth of the cluster the bees began to secrete wax and begin comb building
and by doing so revealed the preferred shape of their nest, i.e. tall rather than broad.
Yet most beehives tend to be constructed in ways which thwart what is more natural
for bees. Beowulf Cooper informed beekeepers that the tall shape of the nest was
evidenced in hives when bees left whole arcs of empty cells in the honey super
directly above a queen excluder. (*Photo: John Phipps*)

DAY	JANUARY 2016 FORAGE	TEMP		WIND		CL'D	RAIN	1	2	3
		MIN	MAX	DIR	B.S			HIVE WEIGHT		
1										
2										
3										
4										
5										
6										
7										
8										
9										
10										
11										
12										
13										
14										
15										
16										
17										
18										
19										
20										
21										
22										
23										
24										
25										
26										
27										
28										
29										
30										
31										

JAN16

	8,FR
1,FR NEW YEAR'S DAY	**9,SA** SR:08:04, SS:04:11
2,SA SR:08:06, SS:04:03	**10,SU**
3,SU	**11,MO**
4,MO	**12,TU**
5,TU ○ 12TH NIGHT	**13,WE**
6,WE EPIPHANY	**14,TH**
7,TH ORTHODOX FEAST OF THE NATIVITY	**15,FR**

16,SA SR:07:59, SS:04:22	24,SU
17,SU	25,MO BURN'S NIGHT
18,MO	26,TU
19,TU	27,WE
20,WE ●	28,TH
21,TH	29,FR
22,FR	30,SA SR:07:43, SS:04:45
23,SA SR:07:52, SS:04:33	31,SU

FEBRUARY

Some beekeepers of Eastern Europe still keep their bees in the same manner as their forest beekeeping antecedents of centuries ago. This must be as near to natural beekeeping as one can get - the bees themselves choosing where to make their nests in the hollows of trees or in cavities made by the beekeepers.

Burzyan Wild-Hive Management in South Ural, BKQ 119, March 2015

DAY	FEBRUARY 2016 FORAGE	TEMP		WIND		CL'D	RAIN	1	2	3
		MIN	MAX	DIR	B.S			HIVE WEIGHT		
1										
2										
3										
4										
5										
6										
7										
8										
9										
10										
11										
12										
13										
14										
15										
16										
17										
18										
19										
20										
21										
22										
23										
24										
25										
26										
27										
28										
29										

FEB16

	8,MO
1,MO	**9,TU** SHROVE TUESDAY , MARDI GRAS
2,TU CANDLEMAS DAY	**10,WE** ASH WEDNESDAY
3,WE ○	**11,TH** ST GOBNAIT, PATRON SAINT OF IRISH BEEKEEPERS
4,TH	**12,FR**
5,FR	**13,SA** SR:07:19, SS:05:11 ST MODMONOC
6,SA SR:07:32, SS:04:58	**14,SU** ST VALENTINE'S DAY
7,SU	**15,MO**

16,TU	**24,WE**
17,WE	**25,TH**
18,TH ●	**26,FR**
19,FR	27,SA SR:06:51, SS:05:36
20,SA SR:07:06, SS:05:24	28,SU
21,SU	**29,MO** LEAP YEAR
22,MO	
23,TU ST KHALAMPII, PATRON SAINT OF BULGARIAN BEEKEEPERS (HIVE-SHAPED PIES BAKED)	

MARCH

Up until the end of the 19th century most colonies in Europe were kept in skeps
which were given extra protection for winter. The colonies were allowed to carry on
their lives with little interference from the beekeeper. Although kept in a natural way,
sadly many colonies were killed each autumn for their honey. However, a movement
which called for 'humanity to bees' led to the driving of bees into other
(already populated) skeps thus saving hundreds of millions of bees from the
sulphur pits each year. *(Anonymous, Bulgaria)*

DAY	MARCH 2016 FORAGE	TEMP		WIND		CL'D	RAIN	1	2	3
		MIN	MAX	DIR	B.S			HIVE WEIGHT		
1										
2										
3										
4										
5										
6										
7										
8										
9										
10										
11										
12										
13										
14										
15										
16										
17										
18										
19										
20										
21										
22										
23										
24										
25										
26										
27										
28										
29										
30										
31										

MAR16

	8,TU
1,TU ST DAVID'S DAY	**9,WE**
2,WE	**10,TH**
3,TH	**11,FR**
4,FR	12,SA SR:06:21, SS:06:01
5,SA ○ SR:06:36, SS:05:48	13,SU
6,SU MOTHERING SUNDAY	**14,MO**
7,MO	**15,TU**

16,WE	**24,TH**
17,TH ST PATRICKS DAY	**25,FR** GOOD FRIDAY, GREEK INDEPENDENCE DAY
18,FR	26,SA SR:05:49, SS:06:24
19,SA SR:06:05, SS:06:13	27,SU EASTER SUNDAY - DST CLOCKS TURNED FORWARD ONE HOUR
20,SU ● SPRING EQUINOX - FIRST DAY OF SPRING, PALM SUNDAY	**28,MO** EASTER MONDAY
21,MO	**29, TU**
22,TU	**30, WE** ST ALEXIUS (UKRAINIAN BEEKEEPERS HANG ICONS OF THEIR PATRON SAINTS OF BEEKEEPING, ST SAVVATY AND ST ZOSIMA IN SHRINES AMONGST THEIR HIVES)
23,WE	**31,TH**

One of the earliest methods of natural beekeeping, still practised by many beekeepers, is the use of top bar hives. Whilst hives of these types were used particularly, at first, in beekeeping development programmes in third world countries, their use became popular not only amongst hobby beekeepers but in some commercial apiaries, too. The use of top bars - maybe with starter strips of wax - allowed the bees to build their combs naturally. The inward sloping sides, usually, but not always, prevented the bees from fastening the sides of the combs to the walls. Whilst these hives can be manipulated with care, naturally-inclined beekeepers allow the colonies to develop without any interference. Hive built by *Ilarai* Baldi, Italy. For a comprehensive manual on top bar hives, W A Mangum's **'Top Bar Hive Beekeeping'** is indispensable. *(Photo: John Phipps)*

The Hive that Ilaria Built, BKQ 87, March 2007

DAY	APRIL 2016 FORAGE	TEMP		WIND		CL'D	RAIN	1	2	3
		MIN	MAX	DIR	B.S			HIVE WEIGHT		
1										
2										
3										
4										
5										
6										
7										
8										
9										
10										
11										
12										
13										
14										
15										
16										
17										
18										
19										
20										
21										
22										
23										
24										
25										
26										
27										
28										
29										
30										

APR16

	8,FR
1,FR	**9,SA** SR:06:17, SS:07:48
2,SA SR:06:33, SS:07:36	**10,SU** PENTECOST
3,SU	**11,MO**
4,MO ○	**12,TU**
5,TU	**13,WE**
6,WE	**14,TH**
7,TH	**15,FR**

16,SA SR:06:02, SS:08:00	24,SU ORTHODOX PALM SUNDAY
17,SU	25,MO
18,MO ●	26,TU
19,TU	27,WE
20,WE	28,TH
21,TH	29,FR
22,FR	30,SA SR:05:34, SS:08:23 ST ZOSIMA - 'GREET THE BEE ON ZOSIMA'S DAY AND THERE WILL BE HIVES AND WAX'.
23,SA SR:05:47, SS:08:11 ST GEORGE'S DAY	

Some beekeepers make the dimensions of their top bar hives so that conventional supers can be placed over them - whilst leaving the bees in the brood area to get on with their lives as they wish. This hive with a strong force of bees has Lansgstroth boxes used as supers. Made by David Dawson, Canada. (Photo: *David Dawson*)

BKQ 121, September, 2015

DAY	MAY 2016 FORAGE	TEMP		WIND		CL'D	RAIN	1	2	3
		MIN	MAX	DIR	B.S			HIVE WEIGHT		
1										
2										
3										
4										
5										
6										
7										
8										
9										
10										
11										
12										
13										
14										
15										
16										
17										
18										
19										
20										
21										
22										
23										
24										
25										
26										
27										
28										
29										
30										

MAY16

	8,SU
1,SU ORTHODOX EASTER SUNDAY, MAY DAY (EASTERN EUROPE)	**9,MO**
2,MO EARLY MAY BANK HOLIDAY ORTHODOX EASTER MONDAY	**10,TU**
3,TU	**11,WE**
4,WE ○	**12,TH**
5,TH ASCENSION DAY	**13,FR**
6,FR	**14,SA** SR:05:10, SS:08:45
7,SA SR:05:21, SS:08:34	**15,SU** PENTACOST

16,MO	**24,TU**
17,TU	25,WE
18,WE ●	**26,TH**
19,TH	**27,FR**
20,FR	28,SA SR:07:38, SS:03:58
21,SA SR:07:27, SS:04:05	29,SU
22,SU	**30,MO** SPRING BANK HOLIDAY
23,MO	**31,TU**

Some beekeepers are reluctant to change their beekeeping to more natural and sustainable ways as they already have many conventional hives. However, as the photos here show, Langstroth boxes can be easily modified to convert them into top bar hives. The additions to the two walls to give the right degree of slope to prevent comb attachment do not reduce the volume of the space available for bees, as the lack of side and bottom bars compensates for this. Hives converted by John Phipps, Greece. *(Photo: John Phipps)*

Make a Langstroth Top Bar Hive, John Phipps: BKQ 102, December 2010

DAY	JUNE 2016 FORAGE	TEMP		WIND		CL'D	RAIN	1	2	3
		MIN	MAX	DIR	B.S			HIVE WEIGHT		
1										
2										
3										
4										
5										
6										
7										
8										
9										
10										
11										
12										
13										
14										
15										
16										
17										
18										
19										
20										
21										
22										
23										
24										
25										
26										
27										
28										
29										
30										

JUN16

	8,WE
1,WE	**9,TH**
2,TH ○	**10,FR**
3,FR	11,SA SR:04:43, SS:09:17
4,SA SR:04:47, SS:09:12	12,SU
5,SU	**13,MO**
6,MO	**14,TU**
7,TU	**15,WE**

16,TH ●	**24,FR**
17,FR	25,SA SR:04:44, SS:09:22
18,SA SR:04:43, SS:09:21	26,SU
19,SU FATHER'S DAY	**27,MO**
20,MO SUMMER SOLSTICE - FIRST DAY OF SUMMER	**28,TU**
21,TU	**29,WE**
22,WE	**30,TH**
23,TH	

JULY

The Warré Hive is becoming increasingly popular especially since David Heaf translated the French priest's 'Beekeeping for All'. Subsequently, he wrote: **'Natural Beekeeping With the Warré Hive - A Manual'** which gives a complete guide to this sustainable method of beekeeping. Compared with long top bar hives, the Warré hive allows the bees to build their nest in boxes giving the structure a narrow/tall profile. Hive made by Gareth John and located at Rye Hill Prison.
(Photo: *Stephen Hammond*)

Bee Friendly Beekeeping with the Warré Hive, David Heaf BKQ 90, December 2007
Towards Sustainable Beekeeping: BKQ 91, February 2008; BKQ 92, June 2008; BKQ 93 September 2008; BKQ 94 November 2008; Ethics in Beekeeping, David Heaf, BKQ 96, June 2009

DAY	JULY 2016 FORAGE	TEMP		WIND		CL'D	RAIN	1	2	3
		MIN	MAX	DIR	B.S			HIVE WEIGHT		
1										
2										
3										
4										
5										
6										
7										
8										
9										
10										
11										
12										
13										
14										
15										
16										
17										
18										
19										
20										
21										
22										
23										
24										
25										
26										
27										
28										
29										
30										
31										

JUL16

	8,FR
1,FR	9,SA SR:04:55, SS:09:16
2,SA ○ SR:04:49, SS:09:20	10,SU
3,SU	**11,MO**
4,MO	12,TU
5,TU	13,WE
6,WE	**14,TH** ST SWITHUN
7,TH	**15,FR**

16,SA ● SR:05:03, SS:09:10	24,SU
17,SU	25,MO
18,MO	26,TU
19,TU	27,WE
20,WE	28,TH
21,TH	29,FR
22,FR	30,SA SR:05:22, SS:08:51
23,SA SR:05:12, SS:09:01	31,SU ○

AUGUST

Vasyl Priyatelenko, in Ukraine, has spent a long time developing a hive which aims to give the same environment as the bees would have in a hollow tree. Thus, the hive has been designed to give the bees a deep space in which to build their combs. Whilst he still uses standard frames he puts them into his hive at right angles to the norm and any supers are aligned with the frames crossways to the ones below. He takes great care to ensure that there is the correct balance between humidity and ventilation of the hive throughout the different seasons.

BKQ 113, September 2013; BKQ 118, December, 2014.

DAY	AUGUST 2016 FORAGE	TEMP		WIND		CL'D	RAIN	1	2	3
		MIN	MAX	DIR	B.S			HIVE WEIGHT		
1										
2										
3										
4										
5										
6										
7										
8										
9										
10										
11										
12										
13										
14										
15										
16										
17										
18										
19										
20										
21										
22										
23										
24										
25										
26										
27										
28										
29										
30										
31										

AUG16

	8,MO
1,MO SUMMER BANK HOLIDAY (SCOTLAND)	**9,TU**
2,TU	**10,WE**
3,WE	**11,TH**
4,TH	**12,FR**
5,FR	**13,SA** SR:05:43, SS:08:26
6,SA SR:05:32, SS:08:39	**14,SU** ●
7,SU	**15,MO** ORTHODOX DORMITION B V MARY

16,TU	**24,WE** ST BARTHOLOMEW (TRADITIONAL DAY FOR HARVESTING HONEY)
17,WE	**25,TH**
18,TH	**26,FR**
19,FR	27,SA SR:06:06, SS:07:57
20,SA SR:05:54, SS:08:12	28,SU
21,SU	**29,MO** ○ SUMMER BANK HOLIDAY (ENG. WALES, NI)
22,MO	**30,TU**
23,TU	**31,WE**

SEPTEMBER

I built the Observation Hive pictured here to correspond with the features in Vasyl Priyatelenko's hive. Whilst the bees are allowed to work unhindered in the deep part of the hive, there is a shallow space above the brood frames for the production of small quantities of comb honey using only top bars, The hive has a mesh floor with a drawer below for monitoring varroa mites.

BKQ 121, September 2015.

DAY	SEPTEMBER 2016 FORAGE	TEMP MIN	TEMP MAX	WIND DIR	WIND B.S	CL'D	RAIN	1	2	3
								HIVE WEIGHT		
1										
2										
3										
4										
5										
6										
7										
8										
9										
10										
11										
12										
13										
14										
15										
16										
17										
18										
19										
20										
21										
22										
23										
24										
25										
26										
27										
28										
29										
30										

SEP16

	8,TH
1,TH	**9,FR**
2,FR	10,SA SR:06:28, SS:07:26
3,SA SR:06:17, SS:07:42	11,SU
4,SU	**12,MO**
5,MO	**13,TU** ●
6,TU	**14,WE**
7,WE	**15,TH**

16,FR	24,SA SR:06:50, SS:06:53
17,SA SR:06:39, SS:07:10	25,SU
18,SU	**26,MO**
19,MO	**27,TU**
20,TU	**28,WE** ○
21,WE	**29,TH**
22,TH AUTUMN EQUINOX - FIRST DAY OF AUTUMN	**30,FR**
23,FR	

OCTOBER

This is a Lazutin-type hive made by Dr Leonid Sharashkin, in the USA. Whilst it
has frames - without wax foundation being fitted - the colony is managed on organic
lines. The late Fedor Lazutin, who lived in Russia, was the author of several books -
'Beekeeping...' 'Vegetable Growing and Fruit Growing With a Smile',
being translated by Leonid Sharashkin.

BKQ 117, September 2014; BKQ 120 May 2104.

DAY	OCTOBER 2016 FORAGE	TEMP		WIND		CL'D	RAIN	1	2	3
		MIN	MAX	DIR	B.S			HIVE WEIGHT		
1										
2										
3										
4										
5										
6										
7										
8										
9										
10										
11										
12										
13										
14										
15										
16										
17										
18										
19										
20										
21										
22										
23										
24										
25										
26										
27										
28										
29										
30										
31										

OCT16

	8,SA SR:05:34, SS:08:37
1,SA SR:05:24, SS:08:49	9,SU
2,SU	10,MO
3,MO	11,TU
4,TU ST FRANCIS - ANIMAL DAY	12,WE
5,WE	13,TH ●
6,TH	14,FR
7,FR	15,SA SR:05:45, SS:08:24

16,SU	24,MO
17,MO	25,TU
18,TU	26,WE
19,WE	27,TH ○
20,TH	28,FR OXI DAY (GREECE)
21,FR	29,SA SR:06:08, SS:07:54
22,SA SR:05:56, SS:08:09	30,SU DST CLOCKS MOVED BACK ONE HOUR
23,SU	31,MO HALLOWEEN

NOVEMBER

The Zest Hive is the creation of Bill Summers. Like Lazutin's hive it is a large horizontal hive with frames. Its principle features include: construction with easily available recyclable materials; excellent insulation for all seasons; and its apparent ability to enable bees to overcome the problems of varroa. Bill Summers has written two books on his hive: '**The Zest Hive**' (2011) and '**Beekeeeping with Zest**' (2015). **The Summers Coffin Hive BKQ 92, June 2008; The Chest Hive BKQ 99, March 2010**

DAY	NOVEMBER 2016 FORAGE	TEMP		WIND		CL'D	RAIN	1	2	3
		MIN	MAX	DIR	B.S			HIVE WEIGHT		
1										
2										
3										
4										
5										
6										
7										
8										
9										
10										
11										
12										
13										
14										
15										
16										
17										
18										
19										
20										
21										
22										
23										
24										
25										
26										
27										
28										
29										
30										

NOV16

	8,TU
1,TU ALL SAINTS' DAY	**9,WE**
2,WE ALL SOULS' DAY	**10,TH**
3,TH	**11,FR** ●
4,FR	12,SA SR:07:14, SS:04:15
5,SA SR:07:02, SS:04:26 GUY FAWKES DAY	13,SU REMBEMBRANCE SUNDAY
6,SU	**14,MO**
7,MO	**15,TU**

16,WE	**24,TH** THANKSGIVING DAY (USA)
17,TH POLYTECHNEIO (GREECE)	**25,FR** ○
18,FR	26,SA SR:07:37, SS:03:58
19,SA SR:07:26, SS:04:06	27,SU FIRST SUNDAY OF ADVENT
20,SU	**28,MO**
21,MO	**29, TU**
22,TU	**30, WE** ST ANDREW'S DAY
23,WE	

DECEMBER

The Sun Hive, designed by Gunthe Munke, originated in Germany and has become an important feature of the worldwide movement of apicentric beekeeping whereby the bees are regarded primarily as pollinators with honey production only being seen as a secondary goal. Sun Hives are based on skeps traditionally used in Europe and the devotees of this type of beekeeping find additional satisfaction in their construction. The Natural Beekeeping Trust hold workshops in making Sun Hives: http://naturalbeekeepingtrust.org A translation of Guenther Mancke's book, "Sun Hive" is also available from the Trust.

BKQ 121, September 2015

DAY	DECEMBER 2016 FORAGE	TEMP		WIND		CL'D	RAIN	1	2	3
		MIN	MAX	DIR	B.S			HIVE WEIGHT		
1										
2										
3										
4										
5										
6										
7										
8										
9										
10										
11										
12										
13										
14										
15										
16										
17										
18										
19										
20										
21										
22										
23										
24										
25										
26										
27										
28										
29										
30										
31										

DEC16

	8,TH
1,TH	**9,FR**
2,FR	10,SA SR:07:55, SS:03:51
3,SA SR:07:47, SS:03:54	11,SU ●
4,SU	**12,MO**
5,MO	**13,TU**
6,TU ST NICHOLAS	**14,WE**
7,WE ST AMBROSE (PATRON SAINT OF BEEKEEPERS)	**15,TH**

16,FR	24,SA SR:08:05, SS:03:55 CHRISTMAS EVE
17,SA SR:08:02, SS:03:52	25,SU ○ CHRISTMAS DAY
18,SU	**26,MO** BOXING EVE
19,MO	**27,TU** BANK HOLIDAY
20,TU	**28,WE**
21,WE WINTER SOLSTICE - FIRST DAY OF WINTER	29,TH
22,TH	**30,FR**
23,FR	31,SA SR:08:06, SS:04:01 NEW YEAR'S EVE

Hive/ Q NO.	Year Q Raised	Frames of Brood Autumn 2014	Combs Covered	Honey Stored- Sugar fed Kg	Combs Covered Spring 2016	Frames of Brood Spring 2016	Spring Feeding Kg	Queens Reared	Nuclei
1									
2									
3									
4									
5									
6									
7									
8									
9									
10									
11									
12									
13									
14									
15									
16									
17									
18									
19									
20									
21									
22									
23									
24									

HONEYBEE COLONIES

1									
2									
3									
4									
5									
6									
7									
8									
9									
10									
11									
12									
13									
14									
15									
16									
17									
18									
19									
20									
21									
22									
23									
24									

BEEEKEEPING RECORDS

Number	items	Est. Value	
		£	P
	Stocks of Bees		
	Empty Hives		
	Combs - Deep - Shallow		
	Frames		
	Foundations		
	Honey Extractor		
	Honey Tanks		
	Other items		
	Honey Jars		
	Honey		

JANUARY 2017

S	M	T	W	T	F	S
1	2	3	4	5	6	7
8	9	10	11	12	13	14
15	16	17	18	19	20	21
22	23	24	25	26	27	28
29	30	31				

FEBRUARY 2017

S	M	T	W	T	F	S
			1	2	3	4
6	7	8	9	10	11	
13	14	15	16	17	18	
20	21	22	23	24	25	
27	28					

MARCH 2017

S	M	T	W	T	F	S
			1	2	3	4
6	7	8	9	10	11	
13	14	15	16	17	18	
20	21	22	23	24	25	
27	28	29	30	31		

APRIL 2017

S	M	T	W	T	F	S
						1
2	3	4	5	6	7	8
9	10	11	12	13	14	15
16	17	18	19	20	21	22
23	24	25	26	27	28	29
30						

MAY 2017

S	M	T	W	T	F	S
	1	2	3	4	5	6
7	8	9	10	11	12	13
14	15	16	17	18	19	20
21	22	23	24	25	26	27
28	29					

JUNE 2017

S	M	T	W	T	F	S
				1	2	3	4
6	7	8	9	10	11	
13	14	15	16	17	18	
20	21	22	23	24	25	
27	28	29	30			

JULY 2017

S	M	T	W	T	F	S
					1	2
3	4	5	6	7	8	9
10	11	12	13	14	15	16
17	18	19	20	21	22	23
24	25	26	27	28	29	30
31						

AUGUST 2017

S	M	T	W	T	F	S
	1	2	3	4	5	6
7	8	9	10	11	12	13
14	15	16	17	18	19	20
21	22	23	24	25	26	27
28	29	30	31			

SEPTEMBER 2017

S	M	T	W	T	F	S
					1	2	3
4	5	6	7	8	9	10
11	12	13	14	15	16	17
18	19	20	21	22	23	24
25	26	27	28	29	30	

OCTOBER 2017

S	M	T	W	T	F	S
						1
2	3	4	5	6	7	8
9	10	11	12	13	14	15
16	17	18	19	20	21	22
23	24	25	26	27	28	29
30	31					

NOVEMBER 2017

S	M	T	W	T	F	S
			1	2	3	4	5
6	7	8	9	10	11	12
13	14	15	16	17	18	19
20	21	22	23	24	25	26
27	28	29	30			

DECEMBER 2017

S	M	T	W	T	F	S
					1	2	3
4	5	6	7	8	9	10
11	12	13	14	15	16	17
18	19	20	21	22	23	24
25	26	27	28	29	30	31

Spring 2016 Convention

Friday 8 April • Saturday 9 April
Sunday 10 April 2016

**Lectures
Courses
Workshops
Trade-show
Accommodation
Dinners**

Tickets on sale and
on-line bookings
January 2016

Harper Adams University
Newport, Shropshire TF10 8NB

enquiries to: tim.lovett@bbka.org.uk

Every effort is made to keep entries up to date but the publishers cannot be held responsible for errors or omissions.
Associations and all other groups listed have been requested (August 2014) to supply updated entries.
Readers who are aware of inaccuracies are asked to send updates to jerry@northernbeebooks.co.uk

DIRECTORY, Associations and Services

Ninemaidens Mead

Award winning mead & honey

visit **www.ninemaidensmead.co.uk**
or tel. 01209 820939 / 860630

APPROVED ORIGIN SCHEME
MADE IN
CORNWALL COUNCIL
Cornwall©

DIRECTORY, ASSOCIATIONS AND SERVICES

BEE-EDU

Bee Educated (BEE-EDU)
e-Learning for Beekeepers

-†beekeeping virtual classroom.

Contact Us
Bee-Edu Administrator
Steven Turner
Email: st@zbee.com

Bee-Edu is a Moodle website set-up specifically for beekeeping tutors and their students.

What is Moodle?
Moodle is a Virtual Learning Environment (VLE) which makes it easy for tutors to provide online support for†their course. It provides†a central space on the web where students can access a set of tools and resources at all times.

What are the Benefits?
1. It is an easy way to communicate with students: The course news automatically emails messages to all students. Forums can also be used to answer commonly asked questions, to provide a space for informal peer to peer student discussion or even online tutorials.

2. It is at quick way to share documents: Moodle provides a place where you can easily create web pages with information about your course and provide links to word, PDF documents, slides, and other resources that your students will want to access.

3. It has easy access to relevant and useful online resources: There is so much information about beekeeping on the Internet which makes it difficult for students to find reliable and trusted resources. You can use your Moodle to provide links directly to these resources in an organised way.

4. Online assignment handling: Online assignment handling can save time and effort for everyone involved, whether it†is just used for student submission with marking

114

done on paper or the whole process is moved online saving time, postage and paper.

5. Other advantages: Making resources available online can save time and money in photocopying. For example keep a central copy of documents†online so everyone can find the latest version of a course handbook etc. Provide handouts online so that students only print out what they really need. It is easy to experiment with new ideas and tools, it's a low risk way to incorporate new tools and ideas into your teaching. Tutors can manage their materials. If all your course information is on Moodle this is easy access this year on year.

6. Other features and tools: Course calendar: use this to flag important events to everyone on your course. Profiles and contact information helps students and tutors get to know each other from the start of the course. Deliver content: add slides and photographs. Video and audio: many tutors find it easy to record lectures as podcasts or even arrange for videos of lectures, posting these online and making it available to students is straight forward with Moodle.

7. Group tools for students. There are many tools that students can use for collaboration with each other such as forums, wiki and chat.

Beekeeping Course Tutors
Bee-Edu are providing a free virtual learning environment (VLE) for beekeeping tutors to complement their existing courses or build new online courses in beekeeping related topics.

Bee-Edu will support those individuals or associations that are keen to try this medium but help will be limited to testing and guidance with the technology rather than organising the teaching resources. There is no time scale and I will not be imposing any rules on tutors who wish do their own thing.

Students
It is†expected that most courses created on Bee-Edu would need enrolment keys and their students would be directed to the site by their tutors.

BEE DISEASES INSURANCE LTD

SECRETARY
Donald Robertson-Adams
Ffosyffin, Ffostrasol,
Llandysul, Ceredigion,
SA44 5JY
07532 336076
secretary@beediseases-
insurance.co.uk

**TREASURER AND
SCHEME B MANAGER**
Mrs Sharon Blake
Stratton Court,
South Petherton,
Somerset TA13 5LQ
01460 242124
treasurer@beediseases-
insurance.co.uk

CLAIMS MANAGER
Bernard Diaper
57 Marfield Close,
Walmley,
Sutton Coldfield B76 1YD
07711456932
claims@beediseasesin-
surance.co.uk

PRESIDENT
Martin Smith
137 Blaguegate Lane
Lathom, Sklemersdale
Lancs WN8 8TX
07831 695732
president@beediseases-
insurance.co.uk

BDI is a small insurance company that specialises in compensating beekeepers in England and Wales, who have had their equipment destroyed by the Bee Inspector as a result of being infected by a notifiable disease. These currently are European Foul Brood (EFB) and American Foul Brood (AFB). as the result of being infested by a notifiable pest (Small Hive Beetle or Tropilaelaps), should they reach England or Wales.

The company is regulated as an insurance company by the Prudential Regulatory Authority and supervised by the Prudential Regulatory Authority and the Financial Conduct Authority.

BDI is owned by most BKAs who are their members. There are no full time employees or premises. BDI is run by a small group of officers on a day – to – day basis from their homes. In addition there is a board of directors who meet regularly.

BDI subscriptions are paid along with the local BKA subscription. This is compulsory if your BKA is a BDI member. You will also be asked to pay premiums for the number of additional colonies you expect to have during the year, above the basic free colonies although you can also top-up during a year.

Further details of current subscription and premium rates together with compensation rates are available on the BDI website.

Research Grants

BDI supports research into the causes of honey bee diseases in a number of ways including the sponsorship

of PhD studentships. Details of the current and past research activities that have been supported by BDI are available on our website.

Training Grants
During 2014, BDI offered a grant of £100 to local associations who organise a practical event, with leaders/demonstrators who are knowledgeable in disease recognition. BDI were pleased to be working with the National Bee Unit to promote bee health. These events covered a range of topics, including for example, maintaining healthy bees, disease recognition, integrated pest management and approved medicines. It is the plan to repeat this grant in the 2015 season.

Further details of the full range of activities carried out can be found on the BDI website HYPERLINK "http://www.beediseasesinsurance. co.uk/"www.beediseasesinsurance.co.uk, or contact via secretary@ beediseasesinsurance.co.uk

Bee Farmers Assocation Limited

BEE FARMERS ASSOCIATION

The BFA represents the professional beekeepers of the UK.
www.beefarmers.co.uk

CHAIRMAN
David Wainwright
Tropical Forest Products
Box 92
Aberystwyth
Dyfed
Wales
SY23 1AA
01970 832511
chair@beefarmers.co.uk

COMPANY SECRETARY
John Howat
8 Olivers Close
West Totton
Southampton
Hampshire
SO40 8FH
023 8090 7850
honsec@beefarmers.co.uk

FINANCE DIRECTOR
John Heard
36 The Green
Long Whatton
Loughborough
Leicestershire
LE12 5DB
01509 646767
financedirector@
beefarmers.co.uk

As the professional trade association for the sector, the Bee Farmers' Association represents around 400 bee farming businesses. Its members produce honey throughout Great Britain and supply products bulk, wholesale and retail. The association is the largest contract pollinator in the UK.

A significant number of members are employed as bee inspectors, responsible for identifying and dealing with notifiable disease.

There is one business meeting a year which follows the Annual General Meeting, held in the spring to coincide with one of the major trade events. There are also twice-yearly regional meetings, usually featuring guest speakers.

The Bee Farmers' Association works with the National Farmers' Union (NFU) and the Honey (Packers) Association to promote ecologically sensitive farming and consumer awareness.

The work of the Bee Farmers' Association

- To monitor and to keep members informed about developments in commercial beekeeping, bee science and UK and EU legislation.
- Liaison with farmers, growers, contractors, consumers and other organisations.
- Liaison and cooperation with UK beekeeping organisations.
- Liaison with UK Government departments dealing with beekeeping, medicines and allied matters.
- Contact with European beekeeping organisations and representation on the EU Honey Working Party (COPA/COGECA) in Brussels.
- Member of the EU Honey Task Force.
- Political lobbying through MPs and MEPs.
- Member of the Confederation of National Beekeeping Associations (CONBA).
- Associate member of the Honey Association.
- Associate member of the National Farmers' Union.

Benefits of membership

- Advice and support on all aspects of honey farming and commercial beekeeping.
- Networking opportunities with others in the sector.
- Insurance for products, third-party liability, and employer's liability.
- Association journal, featuring informative articles, case studies, news and updates on meetings with Defra, Fera, APHA, VMD and the EU, reports on current beekeeping issues and commercial developments worldwide.
- Free classified advertising and discounted display advertising in the association journal.
- Sources of equipment and sundries; product directory of specialist suppliers.
- Supplier discounts through BFA Sales. Discount vehicle purchase scheme.
- Regional meetings which provide networking and trading opportunities.
- UK Spring Conference and overseas visits; these include visits to bee farms and research establishments; lectures and discussions on bee-related matters; sight-seeing and social events.
- Eligibility for the Disease Accreditation Scheme for Honeybees (DASH).
- Free circulation of UK and foreign beekeeping journals.
- Crop and winter loss reports.
- Pollination contracts.

For Membership

Members are expected to have a good level of competence as beekeepers and to maintain a professional approach in their operations.

Full membership is available to those with 40 or more production colonies.

Associate membership is available to those with 20-39 production colonies who wish to progress to operation on a semi-commercial or commercial scale.

Corporate membership

Please contact the General Secretary for details.

How to apply

Further information is available on the Bee Farmers' Association website. Application forms are available from the Membership and Administration Officer.

GENERAL SECRETARY
Margaret Ginman MBA FRSA
Hendal House
Groombridge
Kent
TN3 9NT
01892 864499,
07795 153765
gensec@beefarmers.co.uk

Enquiries in relation to: European Union (EU) and government representation, strategic partnerships, corporate sponsorship, press and public relations, apprenticeship scheme.

MEMBERSHIP AND ADMINISTRATION
Alex Ellis
23 Edgeley Road
Whitchurch
Shropshire
SY13 1EU
01948 510726,
07972 281496
admin@beefarmers.co.uk

Enquiries in relation to: membership, communications, publications, insurance, events and training, Disease Accreditation Scheme for Honeybees (DASH).

POLLINATION SECRETARY
Alan Hart
61 Fakenham Road
Great Witchingham
Norwich
Norfolk
NR9 5AE
01603 308911
07867 523977
pollination@beefarmers.co.uk

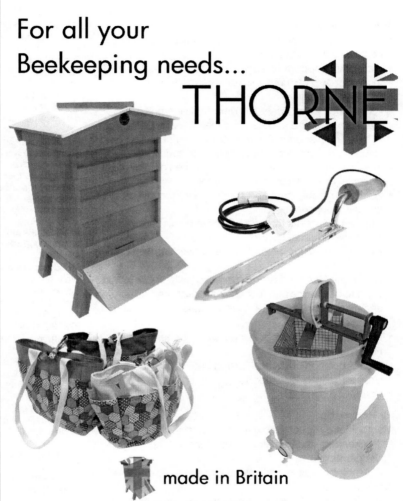

BEES

BEEKEEPING EDITORS'
EXCHANGE SCHEME

BEES is a self-help grouping of local, county and country beekeeping association editors, which operates principally by exchanging journals through a central address. The scheme is supported by Northern Bee Books.

B.E.E.S
Helping Editors
Help Themselves

BEES was founded in 1984 and for many years has been an exchange of paper copy. However, the focus has now changed to an electronic exchange, using the server of one of the participating editors.

Sponsored by
NORTHERN BEE BOOKS

Now fully established as part of the British and Irish beekeeping scene, the scheme brings up to date information to beekeepers throughout the British Isles.

The aims are:
- to exchange ideas for content and production methods
- to aid others by experience
- to communicate matters editorial
- to share information on national beekeeping issues
- to help and reassure those new to the task
- to give a wider readership to the best writing in beekeeping journalism

If you are an editor or potential editor and would like to know more about how we operate write to Chris Jackson
22 Chapter Close, Oakwood, Derby, DE21 2BG
editors-owner@ebees.org.uk

BEES ABROAD UK Ltd

Relieving Poverty through Beekeeping

ADMINISTRATOR:
MRS VERONICA BROWN,
PO Box 2058,
Thornbury
Bristol
BS35 9AF.
0117 230 0231
info@beesabroad.org.uk

Bees Abroad is a UK-registered charity (No 1108464) established in 1999. Its principle aim is the relief of poverty in the developing world using beekeeping and associated skills as tools of individual, group and community empowerment for poverty alleviation and to provide sustainable income. Beekeeping is a valuable tool as it is socially and culturally acceptable for both genders across a wide age range. It can cost very little to set up a beekeeping operation, which will deliver benefits for income, education, health, environment and community. Beekeeping and its associated skills deliver access to gainful self-employment for poor and disadvantaged groups. This enables them to recover social status, improve social interactions, obtain income and acquire new skills to build the confidence to represent their own interests. Bees Abroad receives a high volume of direct appeals for assistance from groups all over the world. In practice, it achieves its aims through a volunteer network of supporters, committee members and project managers. Bees Abroad takes care to ensure that its projects are sustainable and not dependent on constant external input. This is done by supporting community group initiatives, setting up village-based field extension services, running training courses for beekeeping trainers and financing local trainers' wages. All Bees Abroad projects are designed to become self-financing after a defined time period. Its first two projects in Nepal and Cameroon now employ 42 beekeeper trainers and involve many more beekeepers. It currently has projects either running or

seeking funding in Cameroon, Ghana, Kenya, Liberia, Malawi, Nigeria, Uganda, Yemen and Zambia.

Bees Abroad is run by volunteers who are all beekeepers. They currently undertake all activities, including fundraising, though an administrator is employed for one day a week. It also arranges beekeeping holidays to a variety of locations, including Morocco, Poland, Chile and Nepal.

Bees Abroad is delighted to have the support of its patrons: The Most Reverend Justin Welby, Archbishop of Canterbury, Jimmy Doherty (Jimmy's Farm), Martha Kearny (Broadcaster and Journalist), Adam Hart (Professor of Science Communication, University of Gloucestershire), Michael Badger, MBE (Past President, BBKA), Brian Sherriff (BJ Sherriff International), Bill and Paula Stevens (National Bee Supplies), Eric Hiam (Maisemore Apiaries) and Richard Jones (Past Director, IBRA).

For more details of what we do and how you can help, contact Veronica Brown, the Administrator, Bees Abroad (info@beesabroad.org.uk). You can learn more about our work and make a regular or one-off donation through our website, www.beesabroad.org.uk

BEES *for* DEVELOPMENT TRUST

supporting beekeepers in developing countries
www.beesfordevelopment.org

Bees *for* Development
1 Agincourt Street, Monmouth, NP25 3DZ, UK
Tel +44 (0)16007 14848
info@beesfordevelopment.org

YOU CAN HELP US BY:

- **Ensuring** that your group or organisation knows about our work, and supports us if possible
- **Making** a gift of a Resource Box for a training course in a school or project
- **Subscribing** to our magazine, BfD Journal, or Sponsoring a subscription to the Journal for a beekeeper working in a poor country
- **Helping** us to represent our organisation at events
- **Offering** your skills to work with us as a volunteer
- **Giving** a donation
- **Joining** one of our Beekeepers' Safaris
- **Using** our tamper proof seals or labels when you sell or gift your honey
- **Buying** from our special shop in Monmouth or from our on-line store. Proceeds from sales go to support our charitable work.
- **Attending** one of our unique training Courses in UK on Sustainable Beekeeping or on *Strengthening Livelihoods by Means of Beekeeping.* We also run courses at *Humble by Nature* and at *Ragman's Permaculture Farm* in the Wye Valley.

What we do

Bees *for* Development encourages beekeeping to alleviate poverty and to maintain biodiversity in developing countries.

We run practical, community-based projects to develop the skills and knowledge that enable families in poor areas to create reliable income from bees.

We provide educational resources and promote awareness of biodiversity.

Bees *for* Development Journal provides readers in over 130 countries with practical advice, information and articles about how they can keep bees sustainably and increase their incomes.

We always need more help and skills please contact us if you might like to become involved. We are a highly professional organisation, working in the beekeeping development sector for more than 22 years. We are respected and trusted by beekeepers world-wide. Please encourage your beekeeping group or other organisation to support our work: do contact us for more details of our work and current projects.

Charity 1078803

124

BRITISH BEEKEEPERS' ASSOCIATION

www.bbka.org.uk

COMMITTEES OF THE EXECUTIVE AND SECRETARIES

Education & Training

The development of information from practical guidance notes, advisory leaflets, training materials while also undertaking it's own educational initiatives in support of improving the knowledge and skills of beekeepers at all levels. Education & Training liase with the Examination Board to develop training materials to support Association tutors with products such as the Course in a Case.

Examination Board

The BBKA examination board provide a structured range of examinations fulfilling the needs of all beekeepers from Junior Certificate to Master Beekeeper. The board are responsible for all matters relating to the syllabus, content and assessment and operate independently of the BBKA board of Trustees. Where Associations have no Examinations Secretary the Association Secretary deals with examinations. To help future candidates it is suggested that Associations without an Examination Secretary appoint one. Associations are responsible for arranging a suitable room for the written examinations and recommending an invigilator.

Contact Val Frances, Exam Board Secretary
Email: val.frances@bbka.org.uk Tel 01226 286341

FINANCE

This team of Trustees reviews & agrees all budgets, handles all investment matters, finalising insurance policies and sets proposals relating to capitation.

BBKA

PRESIDENT
DR DAVID ASTON
david.aston@bbka.org.uk

CHAIRMAN
DOUG BROWN
doug.brown@bbka.org.uk

VICE CHAIRMAN
MARGARET MURDIN
margaret.murdin@bbka.org.uk

TREASURER
CHRIS LAKE
treasurer@bbka.org.uk

Governance

Primary areas of responsibility are to ensure that we adhere to Charity Commission rules, that we operate within the constitution in addition to ensuring that our Trustees act in the best interests of the BBKA and it's members.

Operations & Membership Services

This team ensures that all Membership Services are administered effectively and on time and that the organisation operates efficiently. It also acts as a co-ordinator for all external fundraising. Contact: jane.moseley@bbka.org.uk

Public Affairs

Whether it be government liason, both UK & EU, or press activity this comes from the Public Affairs team. All enquiries should be made to BBKA Press Officer: gill.maclean@bbka.org.uk

Technical & Environmental

All technical issues and their their potential impact on bees and beekeeping are assessed and monitored within this team. All research projects are reviewed and recommendations made by Technical & Environmental group.

Insurance

Members of BBKA, Area Associations and officials are indemnified against claims for Public Liability to a limit of £10million, Product Liability to a limit of £10 million, Professional Indemnity to a limit of £2 million relating to their beekeeping activities. BBKA Association Officer and Trustee liability insurance also applies to a limit of £10 million. Each new claim carries an excess payable by the member.

An 'All Risks' policy is available to both individuals and Associations, to cover the loss or damage of property & equipment. Details are available via www.bbka.org.uk or the main office: 02476 696679

Publications

- BBKA News is issued monthly free to all members of the BBKA, featuring articles about bees, beekeeping and the other associated articles of interest. Editorial: editorial@bbkanew.org.uk Advertising: advertising@bbkanews.org.uk
- BBKA Year Book is published each June and is for Association use and reference. It contains detailed information on the BBKA including useful reference tools such as a directory of Lecturers and Demonstrators.
- Members Handbook is published annually and sent to Association and Branch Chairman, Secretary, and Treasurer
- BBKA Introduction to Beekeeping

BBKA Website - www.bbka.org.uk

The BBKA Website contains technical information, is easy to navigate and supports both beekeepers and the general public. You can download publications, find help and advice in the discussion forums, purchase merchandise, learn about Bees, use the Bees4kids section, download BBKA exam application forms and the exam syllabus. Within the Members Only area, specific insurance downloads and other member only information is available. Associations beekeeping events are promoted.

A Swarm Collector database is included within the site enabling the general public with a direct link to a local swarm collector.

Events

Area and local associations attend and exhibit at various events within their local throughout the year while the BBKA supports selected national shows. Whether it be village fete or national exhibition these events continue to provide a vital service for the dissemination of knowledge.

BBKA Spring Convention
Held in April every year this is a firmly established major beekeeping event. Lectures and Workshops are staged over 3 days with a trade exhibition. Both Friday and Sunday are member only days which are ticketed. New in 2015 was the instigation of a Trade Day only ticket

Slide Library
The BBKA slide library has been digitised for ease of use and preservation. For a list of slides available and their format please go the BBKA Members Area at www.bbka.org.uk or contact the BBKA office.

Subscriptions & Membership Fees
Individual Membership of the BBKA is £38 per annum, for an Overseas Member the fee is £28.00. All other membership is via local associations.
Friends of the Honeybee Membership is also available via www.bbka.org.uk

Exam Board Footnote
Where Associations have no Examinations Secretary the Association Secretary deals with examinations. To help future candidates it is suggested that Associations without an Examination Secretary appoint one. Associations are responsible for arranging a suitable room for the written examinations and recommending an invigilator.

If you live in an area without a nominated Exam Secretary, you should contact Val Frances, Exam Board Secretary Email: val.frances@bbka.org.uk Tel 01226 286341

BBKA Enterprises
BBKA Enterprises Ltd is a private company, limited by guarantee with all profits from the trading activities being donated to the BBKA. Via the BBKA online shop a range of beekeeping, corporate and related items, specially selected books, gifts, travel items and educational materials are available.

Visit www.thepollenbasket.com, the official BBKA web shop, or call 02476 696679

SOME ASSOCIATION SECRETARIES

AVON
Mr Neil Seymour
The Old School House
Litton
Radstock
BA3 4PW
07921 256120
neil.seymour@gmail.com

BERKSHIRE
Mr John White
6, Horseshoe Road
Pangbourne
Reading
Berkshire
jkwhite70@hotmail.co.uk

**BOURNEMOUTH &
DISTRICT**
Mrs Margaret Davies
57 Leybourne Avenue
Ensbury Park
Bournemouth
BH10 6HE
01202 526077
marg@jdavies.freeserve.
co.uk

BUCKINGHAMSHIRE
Mrs Fiona Matheson
17 Shire Lane
Chorleywood
Hertfordshire
WD3 5NQ
01923 285637
education@buckscounty-
beekeepers.co.uk

CAMBRIDGESHIRE
Mrs Eleanor Witter
177 Hills Road
Cambridge
CB2 8RN
01223 247228
eleanor.witter@tesco.net

CHESHIRE
Mr Graham Royle
7 Symondley Road
Sutton
Macclesfield
SK11 0HT
01260 252 042
g.royle@tiscali.co.uk

CHESTERFIELD
Mrs June Harvey
125 North Road
Clowne
Chesterfield
Derbyshire
S43 4PQ
01246 812115
harveyjex@aol.com

CORNWALL
Mrs Sue Malcolm
Figtree
333 New Road
Saltash
Cornwall
PL12 6HL
01752 845496
suzan@hmalcolm.freeserve.
co.uk

CORNWALL WEST
Mrs Barbara Barnes
Clowance Barton Lodge
Praze-an-Beeble
Camborne
Cornwall
TR14 0PR
07901 977597
bab@barbara-barnes.com

CUMBRIA
Mr Peter Matthews
4 Annan Hill
Back of the Hill
Annan
Dumfries
DG12 6TN
01461 205525
silverhive@hotmail.com

DERBYSHIRE
Mrs Thelma Robinson
72 Church Street
Ockbrook Wood
Derby
Derbyshire
DE72 3SL
01332 662567
thelmaelizabethrobinson@
gmail.com

DEVON
Mrs Lea Bayly
Blowiscombe Barton
Milton Combe
Devon
PL20 6HR
01822 855292
lea.jones2@btinternet.com

DORSET
Mr Terry Payne
Brookmans Farm Bungalow
Dunns Lane
Ewen Minster
Dorset
DT11 8NG
01747 811251
twpayne@btinternet.com

DOVER & DISTRICT
Mrs Jackie Thomas
Quarry House
Agester Lane
Denton Nr Canterbury
Kent
CT4 6NR
01227 831235
jackieaucott@gmail.com

DURHAM
Mr George Eames
11 Sharon Avenue
Kelloe
Durham
DH6 4NE
07970 926250
beeseames@btinternet.com

ESSEX
Mrs Pat Allen
8 Franks Cottages
St Mary's Lane
Upminster
Essex
RM14 3NU
01708 220897
pat.allen@btconnect.com

GLOUCESTERSHIRE
Mr Bernard Danvers
120a Ruspidge Road
Cinderford
GL14 3AG
01594 825063
berniedanvers@hotmail.
co.uk

GWENT
Mrs Janet Bromley
Upper Ty Hir
Monmouth Road
Raglan
Gwent
NP15 2ET
01291 690331
bromleyjan@hotmail.com

HAMPSHIRE
Mrs Jean Frost
5 Pound Close
Upper Wield
Alresford
Hampshire
SO24 9SH
01420 561136
jeanterry@uwclub.net

HARROGATE & RIPON
Mrs Judith Hart
Kintail
Brearton
Harrogate
North Yorkshire
HG3 3BX
01423 865873
jm22.r27@virginmedia.com

BBKA

HEREFORDSHIRE
Mrs Louise Sheppard
The Seggin
Eyton
Leominster
Herefordshire
HR6 0BZ
01568 616692
louisesheppard2@hotmail.com

HERTFORDSHIRE
Mr David Canham
171, London Road
Hertford Heath
Hertfordshire
SG13 7PN
07990 530826
hertsbeeexams@gmail.com

HUNTINGDONSHIRE
Mrs Barbara Woodbine
16 Montagu Gardens
Kimbolton
Cambridgeshire
PE28 0JL
01480 861383
barbara@woodbine16.plus.com

ISLE OF MAN
Mrs Janet Thompson
Cott ny Greiney
Beach Rd
Port St Mary
Isle of Man
IM9 5NF
01624 835524
jthompson@manx.net

KENDAL & SOUTH WEST-MORLAND
Mr. Mick Gander
52 Buttermere Drive
Kendal
Cumbria
LA9 7PH
07515 797899
mickgander@live.com

KENT
Miss S Sharon Bassey
61, Nunhead Lane
London
SE15 3TR
sharonbassey@hotmail.com

NORFOLK WEST AND KINGS LYNN
Mrs Judith Heal
Burgh Parva Hall
Melton Constable
Norfolk
NR24 2PU
01263 862569
judyheal@dsl.pipex.com

LANCASHIRE & NORTH WEST
Mrs Barbarara Roderick
39, Hawksworth Drive
Formby
Liverpool
L73 7EY
01704 877855
beebarb@hotmail.co.uk

LINCOLNSHIRE
Mr Michael Seal
70a, Westfield Drive
North Greetwell
Lincolnshire
LN2 4RB
01522 754435
mikeseal91@sky.com

LONDON
Mr Howard Nichols
45 Selsden Road
West Norwood
London
SE27 0PQ
07809 156185
howard@wrightandco.biz

LUDLOW & DISTRICT
Mr Andy Vanderhook
The Old Forge
Baveney Wood
Cleobury Mortimer
Kidderminster
DY14 8JD

01584 890830
andy.vanderhook@care-4free.net

MANCHESTER & DISTRICT
Mrs Joy Jackson
96a, New Lane
Eccles
Lancashire
M30 7JE
07872 512266
joy.jackson4@hotmail.co.uk

MEDWAY
Mr Terry Clare
89 Chalky Bank Road
Rainham
Gillingham
Kent
ME8 7NP
01634 233748
terryeclare@tinyworld.co.uk

MIDDLESEX
Mrs Jo Telfer
Midwood House
Elm Park Road
Pinner
Middx
HA5 3LH
020 8868 3494
jvtelfer@hotmail.com

MOLE APIARY CLUB
Mr Denis Cutler
70 Hurst Rd
East Molesey
Surrey
KT8 9AG
0208 224 9283
densicutler@ntlworld.com

NEWCASTLE & DISTRICT
Mrs Valerie Hawley
Tindall House
Killingworth Village
Newcastle upon Tyne
Tyne and Wear
NE12 6BL
01912 683949
val.hawley@btinternet.com

NORFOLK
Mrs Carolyne Liston
Ivy Cottage
Dumbs Lane
Hainford
Norwich
NR10 3BH
01603 893330
cliston@ukf.net

NORTHAMPTONSHIRE
Mr Mike Hall
3, Thorpeville
Moulton
Northamptonshire
NN3 7TS
halle3m@gmail.com

NORTHUMBERLAND
Mr Ian Robson
2 Breamish Gardens
Powburn
Alnwick
Northumberland
NE66 4HQ
07833 317399
Ian@kw-porvis.co.uk

NOTTINGHAMSHIRE
Ms Janet Bates
11, Rowan Avenue
Ravenshead
Nottingham
NG15 9GA
01623 794687
janet.bates@ntlworld.com

OXFORDSHIRE
Mr Peter Chaunt
9 Robins Close
Barford St Michael
Banbury
Oxford
OX15 0RP
01869 338625
chaunt@talktalk.com

PETERBOROUGH & DISTRICT
Mr George Newton
65 Queen Street
Yaxley
Peterborough
Cambs
PE7 3JE
01733 243349

SHROPSHIRE
Mrs Liz Williams
35 Ridgebourne Road
Shrewsbury
Shropshire
SY3 9AB
e.williams800@btinternet.
com

SHROPSHIRE NORTH
Mrs Joyce Nisbet
22 Ffordd Ystrad
Coed y Glyn
Wrexham
Shropshire
LL13 7QQ
01978 363168
joycerussell1@hotmail.co.uk

SOMERSET
Mrs B Bridget Knutson
6 Wideatts Road
Cheddar
Somerset
BS27 3AP
01934 742187
bridget_knutson@yahoo.
co.uk

STAFFORDSHIRE NORTH
Ms A Angela Fearon
The Crofters
The Green
Stocton Brook
Staffordshire
ST9 9PD
07764 605663
angelafearon@googlemail.
com

STAFFORDSHIRE SOUTH
Mr Julian Malein
Woodview
School Lane
Admaston nr Rougley
Staffordshire
WS15 3NH
01889 500486
jmalein@yahoo.co.uk

STRATFORD ON AVON
Mr Terry Hitchman
Church View
Pillerton Hersey
Warwickshire
CV35 0QJ
01789 740136
terryhitchman@phonecoop.
coop

SUFFOLK
Mr Adrian Howard
Rondebosch
Lodge Road
Hollesley
Woodbridge
IP12 3RR
01394 4111561
a.howard106@btinternet

SURREY
Mrs Celia Perry
White Gables
68 Broadhurst
Ashstead
KT21 1QF
0790 3991120.
beeexams@hotmail.co.uk

SUSSEX
Mrs Liz Twyford
Westcott
Udimore Road
Broad Oak
Rye
TN31 6DG
01424882361
secretary@sussexbee.
org.uk

SUSSEX WEST
Mr Roger Brooks
23, Lionel Avenue
Bognor Regis
West Sussex
PO22 8LG
01243 584531
rhandm@hotmail.com

THANET
Mrs Rowena Pearce
Summerfield Cottage
Summerfield
Woodnesborough
Sandwich
CT13 0EW
01304 614789
pearcesinsummerfield@
tiscali.co.uk

TWICKENHAM & THAMES VALLEY
Mr Chris Deaves
12 Chatsworth Crescent
Hounslow
TW3 2PB
02085 682869
c_deaves@compuserve.
com

WARWICKSHIRE
Mr Bob Gilbert
66 Sharp Street
Amington
Tamworth
Staffordshire
B77 3HZ
01827 65749
bee1bob1@aol.com

WILTSHIRE
Mrs Sally Wadsworth
57 St Edith's Marsh
Bromham
Chippenham
Wiltshire
SN15 2DF
01380 859052
sally.wadsworth@btinternet.
com

WORCESTERSHIRE
Mr Martin Cracknell
Honeylands
Abberton Road
Bishampton
Worcestershire
WR10 2LU
01386 462385
martyn@cracknellz.
freeserve.co.uk

WYE VALLEY
Mrs Susan Quigley
Newhouse Farm
Michaelchurch Escley
Hereford
Herefordshire
HR2 0PT
01981 510183
quigley.susan@hotmail.
co.uk

YORKSHIRE
Mrs Yvonne Kilvington
Membership
144 93 603 961
10 Banks Avenue
Golcar
Huddersfield
West Yorkshire
HD7 4LZ
01484 643314
ykilvington@btopenworld.
com

SEDBERGH
Mr John Rogers
Holly Bank
Ingleton
Carnforth
LA6 3DR
01524 241364
johnrogers@btinternet.com

VALE & DOWNLAND
Mrs Lilian Valentine
6 Grove Road
Wantage
Oxfordshire
OX12 7BU
01235 767524
jvalentine515@btinternet.
com

NEWBURY
Mr Michael White
17 Donnington Square
Newbury
RG14 1PJ
0163 544945
mpwhite@freegratis.net

BBKA

CLEVELAND
Mr Tom Rettig
Hillcrest Village
Middleton-on-Leven
Yarm
TS15 0JX
01642 596158
t.rettig@btinternet.com

**INSTITUTE OF NI BEEKEEP-
ERS**
Mr Tom Canning
151 Portadown Road
Armagh
BT61 9HL
07867 878474
tjcanning@btinternet.com

RUTLAND
Mr Will Rigby
21 Mill Street
Melton Mowbray
Leicestershire
LE13 1AY
01664 852742
will@gliderman.fsnet.co.uk

LANCASTER
Mr Peter Stephens
49, Redhills Road
Arnside
Cumbria
01524 761445
peterstephens7@btinternet.
com

ISLE OF WIGHT
Mrs Liz Van Wyk
3, Buckingham Road
Ryde
Isle of Wight
PO33 2DP
01983 565839
elizabethvanwyk@aol.com

JERSEY
Mrs Judy Collins
2 Demerara Cottages
Le Mont Sohier
St Brelade
Jersey
JE3 8EA
07797 790420
judybees@collinsje.net

ASSOCIATION EXAMINATION SECRETARIES

10	Ms	R	Taylor	43, High Street, Chew Magna	BRISTOL
11	Mr	M	Moore	19, Armour Hill, Tilehurst	READING
12	Mr	P	Darley	3 Dorset House, 42, The Avenue	POOLE
13	Mrs	S	Carter	74 Whitelands Avenue, Chorleywood	
14	Miss	S	Fenwick	27 Pratt Street, Soham	ELY
15	Mrs	E	Camm	Magpie Manor, Wistaston Green Road	CREWE
16	Mr	R A	Bagnall	21 Ramper Avenue, Clowne, Chesterfield	DERBYSHIRE
17	Mrs	A	Ramsden	1 Wellington Place, Old Carnon Hill, Carnon Downs	TRURO
18	Ms	K	Bowyer	The Nook, Lower Carnkie	REDRUTH
19	Mr	S	Barnes	8 Albermarle Street, Cockermouth	CUMBRIA
20	Mr	M J	Cross	Harlestone, Beggarswell Wood, Ambergate	DERBYSHIRE
21	Mr	B	Neal	Badgers Barn, Withacott, Langtree	TORRINGTON
22	Mrs	L	Rescorla	5, Cowleaze, Martinstown	DORCHESTER
23	Mrs	M E	Harrowell	4 Harton Cottages, Chapel Lane, Ashley	DOVER
24	Mrs	L	Ramsey	Ashes House Farm, Wolsingham	BISHOP AUCKLAND
25	Mr	M	Webb	19 Ingrebourne Gardens, Upminster	ESSEX
26	Mrs	R	Savage	Oak House, Windrush Gardens	LYDNEY
27	Mrs	G	Williams	Green Court, South Row, Redwick, Magor	CALDICOT
28	Ms	Z	Semmens	27 Oak Tree Drive, Hook	HAMPSHIRE
29	Ms	J	Paley	20, Kent Road	HARROGATE
30	Mr	C	Stowell	Clayfoot Farm, Linley Green Road, Whitbourne	WORCESTER
31	Mr	J	Palombo	Field End, Woodside Green, Great Hallingbury BISHOP'S STORTFORD	
32	Mrs	M	Watkin	2, Rusts Lane, Alconbury	HUNTINGDON
33	Mrs	P	Shimmin	66, Ormly Road, Ramsey	ISLE OF MAN
34	Mrs	N	Mumberson	91, Victoria Avenue	SHANKLIN
35	Mrs	J	Bayne	Helm End Farm, Barrows Green, Stainton	KENDAL

36	Mrs J	Spon-Smith	77 Bushey Way	BECKENHAM
37	Mr A	Davies	West Cottage, Swanton Morley Road, Worthing	
				DEREHAM
38	Mr M	Smith	137 Blaguegate Lane, Skelmersdale	LANCASHIRE
39	Ms P	Merriman	19, Greenacre Court	LANCASTER
40	S	Raines	Grange Cottage, 21 Humberstone Avenue	GRIMSBY
41	Ms E	Nye	6 Mayfield House, Rushcroft Road	LONDON
42	Mr A	Jenyon	Oakleigh, Oldwood Road	TENBURY WELLS
43	Mrs J	Jackson	96a, New Lane, Eccles	MANCHESTER
44	Mrs M	Hunter	18, Slades Gardens	ENFIELD
45	Mrs R	Conway	2a, Tippings Lane, Barrowden	OAKHAM
46	Mr V	Cassidy	10, Bankside Close, Ryhope	SUNDERLAND
47	Mrs J	Harrison	Woodgate Barn, Frogs Hall Lane, Swanton Morley	
				DEREHAM
48	Mrs R	Stewart	17, Leys Avenue, Rothwell	KETTERING
49	Mr B	Hopkinson	11 Watershaugh Road, Warkworth	MORPETH
50	Mr MS	Jordan	29 Crow Park Avenue, Sutton-on-Trent,	NOTTINGHAM
51	Miss H C	Raine	37, St Marys Road, Adderbury	BANBURY
52	Mr P G	Newton	65 Queen Street, Yaxley, Peterborough	CAMBS
53	Mrs C	Currier	Churchleigh, Adderley, Market Drayton	SHROPSHIRE
54	Mr N	Hine	Chapel House, Whixall	WHITCHURCH
55	Dr R	Bache	11 Rectory Mews, Hatch Beauchamp	TAUNTON
56	Mr S	Boulton	Middle Banks, Malthouse Road, Alton	STOKE-ON-TRENT
57	Mrs L	Lacey	21, Fisherwick Road	LICHFIELD
58	Mr MJ	Osborne	Oak Lodge, Kings Lane, Snitterfield	
			STRATFORD-UPON-AVON	
59	Mr I J	McQueen	643 Foxhall Road	IPSWICH
60	Mrs S	Rickwood	19 Kenwood Drive, Walton-on-Thames	SURREY
61	Mrs E	Twyford	Westcott, Udimore Road, Broad Oak	RYE
62	Mr G	Elliott	Robins Croft, Chalk Road, Ifold Loxwood	BILLINGSHURST
63	Mrs R	Pearce	Summerfield Cottage, Summerfield, Woodnesborough	SANDWICH
64	Ms S	Crofton	10 Wellesley Avenue, London	
65	Mrs G	Rose	40, Beaudesert Road	BIRMINGHAM
66	Mr B	Wilson	71e, School Lane, Shaw	MELKSHAM
67	Mrs L	Chapman	White House, Warbage Lane, Dodford	BROMSGROVE
68	Mrs S	Quigley	Newhouse Farm, Michaelchurch Escley	HEREFORD
69	Mrs C	Thomson	105, Cidercourt Road	CRUMLIN
70	Mr R	Chappel	4, The Green, Brafferton	DARLINGTON
71	Mrs SJ	Stunell	7, Marshland View, Lower Stoke	ROCHESTER
72	Mrs J	Doyle	1, Cherry Orchard, Great Shefford	HUNGERFORD
73	Mrs J	Greenhalgh	8, Park View, Garston Lane	WANTAGE

74	Mrs	L	Pauley	Croft House, Newby, Clapham	LANCASTER
75	Mr	I	Makinson	36 Montagus Harrier	GUISBOROUGH
76	Ms	P	Kilduff	Rowan House, 4, Le Clos St Sampson	
				La Route Des Quennevais, St Brelade	JERSEY
77	Mr	P	Lythgoe	16, Stockburn Drive, Failsworth	MANCHESTER
95	Ms	L	Pearce	27, The Forstal, Hadlow, tonbridge	OXFORDSHIRE

Where Associations have no Examinations Secretary the Association Secretary deals with examinations. To help future candidates it is suggested that Associations without an Examination Secretary appoint one. Associations are responsible for arranging a suitable room for the written examinations and recommending an invigilator.

If you live in an area without a nominated Exam Secretary, you should contact Mrs Val Frances, 39 Beevor Lane, Gawber, Barnsley, S75 2RP
Tel 01226 286341. e-mail, toval.francis@bbka.org.uk

HOLDERS OF THE BBKA SENIOR JUDGES CERTIFICATE

Mr. Terry Ashley
Meadow Cottage,
11, Elton Lane, Winterley,
Sandbach, Cheshire. CW11 4TN
01270760757

Mr. Dennis Atkinson
4, Fell View, Garstang,
Lancashire. PR3 1WQ
01995602058

Mr. Michael Badger MBE
'Kara', 14, Thorn Lane,
Roundhay, Leeds,
West Yorkshire. LS8 1NN
0113294 5879
buzz.buzz@ntlworld.com

Mrs. Hazel Blackburn
28 Chazey Road, Caversham, Reading,
Berkshire. RG4 7DS
01189475451

Mr Alan Brown
9 The Woodlands, Carleton, Pontefract
Yorkshire. WF8 2RN
01977 796193
alanhoneybees4u@talktalk.net

Mrs. Vivienne Brown
7, Links Way, Flackwell Heath,
High Wycombe,
Buckinghamshire. HP10 9LZ
01628521502

Mr. Martin Buckle
The Little House,
Newton Blossomville,
Bedford, Beds. MK43 8AN
01234881262

Rev'd Francis Capener
1, Baldric Road,
Folkestone, Kent. CT20 2NR
01303254579

Mr. Gerald Collins, NDB
72, Tatenhill Gardens,
Doncaster, Yorkshire. DN4 6TL
01302539873
gerry@collins72.plus.com

Miss Margery Cooper
10, Gaskells End,
Tokers Green, Reading,
Berkshire. RG4 9EW

Mrs. Moyra Davidson
Hazlefield House, Auchencairn,
Castle Douglas DG7 1RF
01556 640597

Mrs. Margaret Davies
57, Leybourne Avenue,
Ensbury Park, Bournemouth,
Dorset. BH10 6ES
01202526077
margaretdavies773@btinternet.com

Mr. Bernard Diaper
57, Marfield Close,
Walmley, Sutton Coldfield,
West Midlands. B76 1YD
07711 456932
b.diaper@tiscali.co.uk

Ms. Fiona Dickson
Didlington Manor, Didlington, Thetford,
Norfolk. IP26 5AT
01842878673

Mr. Mike Duffin
Upper Hurst, Salisbury Road,
Blashford, Ringwood,
Hampshire. BH24 3PB
01425474552

134

Mr. Leo Fielding
Linley, Station Road,
Lichfield, Staffordshire.
WS13 6HZ
01543264427

Mr. Ivor Flatman
15, Waterton Close,
Walton, Wakefield,
West Yorkshire. WF2 6JT
01924257089
ivor.flatman@homecall.co.uk

Mr. Stephen Guest
Bridge House,
Hindheath Road,
Wheelock, Sandbach,
Cheshire. CW11 9LY
01270762226

Mr John Goodwin
Foleshill, Brereton Heath
Congleton , Cheshire. CW12 4SY
01477535032
john.goodwin@virgin.net

Mrs. Mary Hill
Whittington, Selling Road,
Old Wives Lees,
Canterbury, Kent. CT4 8BH
01227730477
mary.hill43@btinternet.com

Mr. Michael MacGiolla
Glengarra Wood,
Burncourt, Cahir,
Co. Tipperary, EIRE.
0035352672053

Mr. Peter Matthews
4, Annanhill, Back of the Hill,
Annan, Dumfries & Galloway,
Scotland. DG12 6TN
01461 205525

Mr. Gerald Moxon
9, Savery Street,
Southcoates Lane,
Kingston upon Hull,
Yorkshire. HU8 8DG
01482782052

Mr. Jim Orton
Occupation Road,
Sibson, Nuneaton,
Warwickshire. CV13 6LD
01827880471

Mrs. Suzette Perkins
Tengore House, Tengore lane
Langport, Somerset
TA10 9JL
01458 250095

Wg Cmdr Tom
Salter MBE C.Eng RAF
Splash Hollow, Five Bells Lane
Nether Wallop, Stockbridge
SO20 8EN
01264 781382
tomasalter@hotmail.co.uk

Mr David Shannon
April Court, High Street, Wroot,
Doncaster, South Yorkshire DN9 2BT
01302 772837
daveshannon.aca@me.com

Mr. Chris Symes
189, Marlow Bottom Road,
Marlow, Buckinghamshire.
SL7 3PL
01628485212

Mr.Arthur Taylor
The Old Pyke Cottage,
Hethelpit Cross, Staunton,
Gloucestershire. GL19 3QJ
01452840522

Mr. Redmond Williams
Tincurry, Cahir,
Co. Tipperary, EIRE.

Mr Alan Woodward
55, Smillie Road
Rossington, Doncaster
South Yorkshire, DN11 0AW
01302868169

Mr. Michael Young MBE
'Mileaway', Carnreagh,
Hillsborough, Northern Ireland.
BT26 6LJ
02892 689724
myoungjudge@yahoo.co.uk

Mr. Derrick Daniels*
Mellifera, 14, Frenches Mead,
Billingshurst, West Sussex.
RH14 9LF
01403784204

Mr. Michael Duggan*
Redstone Wood Cottage,
Philantrophic Lane,
Redhill, Surrey. RH1 4DF
01737762536

Mrs. Elizabeth Rolt*
Ambonne, Northfields Lane,
Aldingbourne, Chichester,
West Sussex. PO20 6UH
01243543599

Mr. Jeff Rounce, NDB*
4, Scarborough Road,
Great Walsingham,
Norfolk. NR22 6AB
01328820241

Mr. GeorgeVickery*
'Ponderosa', Verwood Road,
Three Legged Cross,
Wimborne, Dorset. BH21 6RN
01202825774

* These judges are no longer active.

BEE IMPROVEMENT & BEE BREEDERS' ASSOCIATION

www.bibba.com

SECRETARY
Roy Norris
Llys Gwyn,
Cefn Mawr
Newtown
SY16 3LB
Tel: 01686 622217
E: roy@fulmar.demon.co.uk

MEMBERSHIP SECRETARY
Iain Harley
93 Dunsberry
Bretton
Peterborough
Cambridgeshire
PE3 8LB
01733 700740
iain.harley42@ntlworld.com

BIBBA is an organisation devoted to encouraging beekeepers to breed native or near native bees. The bees more suited to our environmental circumstances than other sub species.

BIBBA's aims are publicised through their magazine 'Bee Improvement', books, workshops, lectures and conferences.

BIBBA co-operates worldwide with Beekeeping and breeding groups interested in conserving and improving their own native bees.

Breeding techniques advocated include:
- Assessment of colonies by observation, recording certain criteria on standard record cards.
- Determination and purity of sub species by measurement of morphometric characters and mitrochondial DNA.
- Use of mini nucs for the mating of queens economically

BIBBA Publications include:
- The Honeybees of the British Isles by Beowulf Cooper
- Breeding Techniques and Selection for Breeding of the Honeybee by Prof. F. Ruttner
- The Dark European Honey Bee by Prof. F. Ruttner, Rev. Eric Milner and John Dews
- Breeding Better Bees using Simple Modern Methods by John E. Dews and Rev.Eric Milner
- Better Beginnings for Beekeepers by Adrian Waring - second edition.

BIBBA encourages the formation of Bee Breeding Groups, and the sharing of knowledge between groups by the provision of genetic material.

Look out for Bee Improvement days and Queen Rearing events in the bee press and on www.bibba.com.

CBDBBRT

THE C.B. DENNIS BRITISH BEEKEEPERS' RESEARCH TRUST

REGISTERED CHARITY NO. 328685

Aims

This independent Charitable Trust awards grants for research at Universities and institutions on the basis of scientific merit and supports young bee scientists by providing funding for studentships and training. Since its inception the Trust has funded work on a wide range of topics related to both honey bees and other bees. Recent projects have focused on gaining a better understanding of the relationship between Varroa destructor and deformed wing virus (DWV) of honey bees and the development of strategies to moderate their damaging effects. Currently the Trust is supporting a number of young scientists who are investigating land use and honey bee bacterial associations, bee pollination in an agricultural landscape and beekeeping and conservation.

Awards

The Trust is administered by a group of seven Trustees all of whom are, or have been career scientists. They therefore have first-hand knowledge of both writing and evaluating research proposals and several have extensive practical experience of working with bees in a professional or hobbyist capacity. This expertise ensures that work funded by the Trust is properly evaluated and provides the greatest possible advantage for bees. Meetings are held twice a year in April and October to evaluate submitted research applications.

Donations

The Trust is pleased to acknowledge the loyal support it already receives from several local beekeeping associations and many individuals. All donations, however small, will be added to the invested capital and bee research in Britain will benefit from the income in perpetuity. Full details of the activities of the Trust, outputs of the research funded and grant application forms can be obtained from www.cbdennistrust.org.uk

CABK

THE CENTRAL ASSOCIATION OF BEEKEEPERS

www.cabk.org.uk

SECRETARY, Pat Allen
8 Frank's Cottages
St Mary's Lane
Upminster, RM14 3NU
pat.allen@btconnect.com

PRESIDENT, Prof. R.S. Pickard
pickard.r@btopenworld.com

TREASURER, Harold Cloutt
Corriemulzie
Netherfield
Battle
Sussex TN33 9PY
bees@cloutthr.plus.com

PROGRAMME SECRETARY
Pam Hunter
Burnthouse
Burnthouse Lane
Cowfold, Horsham
RH13 8DH
pamhunter@burnthouse.org.uk

EDITOR, Pat Allen
8, Frank's Cottages
St. Mary's Lane
Upminster, RM14 3NU

SALES AND DISTRIBUTION,
Bill Fisher
The Old Farmhouse,
Farm Road, Chorleywood,
Hertfordshire
WD3 5QB
theoldfish@hotmail.com
07973 626464

The Central Association of Beekeepers in its present form dates from the time of the reorganisation of the British Beekeepers' Association in 1945. The BBKA was originally made up of private members only. However as County Associations were formed they applied for affiliation and were later permitted to send delegates to meetings of the Central Association, as the private members were then known. This arrangement became unsatisfactory as the voting power of the Central Association greatly outnumbered that of the County Associations and so in 1945 a new Constitution was drawn up whereby the Council comprised Delegates from the Counties and Specialist Member Associations. The private members then formed themselves into a Specialist Member Association with the designation 'The Central Association of the British Beekeepers' Association'; this was later shortened to its present style.

The Association was able to devote itself to its own particular aims, to promote interest in current thought and findings about beekeeping and aspects of entomology related to honey-bees and other social insects. Lectures given by scientists and other specialists are arranged, printed and circulated to members, as has been done since 1879.

A Spring Meeting with three lectures plus Annual General Meeting is held in London, and an Autumn Weekend Conference in the Midlands. In addition a lecture is given at the Social Evening held during the National Honey Show. Subscriptions are £15 per annum for an individual, £18 for dual membership, £20 for corporate membership.

THE EVA CRANE TRUST

www.evacranetrust.org
mail@evacranetrust.org
@evacranetrust

Eva Crane Trust

The Trust was formed by Dr Eva Crane herself. It was enhanced by the residue of her estate bequeathed to the Trust on her death in 2007.

Trust Chairman
Richard Jones

The aim of the Trust is to continue Dr Crane's work in the way she would have liked it to evolve. This includes advancing the understanding of bees and beekeeping by the collection, collation and dissemination of science and research worldwide, as well as recording and propagating a further understanding of beekeeping practices through historical and contemporary discoveries.

The Trust, as well as being Dr Crane's way of ensuring her work continues, is a memorial whereby it may be possible to help fund others who can build on the foundations of sound academic research laid down in her many publications. Grants may be made to individuals and organizations that might otherwise find funding difficult in this specialized field. Applications will be considered from anywhere in the world but must be made in writing in the English language, preferably using the form on the website.

A comprehensive webssite continues to expand with new information on a regular basis. It is intended to be a research portal particularly for those interested in the history and development of bee science and beekeeping.

http://www.EvaCraneTrust.org

Similar information can be obtained by writing to:
The Eva Crane Trust, c/o Withy King Solicitors,
5-6 Northumberland Buildings, Bath, BA1 2JE, UK
Email: mail@evacranetrust.org

CONBA

✉ ☎

CONBA-UK & Ireland
COUNCIL OF NATIONAL BEEKEEPING ASSOCIATIONS IN THE UNITED KINGDOM and IRELAND

Incorporating the beekeeping organisations of :
England, Channel Islands Isle of Man, Wales, Scotland, Ulster, Ireland and The Bee Farmers Association

SECRETARY
Phil McAnespie
12 Monument Road
Ayr KA7 2RL
01292 885660
philmcanespie@btinternet.com

CHAIRMAN,
Margaret Ginman
Hendal House
Groombridge
Kent
TN3 9NT

VICE CHAIR
Doug Brown
3 Willow Close
Little Paxton
St Neots
PE196JH

TREASURER
Phil McAnespie
12 Monument Road
Ayr KA7 2RL
01292 885660
philmcanespie@btinternet.com

CONBA was established in 1978 to promote the aims and objectives of the national beekeeping associations of England, Scotland, Ulster, Wales and Ireland, and the Bee Farmers Association. Its purpose is to represent the interests of beekeepers' with local, national and international authorities. A representative delegate from each of the member country associations occupies the chair for a period of two years, on a rotational basis.

The council meets twice per year, normally at the Spring Convention and at the National Honey Show in London. Council business consists of any matters of common interest to all its members. CONBA provides representation of its membership at the European Union (EU) through two specific committees, COPA and COGECA (COPA – Comite des Organisations Professionelles Agricoles de la CEE); (COGECA Comite de la Cooperation Agricole de la CEE); and the Honey Working Party (HWP).

The Honey Working Party meetings are held at Brussels. This committee liases with the European Commission in relation to apicultural matters concerning the member states of the European Union (EU). These matters are subsequently presented to the European Parliament for its consideration, implementation or revision or rejection. The subsequent approval of such matters results in establishing legislation, government support and possible EC funding relating to the practice of apicultural production in the UK through its membership of the EU.

COUNCILLORS REPRESENTING THE MEMBER ASSOCIATIONS
BFA: Margaret Ginman (Chair)
BBKA: Doug Brown (vice chair), David Aston
SBA: Bron Wright, Phil McAnespie
UBKA: Mervyn Eddie, Susie Hill
FIBKA: Michael Gleeson, Philip McCabe
WBKA: Jenny Shaw, John Bowles

DARG

DEVON APICULTURAL RESEARCH GROUP

CHAIRMAN, Richard Ball
Stoneyford Farmhouse
Colaton Raleigh
Sidmouth, Devon EX10 0HZ
01 395 567 356

HON SECRETARY, Vacant
Contact Chairman

PUBLICATIONS OFFICER, David Loo
25 Woodlands
Newton-St-Cyres, Exeter
Devon EX5 5BP
0139 285 1472

TREASURER, Bob Ogden
Pennymoor Cottage
Pennymoor, Tiverton
Deven EX16 8LJ
01363 866687

All titles cost £2.50 per copy (post free) from the Publications Officer (tel. 01392 851472). Discounts are available for BBKA affiliated Associations **Please contact the Publications Officer for details**

D A R G is an independent group of experienced enthusiastic beekeepers whose primary aim is to collect and analyse data on matters of topical interest which may assist their apicultural education and promote the advancement of beekeeping. At their regular meetings, DARG members discuss various topics in open forum, during which they exchange ideas and information from their personal beekeeping knowledge and experience. They also undertake suitable research projects which further the Group's aims.

TOPICS CURRENTLY BEING UNDERTAKEN
- Use of management (mechanical) methods including shook colonies for varroa control.
- Brood cell size in natural comb.
- A survey of useful bee plants, shrubs and trees in the South West.
- Drone movement between colonies.

In conjunction with Devon BKA
- Survey of Nosema in the County of Devon.
- Survey of drone laying queens in the County of Devon.

PUBLICATIONS AVAILABLE
- **The Beeway Code.** A common sense guide for beginners to help avoid problems with neighbours and produce a safe and peaceful apiary.
- **Seasonal Management**. A useful aid to planning your work effectively
- **Queen Rearing.** Providing detailed help in rearing new queens in order to promote vigorous colonies.
- **The selection of Apiary sites** full of tips for choosing the right sites for your bees.

THE FEDERATION OF IRISH BEEKEEPERS' ASSOCIATIONS

http://www.irishbeekeeping.ie

Secretary: Mr Tom Shaw,
201 Ard Easmuinn, Dundalk, Co. Louth.
Email: tshaw@iol.ie Mobile: 086 236 1286 Home: 042 93 39 619

ANNUAL SUMMER COURSE

The 2015 Beekeeping Summer Course will take place at the Franciscan College, Gormanston, Co Meath from Sunday 25th July to Friday 31st of July. The Guest Speaker will be Professor Ingemar Fries at the Department of Ecology, Swedish University of Agricultural Sciences, Uppsala, Sweden.

For further information and to secure your place, contact the Summer Course Convenor
Mr Michael G Gleeson, Ballinakill, Enfield, Co Meath. Tel No 046-9541433/087-6879584, email mgglee@eircom.net or visit http://www.irishbeekeeping.ie/gormanston/gormprog2014.html

PUBLICATIONS:

Having Healthy Honeybees - Published by F.I.B.K.A. Editor John McMullan, Ph.D.
The aim of this book is to help beekeepers establish healthy honeybee colonies, assess their condition and take appropriate action. Diseases are dealt with in a concise format to improve readability and are referenced to the latest peer-reviewed research. The book emphasises the importance of proper set-up, involving an integrated approach to health management – in effect a preventative system that comes at little extra cost to the beekeeper
Cost €15 + P & P of €2 each
Bulk buying available to Associations In packs of 10 or 20 books, available at €12 each + P & P of €10 for packs of 10 or 20.
The recommended price is €15 per copy.
It is highly recommended for those doing the various FIBKA Examinations.
Available from Mr Michael G Gleeson, Ballinakill, Enfield, Co Meath.

OFFICERS:

President: Mr Eamon Magee, 222 Lower Kilmacud Road, Goatstown, Dublin 14.
Tel No 01-2987611
E-mail eamonmagee222@gmail.com

Vice-President:
Mr Gerry Ryan,
Deerpark, Dundrum, Co Tipperary
Tel No 062-71274/087-1300751, E-mail ryansfancy@gmail.com

P R O:
Paul O'Brien,

Life Vice-Presidents:
Mr P O'Reilly,
11 Our Lady's Place, Naas, Co Kildare
Tel No (045-897568),
E-mail jackieor@indigo.ie

Bee Health officer
Eleanor Attridge

FIBKA

Mr MI Woulfe,
Railway House,
Midleton, Co Cork
Tel No (021-4631011),
E-mail glenanorehoney@
eircom.net

Mrs Frances Kane

Editor: Ms Mary Montaut,
4 Mount Pleasant Villas,
Bray, Co Wicklow.

Tel No 01-2860497. E-mail
mmontaut@iol.ie

Manager: Mr Dermot O'Flaherty,
Rosbeg, Westport,
Co Mayo
Tel No 098-26585/
087-2464045
E-mail:
fibka.manager@anu.ie

Treasurer: Ms Maria Tobin,
Curragh, Donoughmore,
Co. Cork.
email: treasurer@
irishbeekeeping.ie

Education Officer:
Michael Maunsell

Summer Course Convenor:
Mr Michael G Gleeson,
Ballinakill, Enfield,
Co Meath.
Tel No 046-9541433/
087-6879584,
email mgglee@eircom.ne

Tel No (046-9541433) & (087-6879584), E-mail mgglee@ eircom.net

Bees, Hives and Honey - Published by F.I.B.K.A. – Edited by Eddie O'Sullivan
This book has been compiled from writings by some of Ireland's most prominent Beekeepers of the present day. It is an instruction book on beekeeping published as a Millennium project and should prove a modern treatise on the craft of beekeeping and its associated products. There are over 200 pages, also many photographs and illustrations. Price €12.70 (Paperback) or €19 (Hardback) Available from Eddie O'Sullivan, Phone: 021-4542614, Email: eosbee@indigo.ie

The Irish Bee Guide – by Reverend J.D. Digges. First published in 1904, it was proclaimed as an excellent book on beekeeping. It also won a place as a notable production in the literary context. It eventually ran to sixteen editions and sold seventy-six thousand copies overall. The name was changed in the second issue to The Practical Bee Guide.
Now, one hundred years later, a decision has been taken to honour this great work. What better way to do it than to re-issue the book as it was in 1904 when it first entered the literary world. The re-print is an exact replica of the original first edition. The price per copy is Hardback€30 and Softback €20
Available from Eddie O'Sullivan, Phone: 021-4542614, Email: eosbee@indigo.ie

An Beachaire – The Irish Beekeeper the monthly organ of FIBKA, subscription €25.00 (Irish Republic), £25 Stg (Northern Ireland/Great Britain) post free from The Manager
Mr Dermot O'Flaherty, Rosbeg, Westport, Co Mayo Tel No 098-26585/ 087-2464045
E-mail:fibka.manager@anu.ie
Readership of the Journal in Northern Ireland carries third party insurance public liability cover up to €6.500, 000 on any one claim and product liability cover up to €6.500, 000 on any one claim, on payment of £5.00 Stg extra.

LIBRARY

The library is owned and controlled by FIBKA. It contains very many valuable books ancient and modern, available to members for return postage only. The Librarian is Jim Ryan, Innisfail, Kickham Street, Thurles, Co Tipperary. Email jimbee1@eircom.net

EDUCATION

The Federation of Irish Beekeepers' Associations (FIBKA) examination system is run by the Education Officer under the direction of the Examination Board; the Board which is made up of members from the FIBKA and the Ulster Beekeepers' Association (UBKA) is appointed by the Executive Council of the FIBKA.

There are seven levels of examination: Preliminary, Intermediate, Senior, Lecturer and Honey Judge Examinations are held during the Summer Course at Gormanston and Preliminary and Intermediate examinations are also held at Provincial Centres.

The Lecturer's examination takes place in the presence of three Examiners, one of whom is the invited Senior Gormanston Summer Course lecturer and also acts as the Extern Examiner.

The Intermediate Proficiency Apiary Practical Examination, the Practical Beemasters Examination and the Apiary Practical component of the Senior Examination are arranged by the Education Officer and take place in the candidate's own apiary during the beekeeping season and are conducted by two Examiners.

The seven levels of examinations for proficiency certificates and their eligibility requirements are as follows:

Preliminary:

For beginners - no prerequisites.
Intermediate:
The Preliminary Certificate of the FIBKA or the BBKA Basic Certificate must be held for at least one year.

Senior:

Intermediate Certificate and at least five years beekeeping experience.
Intermediate Proficiency Apiary Practical
The Intermediate Proficiency Apiary Practical Examination is intended to be part of a stream that will lead to the Practical Beemasters Certificate. The examination is designed to be less "academic" and there are no written examination papers; (it is not part of the Intermediate Certificate Examination).

The examination will take place in the candidate's own apiary and the Examiners will be two Federation Lecturers appointed by the Executive Council. The pass mark is 70%. 20% of the marks scored may be carried forward to the Practical Beemasters Examination

The prerequisites for Intermediate Proficiency Apiary Practical Examination are: the Preliminary Certificate and at least three years' beekeeping experience satisfactory to the Education Board.

145

The present prerequisites for the Practical Beemasters Certificate are the Preliminary Certificate and at least five years' beekeeping experience satisfactory to the Examination Board - in the future, an additional prerequisite will be the Intermediate Proficiency Apiary Practical Examination.

Practical Beemaster:
Preliminary Certificate and at least five years' beekeeping experience satisfactory to the Examination Board.

Honey Judge:
Intermediate and Practical Beemaster Certificates, successful showing, having obtained a minimum of 200 points at major shows and a record of stewarding under at least four FIBKA Honey Judges.
Lecturer:
Senior Certificate.

Provincial Examinations
Preliminary and Intermediate examinations will be held at provincial centers on the Saturday closest to 6th April (Intermediate) and May 24th (Preliminary). Please note that the minimum number of candidates for a Centre is five for Intermediate and ten for Preliminary. Neighbouring associations may pool their candidates to reach those numbers.
A candidate may sit one Intermediate paper at the Provincial Examination and the other paper at the Summer Course.
The fees for all examinations are valid for the year of application only and are listed on the application forms which may be downloaded from the website. In extreme cases, such as illness (a doctor's certificate must be provided); the examination fee may be held over for one year. There are separate entry forms for the Provincial and Gormanston Summer School Examinations
Fees for Repeat Examinations are the same as for the original examination. Applications to sit the Examinations should be sent to the Education Officer, before the closing dates given above for the Provincial Examinations (applications are however acceptable up to one week after the closing date on payment of a late entry fee which is equal to double the original fee) and before May 1st for the Summer Course Examinations Applications for the Preliminary Examination are also accepted at the Summer Course.

NATIONAL HONEY SHOW

This is held at Gormanston College in conjunction with the annual Beekeeping Course. The Schedule contains 41 Open Classes and 3 Confined classes with €1,000 in prizes. Over 30 Challenge Cups and Trophies are presented for the competition.

Honey Show Secretary: Mr Graham Hall, "Weston", 38 Elton Park, Sandycove, Co Dublin. Tel No (01-2803053) & (087-2406198), E-mail GrahamHall@iolfree.ie

INSURANCE

The limit of indemnity of public liability policy is €6.500, 000 arising from one accident or series of accidents. There is also product liability of €6.500, 000 arising from any one claim. The policy extends to all registered affiliated members whose subscriptions are fully paid up on the 31st December of any one year and whose names are entered in the FIBKA register held by the Treasurer.

ASSOCIATION SECRETARIES

ARMAGH & MONAGH
Mrs. Joanna McGlaughlin
26 Leck Road,
Stewartstown Co Tyrone
BT71 5LS
Tel No 048-87738702/077-
68107984.
secretary@ambka.org

Ashford
Ms Michele O'Connor,
087 2505205
info@wicklowbees.com

Ballyhaunis
Mr Gerry O'Neill,
Drimineen South,
Knock Road, Claremorris,
Co Mayo.
Tel No 087 2553533
ballyhaunisbeekeepers@
gmail.com

Banner
Mr Frank Considine,
Clohanmore Cree,
Kilrush, Co Clare.
Tel No 087-6740462,
bannerbees@gmail.com ,

Beaufort
Mr Padruig O'Sullivan,
Beaufort Bar & Restaurant,
Beaufort, Co Kerry.
Tel No 087-258993006,
beaurest@eircom.net

Carbery
Mr Sean O'Donovan,
Drominidy, Drimoleague,
Co Cork.
Tel No 087-7715001.
seanodonovan10@gmail.
com

Co Cavan
Mr Alan Brady,
Shanakiel House,
Drumnagran, Tullyvin,
Co Cavan
Tel No 086-8127920
alan@alanbrady.ie or Info@
alanbradyelectrical.com

Co Cork
Mr Robert McCutcheon,
Clancoolemore, Bandon,
Co Cork.
Tel No 023-8841714.
bob@cocorkbka.org

Co Donegal
Mr Dan Thompson,
Highfield, Loughnagin,
Letterkenny, Co Donegal
Tel No 074-9125894
dthompson@eircom.net

Co Dublin
Mr Liam McGarry,
24 Quinn's Road,
Shankill, Co. Dublin
Tel No 087 2643492.
mcgarryliam@gmail.com

Co Galway
Dr Anna Jeffrey Gibson,
Ballyclery, Kinvara,
Co Galway
secretary@
galwaybeekeepers.com

Co Kerry
Mr Ruary Rudd,
Westgate, Waterville,
Co Kerry.
Tel No 066-9474251.
rrudd@eircom.net

Co Limerick
Mr Gus McCoy,
Mount Catherine Clonlara
Co. Clare
Tel No 087 1390039 :
gusmccoy1@eircom.net

Co Louth
Mr Tom Shaw,
201 Ard Easmuinn, Dundalk,
Co Louth
Tel No 042-9339619/
086-2361286,
tshaw@iol.ie

Co Longford
Mr Joe McEntegart,
Cleanrath, Aughnacliffe,
Co Longford.
Tel No 087-2481340.
josephmcentegart@yahoo.
com

Co Mayo
Ms Helen Thompson,
Graffy, Killasser,
Swinford, Co. Mayo.
Tel No 087-7584835
info@mayobeekeepers.com
or helen.mmooney@gmail.
com

Co Offaly
Mrs Geraldine Byrne,
4 Sheena, Charleville Rd,
Tullamore, Co Offaly
Tel 086-3464545,
loureiro.byrne@gmail.com

Co Waterford
Ms Colette O'Connell,
4 Davis Street, Dungarvan,
Co Waterford
Tel No 058-41910,
coletteoconnell@ymail.com

Co Wexford
Mr John Cloney,
Ballymotey Beg,
Enniscorthy, Co.Wexford.
Tel No 087 9801015
countywexfordbeekeepers@
gmail.com

Chorca Dhuibhne
Ms Juli Ni Mhaoileoin,
Burnham, Dingle,
Co Kerry
Tel No 086-8337733,
julimaloneconnolly@
gmail.com

Chonamara
Mr Billy Gilmore,
Maam West, Leenane,
Co. Galway
Tel No 091-571183/087-
7942028,
b.gilmore@
connemarabeekeepers.ie

Digges & Dist
Mr Walter Sharpley,
Aughayoula, Ballinamore
Co. Leitrim
Tel No 086 1236207
waltersharpley@gmail.com

Duhallow
Mr Andrew Bourke,
Pallas, Lombardstown,
Mallow, Co Cork
Tel No 087-2783807.
bourke.andy@gmail.com

Dunamaise
Mr Thomas Hussey,
Glenside Portlaoise,
Co. Laois
thomasjhussey@eircom.net

Dunmanway
Elke Hasner,
Kilnarovanagh, Toames,
Macroom, Co.Cork
026 46312/ 087 2525771
elkehasner@gmail.com

East Cork
Mrs Bridie Terry,
Ait na Greine, Coolbay,
Cloyne, Co Cork.
Tel No 021-4652141.
aitnagreine@gmail.com

East Waterford
Mr Michael Hughes,
51 Woodlawn Grove, Cork
Road, Waterford
Tel No 051-373461.
waterfordbees@gmail.com

Fingal
Mr John McMullan,
34 Ard na Mara Crescent,
Malahide, Co Dublin
Tel No 01-8450193.
jmcmullan@eircom.net

Foyle
Mr Martin Coleman,
Greencastle,
Co. Donegal
foylebeekeepers@
gmail.com

Gorey
C/O President,
Gerard M Williams,
Carrigbeg,
Gorey Co. Wexford
Tel No 053-9421823/086-
3634134 e-mail
geraldandvera@eircom.net

Inishowen
Mr Paddy McDonagh,
Milltown, Carndonagh,
Co Donegal.
Tel No 074-9374881.
paddymcdonough@eircom.
net

Iveragh
Mr Shannon
Ware, 4 Ballinskelligs
Holiday Homes,
Ballinskelligs,
County Kerry.
Tel No: 083-3862345
research@gamelab.ca

Killorglin
Mr Declan Evans,
Reeks View Lodge,
Killorglin, Co Kerry.
Tel: 087 175 4078, :
declanjevans@gmail.com

Kilternan
Ms Mary Montaut,
4 Mount Pleasant Villas,
Bray, Co Wicklow.
Tel No 01-2860497.
mmontaut@iol.ie

Mid-Kilkenny
Jer Keohane,
Jenkinstown Park, Kilkenny.
Tel. 056-7767195 / 087-
2523265 /
jkeohane@iece.ie

New Ross
Mr Seamus Kennedy,
Churchtown,
Feathard-on Sea,
New Ross, Wexford
Tel No 051-397259/
086- 3204236.
seamus.kennedy@yahoo.
co.uk

North Cork
Mr. Eamon Nelligan
3 Carriagroghera
Fermoy Co. Cork.
ciaranneligan@gmail.com

North Kildare
Mr Norman Camier,
34 Lansdowne Park,
Templeogue, Dublin 16.
Tel No 01-4932977/
087-2848938,
norman.camier@gmail.com

Nth Tipperary
Mr Jim Ryan,
"Innisfail", Kickham Street,
Thurles, Co Tipperary.
Tel No 0504-22228.
jimbee1@eircom.net

Roundwood
Mr John Coleman,
Hillside Cottage,
Roundhill Haven, Clara
Beg, Roundwood, Co.
Wicklow Tel No 087-795
4385, colemanjkc@gmail.
com
Sliabh Luachra
Mr Billy O'Rourke,
Dooneen, Castleisland,
Co Kerry
Tel No 066-7141870,
siobhancorourke@eircom.
net
Sligo/Leitrim
Mr Peter Carter,
Doon West, Gurteen,
Co.Sligo
slbasecretary@gmail.com
Sneem
Mr Frank Wallace,
Boolananave, Sneem.
County Kerry.
Tel No 086 3522205,
franksneem@hotmail.com
South Donegal
Mr Derek Byrne,
Carrick West, Laghey,
Co Donegal.
Tel No 074-9722340.
dcbyrne@eircom.ie
South Kildare
Mr Liam Nolan,
Newtown, Bagnelstown,
Co Carlow.
Tel No 059-9727281.
liamnolannt@gmail.com

Sth Kilkenny
Mr John Langton,
Coolrainey,
Graiguemanagh,
Co Kilkenny
Tel No 086-1089652,
jjlangton@eircom.net
Sth Tipperary
Mr P J Fegan,
Tickinor, Clonmel,
Co Tipperary.
Tel No 086 1089652,
feganpj@eircom.net
Sth West Cork
Ms Gobnait O'Donovan,
38 McCurtain Hill,
Clonakilty, Co Cork.
Tel No 023-
8833416/083-3069797
gobnaitodonovan@gmail.
com
Sth Wexford
Mr. Dermot O'Grady,
Linden House, Horetown
North, Foulksmills, Co.
Wexford Tel: (051) 565651,
dermaloid@gmail.com
Suck Valley
Ms Anne Towers,
Doonwood,
Mount Bellew, Co Galway.
Tel No 0909-684547/
087-6305714,
annevtravers@gmail.com
The Kingdom
Ms Rebecca Coffey,
75 Ashgrove, Tralee,
Co Kerry
Tel No 066- 7169554,
bexk8@yahoo.co.uk

The Royal Co
Ms Geraldine McCann,
Mooretown, Ratoath,
Co. Meath.
geraldine.toole@ucd.ie
The Tribes
Mr Eoghan O'Riordan,
28 Arbutus Avenue,
Renmore, Galway.
Tel No 091-753470/
087-6184132,
landservices@eircom.net
West Cork
Ms Jacqueline Glisson,
Costa Maningi, Derrymihane
East, Castletownbere,
Co Cork. Tel No 086-
3638249,
jglisson@eircom.net
Westport
Mr Dermot O Flaherty,
Rosbeg, Westport,
Co Mayo
Tel No 098 26585/
087-2464045,
info@mayo-westport.com

INTERNATIONAL BEE RESEARCH
ASSOCIATION WEB http://www.ibra.org.uk

The International Bee Research Association (IBRA) promotes the value of bees by providing information on bee science and beekeeping worldwide. This Registered Charity was founded in 1949 and is supported by members from around the world. IBRA publishes books, journals and other information and organises conferences on all species of bees, beekeeping and bee conservation. IBRA has one of the largest international collections of bee books and journals, as well as the Eva Crane / IBRA historical collection and a photographic collection.

PUBLICATIONS
Journal of Apicultural Research
A peer reviewed scientific journal that is worldwide and world class. JAR is edited by Senior Editor Norman Carreck and our team of editors in Argentina, Germany, Greece, Switzerland, Turkey and the USA. It is published for IBRA by Taylor & Francis and available both print and online. Published five times a year it contains the latest high quality original research from around the world, covering all aspects of the biology, ecology, natural history, culture and conservation of all types of bee.

Bee World
IBRA's quarterly international popular journal provides a world view on bees and beekeeping. It is edited by Kirsten Traynor in the USA and published for IBRA by Taylor & Francis and available both print and online. It covers all topics from bee history to the latest findings in bee science in a digestible form.

SCIENCE DIRECTOR
Norman Carreck
Laboratory of Apiculture and Social Insects,
University of Sussex
Falmer
Brighton
East Sussex
BN1 9QG
01273 872587
norman.carreck@btinternet.com

SECRETARY
Margaret Ginman
Hendal House
Hendal Hill
Groombridge
Tunbridge Wells
Kent
TN3 9NT
margaret.hendal@btconnect.com

Correspondence to:
mail@ibra.org.uk

www.ibra.org.uk
https://www.facebook.com/
IBRAssociation
https://twitter.com/IBRA_Bee

The IBRA BOOKSHOP
Through our online bookshop IBRA sells IBRA publications, together with a wide range of other publications at competitive prices as well as posters, gifts, DVD's and sundries. Our bookshop also visits the BBKA Spring Convention, the National Honey Show and other events for you to browse before you buy and purchase items post free.
http://ibrabee.org.uk/index.php/our-shop

MEMBERSHIP
IBRA is a truly international organisation, with members all over the world. IBRA Members receive Bee World free of charge, together with discounts on IBRA publications and other benefits. For details on current membership rates and how to join please visit our website.

The International Bee Research Association is a Company limited by Guarantee,

Registered in England and Wales, Reg. No. 463819,
Registered Office: Hendal House, Hendal Hill, Groombridge,
East Sussex, TN3 9NT, UK, and is a Registered Charity No. 209222.

Information about all IBRA publications and services can be found via our web site: www.ibra.org.uk

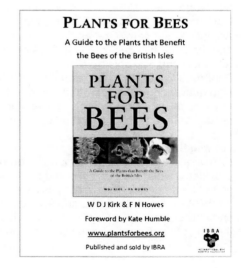

Available and published by IBRA but also available from Northern Bee Books at www.northernbeebooks.co.uk

THE INSTITUTE OF NORTHERN IRELAND BEEKEEPERS (INIB)

www.inibeekeepers.com

Annual Conference and Honey Show. Saturday 24th October 2015
Speakers: Jennifer Berry, Dr. Deborah Delaney and Dr. Jim Loughrey
Lough Neagh Discovery Discovery Centre, Oxford Island, Lurgan, BT66 6NJ

Objectives of the Institute
The Institute is established to advance the service of apiculture and to promote and foster the education of the people of Northern Ireland and surrounding environs without distinction of age, gender, disability, sexual orientation, nationality, ethnic identity, political or religious opinion, by associating the statutory authorities, community and voluntary organisations and the inhabitants in a common effort to advance education, and in particular:

- to raise awareness amongst the beneficiaries about bees, bee-keeping and methods of management;
- to foster an atmosphere of mutual support among bee-keepers and to encourage the
- sharing of information and provision of helpful assistance amongst each other.

Affiliation
INIB is affiliated to the British Beekeepers Association.
With 24,000 members the British Beekeepers Association (BBKA) is the leading organisation representing beekeepers within the UK.
As an INIB member, affiliation gives the following benefits.

- BBKA News
- Public Liability Insurance
- Product Liability Insurance
- Bee Disease Insurance available
- Free Information Leaflets to Download
- Members Password Protected Area and Discussion Forum
- Correspondence Courses
- Examination and Assessment Programme
- Telephone Information
- Research Support
- Legal advice
- Representation and lobbying of Government, EU and official bodies.

Events

The Institute holds an annual conference, bringing to Northern Ireland a variety of world renowned expert beekeepers from the USA and Europe. The annual conference is accompanied by an annual honey show which attracts exhibitors from across the UK and Ireland. A variety of social and charitable events are hosted by the INIB.

Education

The INIB attends numerous events annually in an effort to educate the public about honeybees and the craft of beekeeping. The Institute also hosts an annual "Beekeeping for Beginners Day" which we open to the public.

Honey Bees On Line Studies

INIB has a strong relationship with Professor Jurgen Tautz's of BEEgrouup Biozentrum Universitaet Wuerzburg and his Honey Bee On Line Studies project which continues to develop.

MEMBERSHIP SECRETARY
Lyndon Wortley
Teemore Grange
224 Marlacoo Rd,
Portadown,
BT62 3TD
Membershipsecretary@
inibeekeepers.com

CHAIRMAN
Michael Young MBE
101 Carnreagh,
Hillsborough
BT26 6LJ
02892689724
chairman@
inibeekeepers.com

Holders of the Institute of Northern Ireland Beekeepers Honey Judge Certificate

001.	MICHAEL BADGER MBE	01132 945879	buzz.buzz@ntlworld.com
002.	GAIL ORR	02892 638363	gail.orr@belfasttrust.hscni.net
003.	CECIL MCMULLAN	02892 638675	Madeline.mcmullan@hotmail.co.uK
004.	HUGH MCBRIDE	02825 640872	lorraine.mcbride@care4free.net
005.	LORRAINE MC BRIDE	02825 640872	lorraine.mcbride@care4free.net
006.	BILLY DOUGLAS	02897 562926	
007.	MICHAEL YOUNG MBE	02892 689724	chairman@ inibeekeepers.com
008.	FRANCIS CAPENER	01303 254579	francis@honeyshow.freeserve.co.uk
009.	MARGARET DAVIES	01202 526077	marg@jdavies.freeserve.co.uk
010.	IAN CRAIG	01505 322684	ian'at'iancraig.wanadoo.co.uk
011.	DINAH SWEET	02920 756483	
013.	LESLIE M WEBSTER	01466 771351	leswebster@microgram.co.uk
014.	REDMOND WILLIAMS	003535242617	emwilliams@eircom.net
015.	TERRY ASHLEY	01270 760757	terry.ashley@fera.gsi.gov.uk
016.	IVOR FLATMAN	01924 257089	ivorflatman@supanet.com
017.	ALAN WOODWARD	01302 868169	janet.woodward@virgin.net
018.	DENNIS ATKINSON	01995 602058	dhmatkinson@tesco.net
019	LEO MCGUINNESS	028711 811043	pmcguinness@glendermott.com
020	TOM CANNING		tjcanning@btinternet.com
023	ALAN BROWN	01977 776193	alanhoneybees4u@talktalk.net
024	DAVID SHANNON	01302772837	dave_aca@tiscali.co.uk

USA

021	ROBERT BREWER	rbrewer@arches.uga.edu
022	BOB COLE	
023	ANN HARMAN	

LABRATORY OF APICULTURE & SOCIAL INSECTS (LASI)

UNIVERSITY OF SUSSEX

FURTHER INFORMATION CONTACT
Francis L. W. Ratnieks,
Professor of Apiculture
Laboratory of Apiculture &
Social Insects (LASI)
Department of Biological &
Environmental Science
University of Sussex, Falmer,
Brighton BN1 9QG, UK

01273 872954 (landline),
07766270434 (mob)
F.Ratnieks@Sussex.ac.uk
www.sussex.ac.uk/lasi

Youtube:
LASI Bee Research
& Outreach

LASI was founded in 1995 and is headed by Francis Ratnieks, who is the UK's only Professor of Apiculture. Prof. Ratnieks received his training in honey bee biology at Cornell University and the University of California in the USA. Whilst in the USA he was also a part-time commercial beekeeper with up to 180 hives used for almond pollination and comb honey production.

From 1995 to 2007, LASI was based at the University of Sheffield. In 2008 Prof. Ratnieks moved to the University of Sussex, which provided LASI with excellent facilities for honey bee research. There is an integrated lab space and offices sufficient for 13 researchers with an adjoining apiary, garden, equipment shed and workshop. There are further apiaries on the university campus and in the surrounding countryside.

LASI is the largest university-based laboratory studying honey bees in the UK and is set up both to undertake research and to train the next generation of honey bee scientists. Undergraduate students receive lectures on honey bee biology and can also do research projects on honey bee biology in their final year and assist LASI research via summer bursaries. Graduate students take a PhD that focuses in a particular area of research. Postdoctoral researchers can learn new skills to complement the training they received during their PhD.

LASI research focuses on both basic and applied questions in bee biology and beekeeping. Basic research areas include communication, foraging, colony organization, nestmate recognition and guarding, and conflict resolution. Applied research areas include improved beekeeping techniques, studies of bee foraging and the value of different plants for honey bees and other pollinators, crop pollination, practical

studies of honey bee diseases and their management, and practical measures for bee conservation. Collectively, the LASI team has 80 years of research experience with honey bees.

As well as research and teaching, LASI places great emphasis on outreach and communication. Each year LASI runs workshops, gives talks and writes many outreach articles so that research results are also transferred to beekeepers, gardeners, farmers, land owners, the media, the general public, and policy makers.

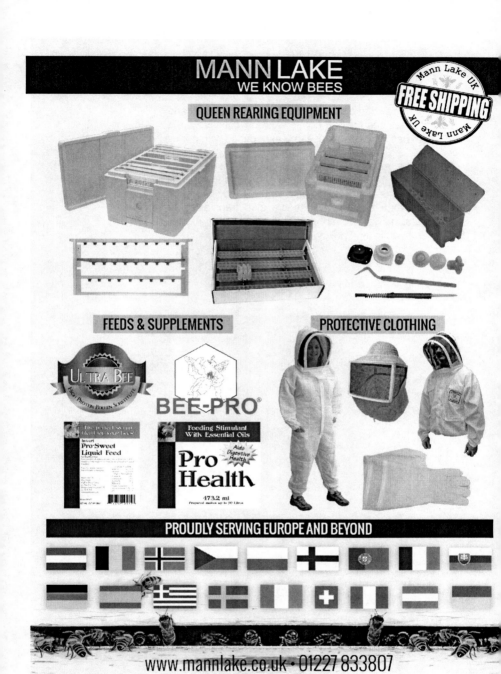

THE NATIONAL DIPLOMA IN BEEKEEPING

The Examinations Board for the National Diploma in Beekeeping was set up in 1954 to meet a need for a beekeeping qualification above the level of the highest certificate awarded by the British, Scottish, Welsh and Ulster Associations.

The Diploma Examination, as designed by the Board, was considered to be an appropriate qualification for a County Beekeeping Lecturer or a specialist appointment requiring a high level of academic and practical ability in beekeeping. It is the highest beekeeping qualification recognised in the British Isles and a high percentage of the past and present holders of the Diploma have given distinguished service to beekeeping education at all levels.

Although the post of County Beekeeping Lecturer has now disappeared, this has merely emphasised the need for some beekeepers to face the challenge of this examination and maintain the high level skills and knowledge needed to keep pace with the increased problems facing all beekeepers at the present time.

The Board consists of representatives from a wide range of organisations and from Government Departments and together form an impressive amalgam of expert knowledge in Beekeeping and Education. Although the National Beekeeping Associations are represented on the Board it is entirely independent of them.

Normally the highest certificate of one of the National Associations is a necessary criterion for eligibility to take the Examination for the Diploma which is held in alternate years. The Written Examination is taken in March, and the Practical, in three sections plus a viva-voce is held in later in the same year.

The Board also organises an annual Advanced Beekeeping Course covering various parts of the syllabus that are difficult to cover by independent study. Lasting

HON. SECRETARY
Mrs Margaret Thomas NDB
Tig na Bruaich,
Taybridge Terrace,
Aberfeldy, Perthshire,
PH15 2BS.

CHAIRMAN,
Ivor Davis NDB
91 Brinsea Road,,
Congresbury
BS49 5JJ
07831 379222

a working week, they cover the main sections of the Syllabus and represent the highest level of training available to British Beekeepers at the present time. The outside lecturers are each acknowledged experts in their particular field. In recent years the Board have been privileged to hold their course at the Fera National Bee Unit at Sand Hutton, York.

In addition the Board organize various short courses at locations in the UK on a number of topics. These are advertised in the bee press and the web site.

For further details regarding the Diploma write, enclosing a stamped A4 SAE to the Secretary, or visit our website: http://www.national-diploma-bees.org.uk/

Those who have gained the National Diploma in Beekeeping

Matthew Allan
*Harry Allen
*Harrison Ashforth
*John Ashton
Dianne Askquith-Ellis
David Aston
*John Atkinson
*Miss E.E. Avey
Dan Basterfield
Ken Basterfield
Bridget Beattie
*Brig. H.T. Bell
R.W. Brooke
Norman Carreck
*Rosina Clark
Charles Collins
Gerry Collins
*Tom Collins
*Robert Couston
John Cowan
S. J. Cox
Jim Crundwell
Beulah Cullen

Celia Davis
Ivor Davis
*Alec S.C. Deans
Clive De Bruyn
A.P. Draycott
M. Feeley
*Barry Fletcher
* David Frimston
Oonagh Gabriel
George Gill
*Reg Gove
*Eric Greenwood
Pam Gregory
Anthony R.W. Griffin
* Robert Hammond
Ben Harden
Tony Harris
C.A. Harwood
*Leslie Hender
*Alf Hebden
*Ted Hooper MBE
Geoff Hopkinson BEM
*G. Howatson

* Geoff Ingold
George Jenner
C. F. Jesson
Simon Jones
A.C. Kessel
W.E.Large
Adam Leitch
G.W. Lumsden
*Henry Luxton
A.S. Mcclymont
J.I. Macgregor
Ian Mclean
Ian A. Maxwell
Paul Metcalf
J.Mills
*Bernhard Mobus
Margaret Murdin
G. N'Tonga
*Peter Oldrieve
Gillian Partridge
* E.H. Pee
I.E. Perera
E.R. Poole

Bill Reynolds
Pat Rich
*Fred Richards
E. Roberts
*Arthur Rolt
*Jeff Rounce
Graham Royle
J. Ryding
J.H. Savage
*Donald Sims
F.G. Smith
*George Smith
J.H.F. Smith
Robert Smith
*Ken Stevens
*J. Swarbrick
Margaret Thomas
Adrian Waring
Alastair Welch
Brian Welch
J. Wilbraham

* - deceased

THE NATIONAL HONEY SHOW

www.honeyshow.co.uk

29TH – 31ST OCTOBER 2015.

This venue is excellent with Free car parking
Just off the M25 junction 11
Rail from Waterloo to Weybridge or Addlestone

The Show itself is a wonderful competitive exhibition
of all the products of the bee-hive, coupled with an
excellent series of lectures, workshops and a wide
variety of trade and educational stands.

We recommend that you attend all three days, and
suggest that you become a member of the Show –
just **£15.00** per annum

For further information, please write to the Hon General
Secretary, or Email: showsec@zbee.com or visit our
website www.honeyshow.co.uk

- The National Honey Show is the premier honey
  show within the United Kingdom.

- Although it is named the "National Honey Show",
  it includes a strong international element.

- As well as the competitive content of the Show,
  there is also a full programme of lectures and
  workshops.

- In the Sales Hall, all the major traders and
  educational organisations are present.

- Further information is readily available on the
  website www.honeyshow.co.uk or from the Hon
  General Secretary showsec@zbee.com

HON SECRETARY
J.D. Hendry
26 Coldharbour Lane
Hildenborough
Tonbridge
TN11 9JT
01732 833894

NIHBS

The Native Irish
Honey Bee Society
Apis mellifera mellifera

NATIVE IRISH
HONEY BEE SOCIETY

CHAIRPERSON:
Mr. Gerard Coyne
Chairperson@nihbs.org

HON. SECRETARY:
Mr. Seamus Meade
Secretary@nihbs.org

TREASURER;
Mr. Pat Deasy
treasurer@nihbs.org

PUBLIC RELATIONS OFFICER:
Mr. Gerard Coyne
pro@nihbs.org

WEBMASTER:
Mr. Jonathan Getty
webmaster@nihbs.org
www.nihbs.org

FACEBOOK PAGE
www.facebook.com/native-
irish-honey bee-societyy

What is the Native Irish Honey Bee Society?
NIHBS was established in November 2012 by a group of beekeepers who wish to support the various strains of Native Irish Honey Bee (Apis mellifera mellifera) throughout the country. It is a cross border organisation and is open to all. It consists of members and representatives from all corners of the island of Ireland.

Aims and Objectives -
To promote the conservation, study, improvement and re-introduction of Apis mellifera mellifera (Native Irish Honey Bee), throughout the island of Ireland.
- To establish areas of conservation throughout the island for the conservation of the Native Honey Bee.
- To promote formation of bee improvement groups.
- To provide education on bee improvement and to increase public awareness of the native honey bee.
- To act in an advisory capacity to groups and individuals who wish to promote it.
- To co-operate with other beekeeping organisations with similar aims.
- To seek the help of the scientific community and other stake holders in achieving our aims and objectives.

NIHBS - Plans for the future -
Liaise with groups interested in Native Honey Bees
- Will apply for funding -
- Will help to co-ordinate projects -
- Will raise awareness to beekeepers and the public about Native Honey Bees -
- Talks and lectures

Why Join NIHBS?
- Information on beekeeping events around Ireland – North and South
- queen rearing workshops, talks and lectures.
- Information on how to obtain Native Honey Bees
- Conference discounts
- Discounted entrance fees to events run by NIHBS
- Eligibility to schemes coordinated by NIHBS
- A network of beekeepers interested in our native honeybee

1 years membership costs 20 euro or 20 pounds sterling.
A membership form can be downloaded from website and sent to treasurer or payment can be made on website via paypal.

ROTHAMSTED RESEARCH

www.rothamsted.ac.uk

ROTHAMSTED RESEARCH
Department of AgroEcology,
Rothamsted Research
Harpenden,
Hertfordshire.
AL5 2JQ

STAFF
DR ALISON HAUGHTON
DR JASON LIM
DR SAMANTHA COOK
DR TRISH WELLS
JENNY SWAIN
JONATHAN CARRUTHERS
(PHD STUDENT)
THOMAS DAVID (PHD STUDENT)
STEVE KENNEDY (BEEKEEPER)

The Rothamsted site provides a unique working environment with specialist modern equipment facilitating research on plant and microbial metabolites, molecular biology and synthetic and analytical chemistry. There is an experimental farm for complex field experiments, and there is a suite of glasshouses, controlled environment facilities, an insectary and a state-of-the-art bioimaging suite housing three new electron microscopes and a confocal laser scanning microscope. Experimental design and analysis are backed up by excellent statistical, computing and library support.

BEE BEHAVIOUR AND POLLINATION ECOLOGY

We are investigating the interaction between bees, crops and the agricultural environment. The spatial and temporal foraging behaviour of honey bees and bumble bees within agricultural areas is being compared. Harmonic radar is being used to track flying bees, and other pollinators such as butterflies, to obtain new information about their flight paths, forage ranges, food preferences and orientation mechanisms.

An integrated model for predicting bumblebee population success and pollination services in agro-ecosystems will be developed by Rothamsted and colleagues at the Environment & Sustainability Institute at the University of Exeter and the University of Sussex, and will provide a powerful tool for shaping recommendations for land managers and policy makers for the sustainable spatial management of pollination within arable and horticultural production systems.

Various qualities of different varieties of crops (oilseed rape and short rotation coppice willows) as important resources for bees are being investigated. The nutritional

value of the nectars and pollens, effects on bee fitness and behaviour are key areas of interest.

HONEY BEE PATHOLOGY

Rothamsted's research on the natural history and epidemiology of the infections and parasites of bees has had wide international recognition. However, research on honey bee pathology is currently suspended due to changes in funding available from Defra for bee health. Over the last 20 years, this work focused on *Varroa destructor* and the losses caused by honey bee virus infections that the mite transmits. In a collaborative project with Horticulture Research International (at University of Warwick), investigating potential biological control agents of *V. destructor*, the research identified and characterised fungal pathogens which are active against the mite but which are relatively safe for bees and other beneficial insects. Biological control offers an environmentally acceptable approach to the problem that could have considerable economic benefits, and we are actively seeking funding to continue this work.

We are currently analysing data from an Insect Pollinator Initiative funded project that assessed the impact of emergent diseases, including the Varroa associated Deformed wing virus, and the Microsporidian Nosema ceranae on the flight performance and orientation ability of honeybees and bumblebees and its consequences for bee populations.

HARMONIC RADAR

The use of harmonic radar in insect behaviour studies has been pioneered at Rothamsted. A transponder weighing just a few milligrams fitted to the thorax of bees picks up the interrogation radar signal and immediately emits a signal at a different frequency, which is then received by the radar. A recently awarded European Research Council grant will now enable cutting-edge development of the harmonic radar to allow us to collect data for entire adult life-spans and foraging ranges for multiple individuals of bee species, thus allowing us whole new insights into bee behaviour and pollination ecology.

INFORMATION EXCHANGE

Expertise in bee research is drawn upon by scientific colleagues world-wide and there are research links with institutes and universities in this country and abroad. Research findings are published in scientific journals but popular articles are also written for the beekeeping and agricultural press. Effective communication of our science by staff members is delivered via a vigorous programme of lectures presenting to national and local beekeeping associations and participation in various public media, including BBC programmes.

FUNDING

Rothamsted receives funds for research from the Biotechnology and Biological Sciences Research Council, through competitions and contracts from the Department for Environment, Food and Rural Affairs, the European Community, from Levy boards, commercial and other organisations. The support of the bee research programme in recent years by grants from the British Beekeepers Association, C. B. Dennis British Beekeepers Research Trust, the Eastern Association of Beekeepers and the Bedfordshire, Cambridgeshire, Norfolk, St Albans and Hertfordshire and High Wycombe Beekeepers Associations is gratefully acknowledged.

For more information visit: **http://www.rothamsted.ac.uk**

THE SCOTTISH BEEKEEPERS' ASSOCIATION

Purposes of the Association

The organisation's purposes are to support honeybees and beekeepers, to improve the standard of beekeeping, and to promote honeybee products in Scotland through:

The advancement of education in relation to the craft of beekeeping; The advancement of the heritage, culture and science of beekeeping; and The advancement of environmental protection by conservation of the honeybee.

The SBA arranges courses and awards certificates to successful candidates in a comprehensive education system. It also actively promotes beekeeping by informing the public, including the young, about bees and their benefits to the environment.

INSURANCE AND THE COMPENSATION SCHEME

All members of the SBA have insurance against Public Liability. The SBA Compensation Scheme is restricted to bee colonies located in Scotland and allocates part-replacement value for damage by vandalism, fire, theft and certain brood diseases.

LIBRARY

The SBA Moir Library in Edinburgh has one of the world's finest collections of beekeeping books. A library card is issued annually to every member who can borrow books at the cost of return postage only. Details may be obtained from the Library Officer.

MARKETS

Advice is given on all aspects of marketing honey products at appropriate times. Suggested bulk, wholesale and retail prices are notified in the magazine.

GENERAL SECRETARY
Tony Harris,
Cowiemuir,
Fochabers,
Moray
IV32 7PS
07884 496246
secretary@
scottishbeekeepers.org.uk

HON PRESIDENT
The Rt. Hon. Earl of Mansfield D.L, J.P
Scone Palace
Perth PH2 6BE

HON. VICE PRES,
Iain F Steven
4 Craigie View
Perth
PH2 0DP
01738 621100

Ian Craig
30 Burnside Ave, Brookfield,
Johnstone, Renfrewshire,
PA5 8UT
01505 322684
beekeeper30@btinternet.
com

HON. LIBRARIAN
Mrs. Margaret M. Sharp
City Librarian, City Library
George IV Bridge, Edinburgh

SBA

PUBLICATIONS

The Scottish Beekeeper is published monthly and sent post free as part of the annual membership fee of £30 payable to the Membership Officer. Introduction to Bees and Beekeeping is £6.00 plus postage and may be obtained from the Advertising and Publicity Officer.

PUBLICITY

Members can purchase the Association tie, lapel badge, car sticker etc. Details may be obtained from the Shows and Publicity Officer.

SHOWS

Two major annual honey shows are held in Scotland. A honey competition and show with educational displays is held at the Royal Highland Show, Ingleston, Edinburgh in June and the Scottish National Honey Show is conducted at the Dundee Food and Flower Festival in September. Other Honey Shows are run in Ayr, Fife, Inverness, Turiff and at many other locations in Scotland as organised by Local Associations.

TRUSTEES

SBA

S.B.A LECTURERS   ★Addresses in SBA Honey Judges List

All those listed may claim expenses except G. Sharpe, Scottish Bee Inspectors and Stephen Sunderland, all funded by SGRPID. All speakers accompany talks with visual aids

Miss. E. Brown (General)★
01592 840542

A. Chilcott (Observation at the Hive Entrance)
Sonas
Piperhill
Nairn
IV12 5SD
01667 404606

I. Craig (General)★
01505 322684

P.I Gibson
7 Shielswood Court
Galashiels
Selkirkshire
TD1 3RH
01896 750110

T. Harris NDB★
(General, Botany for Beekeepers, Bumble and Solitary Bees of Britain)
01343 821282

C. Irwin (General)★
0141 7791333

M.M. Peterson
(Bee genetics)
Balhaldie House,
High street, Dunblane
FK15 0ER
01786 822093

Dr G Ramsay
(Beekeeping on the Internet / Can Bees fight Varroa?)
Parkview, Station Road
Errol, Perth
PH2 7SN
01821 642385

A Riach★
(Beehives through the Ages, Microscopy))

Bryce Reynard, ★Making Skeps)
39 Old Mill Lane, Inverness
IV2 3XP
01463 225887

G. Sharpe (SAC) (Varroa Management: My apiary management system)
Apiculture Specialist
Life Science Technology Group, SAC Auchincruive
Ayr
KA6 5HW
01292 525375

Mrs M Thomas NDB (General)
Tighnabraich, Taybridge
Terrace, Aberfeldy
Perthshire PH15 2BS
01887 829710

Scottish Bee Inspectors,
SGRPID, P Spur,
Saughton House,
Broomhouse, Edinburgh
EH11 3XD
0300 244 6672
beesmailbox@scotland.gsi.
gov.uk

Dr Peter Stromberg,
21 Woodside, Houston,
Renfrewshire,
PA6 7DD
01505 613 830
pstromberg1@aol.com

Stephen Sunderland,
Lead Bee Inspector,
SGRPID, P Spur,
Saughton House,
Broomhouse, Edinburgh
EH11 3XD
0300 244 6672
steve.sunderland@
scotland.gsi.gov.uk

Dr David Wright,
20 Lennox Row,
Edinburgh
EH5 3JW
0131 552 3439
bdwright20lr@btinternet.
com

SBA

MEMBER ASSOCIATIONS AND THEIR SECRETARIES

Aberdeen, Rosie Crighton
29 Marcus Cresc
Blackburn, Aberdeen
AB21 0SZ
01224 791181
aberdeenbeekeepers@
gmail.com
Arran Bee Group, W K McNeish
Seafield, Kildonan,
Isle of Arran,
KA27 8SE
01770 820357
wmcnsh@aol.com
Ayr, Mrs L Baillie
Windyhill Cottage
Uplands Rd, Sundrum
Ayre, KA6 5JU
01292 570659
lbaillie@sundrum.demon.
co.uk
Border, Liz Howell
Oatlands, Houndridge,
Kelso
TD5 7QN
01573 470747
kevhwl@aol.com
**Caddonfoot, Mrs Brenda
Lambert**
1 High Cottage,
Walkerburn
EH43 6AZ
01896 870428
blambert1962@outlook.
com
**Covington and Thankerton,
Angus Milner-Brown**
Covington House,
Covington Road,
Biggar
ML12 6NE
01899 308024
angus@therathouse.com

Cowal, Ceci Alderton
2 Stronechrevich
Strachur
Argyll
PA27 8DF
01369 860445
cecis.farmlet@gmail.com
Dingwall, Alpin Stewart
Rowan Cottage, Fasaig,
Torridon by Achnasheen,
Ross-shire
IV22 2EZ
01445 791450
dingwall.beekeeping@
googlemail.com
**Dunblane & Stirling, Fiona
Fernie**
Greystones Dunira,
By Comtie
PH6 2JZ
01764 679152
secretary@
dunblanebeekeepers.com
**Dunfermline & West Fife
Liz Wyatt**
Hollytree Lodge,
Muckhart,
Dollar,
FK14 7JW
01259 781214
dwf@fifebeekeepers.couk
East Lothian, Deborah Mackay
5 Goshen Farm
Steading,
Musselburgh, East Lothian
EH21 8JL
0131 665 8939
eastlothianbeekeepers@
googemail.com
East of Scotland, Colin Smith
The Laundry House,
Ethie, Inverkielor, Arbroath,
DD1 5SP
secretary@
eastofscotlandbeekeepers.
org.uk

Easter Ross, Colin Ridley
Stirling Cottage,
Lamington Park,
Kildray,
Ross-shire
IV18 0PE
01862 842410
colinr031@googlemail.com
Eastwood, Robert Gordon
10 Caribar Drive,
Barrhead, Glasgow
G78 1BQ
0141 5716498
Robert.gordon@ntworld.
com
**Edinburgh & Midlothian
Gordon Jardine**
20 Pentland Grove,
Edinburgh,
EH10 6NR
07703 528801
gordieric@hotmail.com
Fife, Janice Furness
The Dirdale, Boarhills
St. Andrews,
Fife
KY16 8PP
01334 880 469
jcfurness@dirdale.fsnet.
co.uk
Fortingall, Mrs Sharon Martin
Gardeners Cottage,
Grand Tully,
PH15 2EG
01887840407
ssharon.x.martin@
btinternet.com
Glasgow District,
Mhairi Neill
3 Machan Ave,
Larkhall,
ML9 2HE
01698 881602
glasgowbeeksec@hotmail.
co.uk

171

SBA

Helensburgh, Cameron Macallum,
The Old Police Station,
Arrochar, Argyll.
G83 7AA.
Tel. No. 01301702295.
secretary@helensburghbees.
com

Honeypotz (West Lothian),
Shiona Airlie
Blair House, Hirst Road,
Near Harthill, Shotts,
North Lanarkshire,
ML7 5TL.
07722431987
honeypotzbees@aol.com

Inverness, Julia Moran
Woodend Cottage,
Dunloit, Drumnadrochit,
IV36 6XF
01456 450463
woodendcottage@homecall.
couk

Kelvin Valley, I Ferguson
4 South Glassford Street
Milngavie
G62 6AT
0141 956 3963
jeanian@ferguson2007.plus.
com

**Kilbarchan and District,
I. Craig**
30 Burnside Ave
Brookfield
Johnstone
PA5 8UT
01505 322684
beekeeper30@btinternet.
com

**Kilmarnock & District,
J. Campbell**
North Kilbryde House,
Stewarton, Kilmarnock,
KA3 3EP
01560 482489
john.d.campbell@talktalk.net

Kintyre & Mid Argyll, Zoe Weir
1 Lagnagorton,
Clachan, Tarbert,
Argyll, PA29 6XW
lagnagortan@aol.com

Lochaber, Sarah Kennedy
Tigh na Feid,
Achintore Road,
Fort William
PH33 6RN
secretary@
lochaberbeekeepers.org

Moray, Anne Black
Four winds,
Prospect Terrace,
Lossiemouth, Moray
IV31 6JS
01343 810899
secretary@
moraybeekeepers.co.ukcom

Mull, Mrs. S. Barnard
Viewmount, Tobermory
Isle of Mull
PA75 6PG
01688 302008
tim-barnard@lineone.net

Nairn & District, Ruth Burkhill
2 Cloves Cottage,
Alves, Moray
IV36 2RA
01343 850041
ruthburkhill@gmail.com

Newbattle, Joyce Jack,
23 South Park West,
Peebles EH45 9EF
01721 722444
joycecjack@aol.com

North Ayrshire, Ruth Anderson
07773 776253
Ruthanderson7@googlemail.
com

Oban & District, Nigel Mitchell
Barochreal
Kilninver
Oban,
PA34 4UT
01852 316151
nigel@the mitchells.co.uk

Olrig and District, Robin Inglis
Roadside Skirza
Freswick,
Wick
KW1 4XX
01955 611260
gailinglis@btinternet.com

Orkney, Sue Spence
Alton House,
Berstane Road,
Kikwall,
Orkney
KW15 1NA
01856 873920
bs3920@yahoo.com

Peebles-shire, Amanda Clydesdale
20 Kingsmeadows Gardens
Peebles
EH45 9LB
01721 720563
amanda.clydesdale@
btinternet.com

Perth and District, Brian Clelland
12 Albert Road,
Scone, Perth,
PH2 6QH
07845375298
info@
perthanddistrictbeekeepers.
co.uk

Skye & Lochalsh, Joe Grimson
1 Riverside Cottage,
Braeintra, Stromeferry,
IV53 8UP
j.grimson@btinternet.com

South of Scotland,
Debbie Park
Crofthead,
Dalswinton,
Dumfries
DG2 0XY
01387740030
d.parke@yahoo.co.uk

Speyside, Gerry Thompson
Highland House,
Knockando,
Aberlour, Moray,
AB53 7RP
01340810229
gjthom@sky.com

Sunart, Ardnamurchan, Moidart and Morvern
Kate Atchley
Anasmara,
Mingarry, Acharacle,
Argyll & Bute
PH36 4XJ
07774807645
bees@kateatchley.co.uk
Sutherland, Sue Steven
Mulberry Croft,
2 East Newport,
Berriedale
Caithness
KW7 6HA
01539 751 245

SBA ACTIVE HONEY JUDGES

Miss E. Brown
Milton House,
Main Street,
Scotlandwell,
Kinross
KY13 9JA
01592 840582
01397 712730
M. Canham
Whinhill Farm House
Nairn IV12 5RF
01667 404314
I. Craig
30 Burnside Avenue
Brookfield,
Johnstone
Renfrewshire,
PA5 8UT
01505 322684
H Donohoe
7 Grant Road
Banchory
AB31 5UW
01330 823502

T. Harris NDB
Cowiemuir
Fochabers,
Moray IV32 7PS
01343 821282
C. E. Irwin
55 Lindsaybeg Road
Chryston, Glasgow
G69 9DW
0141 7791333
Dr F. Isles
"Gardenhurst",
Newbigging
Broughty Ferry
Dundee DD5 3RH
01382 370315
P Mathews
Mrs C Mathews
4 Annanhill
Annan, Dumfries-shire
DG12 6TN
01461 205525

A. Riach
7 Newlands Avenue,
Bathgate
EH48 1EE
01506 653389
C. Wilson
Cedarhill,
Auchencloch,
Banknock,
Bonnybridge
FK4 1VA
01324 840227
Dr D Wright
Mrs B Wright
20 Lennox Row
Edinburgh
EH3 5JW
0131 552 3439

173

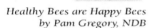

ULSTER BEEKEEPERS' ASSOCIATION

www.ubka.org

OBJECTS OF THE ASSOCIATION

The objects of the Association are to unite beekeepers for their mutual benefit to serve the best interests of beekeeping by all means within its power and to foster its healthy development.

For the purpose of achieving these objects the Association will:

- promote the formation of local Beekeepers' Associations
- disseminate information and advice about beekeeping
- provide examination facilities in the craft of beekeeping
- encourage maintenance and improvement of the beekeeping environment.

EDUCATION

In conjunction with the College of Agriculture, Food & Enterprise (CAFRE), the U.B.K.A. assists in organising classes for Preliminary, Intermediate and Senior Certificate Examinations in Beekeeping following the syllabus of the Federation of Irish Beekeepers' Associations (FIBKA).

INSURANCE

Affiliated local Associations and their individual members have access to the UBKA group public and product liability insurance scheme.

APIARY SITES

Almost all twelve local Associations and CAFRE's Greenmount Campus have access to apiary sites and, for some sites, access to observation houses provided with help from Leader 2 funding, for use in demonstrating and promoting good practice to members, schools and other interested groups.

PRESIDENT,
David Wright
24 Quarry Road
Lisbane, Comber,
Newtownards
Co Down BT23 5NF

SECRETARY,
Lorraine McBride,
11 Ballyloughan Park,
Ballymena,
BT43 5HW.
email:
ubkasecretary@gmail.com

TREASURER,
Gail Orr.
64 Ballycrune Rd.,
Hillsborough,
BT26 6NH

LECTURERS
Vanessa Drew,
40 Lacken Rd.,
Ballyroney,
Banbridge,
Down BT32 5JA

Jim Fletcher
26 Coach Road, Comber
Co.Down. BT23 5QX

175

UBKA

Lecturers continued
Ethel Irvine
2 Laragh Lee
Ballycassidy
ENNISKILLEN
BT94 2JT

Lorraine McBride
11, Ballyloughan Park
Ballymena, Co.Antrim,
BT43 5HW

Gemma Hutton
gemma45@hotmail.co.uk

Norman Walsh
43, Edentrillick Rd
Hillsborough, Co. Down
BT26 6PG

HONEY SHOWS

Local Associations stage honey shows throughout Northern Ireland. The Northern Ireland Honey Show, hosted by the Belfast City Parks Department, is held annually in September in the Botanic Gardens Belfast.

CONFERENCE

The 71st UBKA Annual Conference will be held on 20th – 21st March 2015 at CAFRE's Greenmount Campus, Antrim. Contact the U.B.K.A. Conference Secretary at 07871 161303 and www.ubka.org for details.

SECRETARIES OF ASSOCIATIONS

Belfast,
Jonathan Getty
80 Locksley Park,
Belfast,
BT10 0AS
email: bbkasecretary@
googlemail.com

Clogher Valley,
Chester Roulston
10 Ednagee Rd,
Garvetagh, Castlederg,
Co. Tyrone
BT81 7QF
email: chester.roulston@
hotmail.co.uk.

Derry City, Jen Simpson
4 Cullinean Manor,
Redcastle,
Nr Lifford
Co. Donegal
email: jennifersimpson163@
yahoo.com.

Dromore, Patrick Lundy
116 Dromore Road,
Ballynahinch,
Co.Down
BT24 8HK
email: patrickjlundy@
gmail.com

East Antrim, Stephen Robinson
53 Wellington Ave.,
Larne, Co Antrim
BT40 1EH
email: admin@sgrobinson.
co.uk.

Fermanagh,
Jorgen Pedderson
email: enniskillencc@
gmail.com.

Killinchy, Dawn Stocking
Ballycruttle House,
7 Tullynaskeagh Road
Downpatrick
Co. Down
BT30 7EJ
email: kbkasecretary@
gmail.com

Mid Antrim, Angela Morrow
23 Beechwood Drive
Ahogill
Ballymena
BT42 1NB
email: midantrimbka@
btinternet.com

Mid Ulster, Anne Milligan
61 Blackisland Road ,
Annaghmore,
Portadown
BT62 1NE
email: annpmilligan@
gmail.com

Randalstown, Brian Gillanders
email: hightown@live.co.uk

Roe Valley, Sandra Logan
22 Knocknougher Road,
Macosquin,
Coleraine,
Co. Londonderry.
email: alexandramlogan@
aol.com

The Three Rivers,
Daniel McMenamin
email: daniel@urney.info.

Rostrevor & Warrenpoint,
Darren Nugent,
email: biglongdarren@
hotmail.com

Honey Judges
Jim Fletcher
26 Coach Road,
Comber
BT23 5QX

Michael Young
Mileaway, Carnreagh
Road
Hillsborough
Co. Down
BT26 6LJ

Norman Walsh
43 Edentrillick Rd
Hillsborough
Co. Down
BT26 6NH

CYMDEITHAS GWENYNWYR

CYMRU WELSH BEEKEEPERS' ASSOCIATION

AMCANION Y GYMDEITHAS / AIMS OF THE ASSOCIATION
- Promote and develop beekeeping in Wales
- Conduct examinations in beekeeping
- Liaise with organisations and bodies for the benefit of beekeeping in Wales

AELODAETH UNIGOL / INDIVIDUAL MEMBERSHIP
Individual membership of the WBKA is provided for persons who do not live within the areas of branch associations, and wish to support the association. Information relating to benefits and facilities provided for individual members is available from the Individual Membership Secretary.

ARHOLIADAU / EXAMINATIONS
The Examinations Board conducts six grades of examinations: Junior, Primary, Intermediate, Practical, Honey Show Judges, Senior. Information is available from the Examination Board Secretary.

Candidates following the Duke of Edinburgh Award Scheme may receive information regarding the inclusion of beekeeping as a course submission from the Examinations Secretary.

CYNHADLEDD/ CONVENTION
At the Royal Welsh Agricultural Society's Showground, Llanelwedd. This event is normally held during Late March/ Early April. Information relating to this event is available from the convention secretary.

YSWIRIANT / INSURANCE
All individual and fully paid up members of beekeeping associations affiliated to WBKA are covered against 'Public and Product' liability claims. All affiliated associations are covered against public liability during conventions officially organised by the association.

WBKA/CGC

TRYSORYDD/TREASURER
Margaret Jones

GWEFEISTR/WEBMASTER
Grant Williams

AND GOLYGYDD/EDITOR
Sue Closs
editor@wbka.com

IS-OLYGYDD (ERTHYGLAU
CYMRAEG)/SUB EDITOR
Dewi Morris Jones
Llwynderw, Bronant
Aberystwyth SY23 4TG
(01974 251264)

ARHOLIADAU/EXAMINATIONS
Lynfa Davies

The WBKA Individual Membership benefits include cover under the BDI Scheme against the loss, due to foul brood diseases, of a minimum number of stocks (determined by BDI). Affiliated Associations provide this cover for their members.

LLYFRGELL / LIBRARY

The reference sections of all county libraries in Wales have details of the names and addresses of Secretaries of Associations affiliated to WBKA.

Books on beekeeping can be borrowed from county, branch and mobile libraries. The Library, Ffordd y Bala, Dolgellau LL40 2YS, has been nominated to stock beekeeping books.

Members of associations affiliated to IBRA may borrow books/documents from its library.

GWENYNWYR CYMRU - The Welsh Beekeeper

A publication of the Welsh Beekeepers Association, giving news and views of beekeeping and related subjects. Articles and advertisements enquiries should be sent to the Editor. Articles written in Welsh should be sent to the Sub Editor. Gwenynwyr Cymru is provided free to members of Affiliated Associations and Individual Members. Information regarding subscriptions is available from the Individual Membership / Subscription Secretary.

DARLITHWYR / DANGOSWYR, LECTURERS / DEMONSTRATORS

The names and addresses of lecturers and demonstrators, recommended by associations affiliated to the WBKA, are available from the General Secretary.

CYNLLUN CYSWLLT CHWYSTRELLU / SPRAY LIAISON SCHEME

Information is available from the General secretary

WBKA/CGC

SIOEAU / SHOWS

Honey/beekeeping sections are included at the Royal Welsh Agricultural Show, Llanelwedd, (OS ref: SO040520) during July, and at county, town and village shows throughout Wales. Information relating to these events may be obtained from secretaries of associations in the locality of the shows.

The historic FFAIR FEL ABERCONWY is held annually in the main street of the town, (OS ref: SH278378), on 13th September. Further information is available from the secretary of Conwy Association.

RHEOLAU CYFREITHIOL / STATUTORY REGULATIONS

The administration of the statutory regulations governing all aspects of beekeeping in Wales, is the responsibility of the Wales National Assembly, Caerdydd, CF99 1NA Phone (02920) 825111 Fax: (02920) 823352 Matters concerning statutory regulations, their implications and execution, should be addressed to the Minister of Agriculture and Rural Affairs, Wales National Assembly, at the above address.

AELODAETH UNIGOL-TANYSGRIFAU/ INDIVIDUAL MEMBERSHIP SUBSCRIPTIONS
Ian Hubbuck
White Cottage
Berriew
SY21 8BB
01686 640205
ianhubbuck@hotmail.com

INSURANCE:
John Bowles
insurance@wbka.com

CONVENTION SECRETARY:
Jill Wheeler
mertyndowning@
btinternet.com

CONVENTION TRADE STANDS SECRETARY:
Wally Shaw
Llwyn Ysgaw, Dwyran,
Llanfairpwll, Anglesey
LL61 6RH 01248 430811
waltershaw301@
btinternet.com

WBKA/CGC

CYMDEITHASAU TADOGOL A'U YSGRIFENYDDION / AFFILIATED ASSOCIATIONS AND SECRETARIES

ABERYSTWYTH, Ann Ovens,
Tan-y-Cae, Nr Talybont,
Ceredigion,
SY24 5DP
01970 832359
ann.ovens@btinternet.com

ANGLESEY, John Bowles,
Penrhos
Llanfaglan
Caernarfon
LL54 5RB
07449 021219
secretaryabka@gmail.com

BRECKNOCK AND RADNOR,
Diane Williams,
7 Diggedi Villas
Llanigon
Hay on Wye
Hereford
HR3 5PZ
dw.6@hotmail.co.uk

BRIDGEND, Shirley Myall
Distant View
Penylan Road
St Brides Mayor
Bridgend
CF32 0SA
shirley.myall@btinternet.com

CARDIFF AND VALE,
Annie Newsam
Stonecroft, Mountain Road,
Bedwas, Caerphilly, CF83 8ER
annienewsam@hotmail.co.uk

CARMARTHEN, Stephen Cox
Pen-Y-Maes
Ostrey Hill
St Clears
SA33 4AJ
steve_p_cox30@hotmail.com
07906 515996

CONWY, Mr Peter McFadden,
Ynys Goch
Ty'n y Groes,
Conwy LL32 8UH
01492 650851
peter@honeyfair.freeserve.co.uk

EAST CARMARTHEN
Doug Taylor,
Rhydgoch
Golden Grove
Carmarthen
SA32 8ND
01558 668339
doug@rhydgoch.co.uk

FLINT AND DISTRICT,
Jill and Graham Wheeler,
Mertyn Downing, Whitford
Holywell, Flintshire,
CH8 9EP.
01745 560557
mertyndowning@btinternet.com

GWENYNWYR CYMRAEG
CEREDIGION W.I.Griffiths,
Llain Deg, Comins Coch,
Aberystwyth, SY23 3BG
01970 623334
wilmair@btinternet.com

LAMPETER AND DISTRICT
Mr Gordon Lumby,
Gwynfryn, Brynteg,
Llanybydder,
SA40 9UX
01570 480571
g.lumby@btopenworld.com

LLEYN AC EIFIONYDD
Amanda Bristow,
Bryngwydion, Pontllyfni,
Gwynedd
LL54 5EY 01286 831328
amanda.bristow@egnitec.com

MEIRIONNYDD,
Sue Davies
Nant Ddu
Arenig
Bala
LL23 7PA
suedavies0117@gmail.com
01766 540790

MONTGOMERYSHIRE,
Keith Rimmer,
Beudy Clyd, Maesmawr,
Caersws SW17 5SB,
01686 689061
secretary@montybees.org.uk

PEMBROKESHIRE,
Lesley Williams
Tanffynnon
Blaenffos
Boncath
SA37 0HT
SOUTH CLWYD,

WBKA/CGC

✉ ☎

David P. Evans
Cwellyn
Dinmael
Corwen
LL21 0NY
dinmaelbees@btinternet.com
01490 460329

SWANSEA,
Julian Caruana
61 Glanyrafon Road
Pontarddulais
Swansea
SA4 8LT
07985 328910
sdbks.secretary@gmail.com
TEIFISIDE

Donald Robertson-Adam
Ffos y Ffin
Ffostrasol
Llandysul
SA44 5JY
donald@theoldmill.fsnet.co.uk

WEST GLAMORGAN
John Beynon
48 Whitestone Avenue
Bishopston
Swansea
SA3 3DA
jakbeynon@btinternet.com

HEB DADOGU/NON
AFFILIATED:
Mrs J Bromley
Ty Hir, Monmouth Road
Raglan, Usk. NP15 2ET
01291 690331
bromleyjan@hotmail.com

BEIRNIAID SIOE FÊL TRWYDDEDIG / WBKA QUALIFIED HONEY SHOW

TERRY E. ASHLEY
Meadow Cottage,
11 Elton Lane, Winterley
Sandbach CW11 4TN
M. J. BADGER MBE
14 Thorn Lane, Leeds
LS8 1NN
M BESSANT
Gwili Lodge, Heol
Lotwen, Rhydaman
SA18 3RP
ROBERT BREWER
PO Box 369, Hiawassee,
Georgia, USA
TOM CANNING
151 Portadown Road,
Armagh, Co Armagh
BT61 9HL
LES CHIRNSIDE
Bryn-y-Pant Cottage,
Upper Llanover,
Abergavenny NP7 9ES

CARYS EDWARDS
Ty Cerrig, Ganllwyd,
Dolgellau LL40 2TN
IFOR C. EDWARDS
Lleifior, Pontrhydygroes,
Ystrad Meurig SY25 6DN
STEVEN GUEST
Bridge House, Hind
Heath Road, Sandbach,
CW11 3LY
HUGH MCBRIDE
11 Ballyloughan Park
Antrim BT43 5HW
LORRAINE MCBRIDE
11 Ballyloughan Park
Antrim BT43 5HW

CECIL MCMULLAN
33 Glebe Road,
Hillsborough, County
Down
LEO MCGUINESS
89 Dunlade Road, Grey
Steel BT47 4QL
GAIL ORR
64 Ballycrone Road,
Hillsborough BT26 6NH
DINAH SWEET
Graig Fawr Lodge,
Caerphilly, CF83 1NF
REDMOND WILLIAMS
Tincurry, Cahir, Co
Tipperary Eire
MICHAEL YOUNG MBE
Mileaway, Carnreagh,
Hillsborough BT26 6LJ

NATIONAL BEE UNIT,
Animal and Plant Health Agency
(APHA)

www.nationalbeeunit.com

National Bee Unit
APHA, National Agri-Food Innovation Campus
Sand Hutton, York, YO41 1LZ, UK

Tel.No: 0300 3030094
Fax.No: 01904 462240
E-Mail: nbu@apha.gsi.gov.uk
Website: www.nationalbeeunit.com

NATIONAL BEE UNIT TECHNICAL STAFF, HEAD OF UNIT
Mike Brown

NATIONAL BEE INSPECTOR
Andy Wattam
01522 789726
07775 027524

National Bee Unit

The National Bee Unit (NBU) is part of the Animal and Plant Health Agency (APHA), an agency of the Department for Environment, Food and Rural Affairs (Defra), and is based just outside of York. The NBU is an element of APHA and its work covers all aspects of bee health and husbandry in England and Wales, on behalf of Defra in England and for the Welsh Government in Wales. The work of the unit includes disease and pest diagnosis, research into bee health matters, development of contingency plans for emerging threats, import risk analysis, related extension work and consultancy services to both Government and industry.

Bee Health Inspection Service

The NBU has a long track record in bee husbandry and bee disease control (since 1946) and has been directly responsible for the Bee Inspection services in England and Wales since 1994. The NBU consists of a home-based Inspectorate team, and the laboratory diagnostic and research team based at National Agri-Food Innovation Campus, Sand Hutton. In addition colleagues across Fera contribute to the programme and research projects. The Bee Health Inspectorate team consists of approximately 60 home-based members of staff. It is headed by the National Bee Inspector (NBI), whose role it is to manage the statutory disease control and training programmes. The NBI has management responsibility for eight home-based Regional Bee Inspectors (RBIs), one heading each of the seven regions in England and one covering Wales. The RBI in turn manages a number of Seasonal Bee Inspectors (SBIs). The RBIs

and SBIs organise inspections under EU and UK legislation, submit suspect samples for diagnosis, treat colonies for foulbrood and train beekeepers in bee husbandry for better disease control and greater self-sufficiency. In addition the Bee Inspectors also collect honey samples for residue analysis under the Statutory Honey collection agreement with Defra Veterinary Medicines Directorate (VMD). With *Aethina tumida* (Small hive beetle (SHB)) and *Tropilaelaps spp.* both notifiable under UK and EU law, Inspectors also undertake surveillance for these exotics in "Sentinel Apiaries (SA)" close to identified high risk areas. Beekeepers who manage SA's represent a valuable front line defence against an exotic pest incursion.

Bee Disease Diagnostic Team

The NBU's diagnostic team provides a rapid, modern service for both the Inspection team and beekeepers. The NBU laboratory adheres to ISO 9001 quality schemes to ensure a high professional standard. All diagnostic tests are conducted according to the OIE (Office International des Epizooties) Manual of Standard Diagnostic Tests and Vaccines. The OIE is the World Organisation for Animal Health and produce internationally recognised disease diagnosis guidelines (http//www.oie.int.). Across Fera, diagnostic support is provided from teams of microbiologists, acarologists, insect virologists and molecular specialists.

Bees and the Law

The 1980 Bees Act empowers Ministers to make Orders to control pests and diseases affecting bees, and provides powers of entry for Authorised Persons. Under the Bees Act, The Bee Diseases and Pests Control Order 2006 for England (as amended) and Wales, (there is similar legislation for Scotland and Northern Ireland) designates American foulbrood (AFB), European foulbrood (EFB), *A. tumida* (SHB) and *Tropilaelaps* mites (all species) as notifiable pests and defines the action which may be taken in the event of outbreaks. The Trade in Animals and Related Products Regulations 2011 (TARP) give effect to EU legislation concerning trade in animals and animal products

REGIONAL BEE INSPECTORS

Ian Molyneux
Northern Region
01204 381186
07775 119442

Jo Schup
Western Region
01948 710731
07979 119368

Nigel Semmence
Southern Region
01264 338694
07776 493649

Julian Parker
South East Region
01494 578505
07775 119469

Simon Jones
South West Region
01823 442228
07775 119459

Keith Morgan
Eastern Region
01485 520838
07919 004215

Ivor Flatman
North East Region
01924 252795
07775 119436

Frank Gellatly
Wales
01558 650663
07775 119480

To find details of Seasonal / Bee Inspectors please see BeeBase: https://secure.fera.defra.gov.uk/beebase/index.cfm . Remember that Seasonal Inspectors only work from April to September

NBU

Research Co-ordinator
Kat Roberts

Laboratory
Ben Jones (laboratory manager)
Ruth Grant
Ilex Whiting
Victoria Tomkies

Apiarists
Jack Wilford

Technical Advisor
Jason Learner

Administrative Programme Support
Kate Parker,
Lesley Debenham
& Jenna Cook

from other Member States and the importation of animals and animal products from Third Countries. Consolidated in TARP is the Directive on animal health requirements for trade in bees (the Balai Directive (92/65/EEC)). The Balai Directive specifically describes the intra-trade certification requirements for honey bees. Annexes A and B list the pests and diseases of animals, including those that affect honey bees, which are considered highest risk. Annex A lists the notifiable organisms throughout the Union. These are American foulbrood (AFB), the Small hive beetle (*A. tumida*) and *Tropilaelaps* mites. Annex B lists organisms that are not notifiable across the EU, but which Member States may choose to cover under their own domestic legislation. At the time of writing *Tropilaelaps* has not been confirmed in Europe.

The Importation of Bees

Beekeepers may legally import Queen honey bees from listed Third Countries as set out in the Commission Regulation (EU) 206/2010 . There are three countries outside of the EU, that we are aware of, whom can comply with the Decision: Argentina, Australia and New Zealand. Honey bee queens and packages may be imported from the EU, however, the beekeeper must make themselves aware of and adhere to the importation guidelines which can be found on BeeBase: http://www.nationalbeeunit.com/index.cfm?sectionid=47.

Under the Balai directive consignments of bees moved between Member States must be accompanied by an original health certificate confirming freedom from notifiable pests and diseases. In addition, colonies may be subject to controls aimed at preventing the spread of Fireblight between 15th March and 30th June. More information about this can be found on BeeBase http://www.nationalbeeunit.com/index.cfm?pageId=103

American and European foulbrood

American and European foulbrood are both serious diseases of European honey bees and are subject to

statutory control in the United Kingdom.

Any beekeeper who suspects their colonies to be infected with foulbrood should contact their nearest Appointed Bee Inspector (ABI) to report this.

Those apiaries that are suspected or confirmed to have a notifiable disease will be issued with a Standstill notice prohibiting the movement of any hive, bees, combs, bee products, bee pests, hive debris, appliances or other things liable to spread a suspected notifiable disease or pest on those premises or vehicle except under licence. More information about foulbrood disease is available on our website or in our advisory leaflet 'Foulbrood Disease of Honey Bees and other common brood disorders' http://www.nationalbeeunit.com/index. cfm?pageid=167.

Varroa

As part of the NBU's routine field screening programme the first known case of pyrethroid resistant Varroa mites in the UK was discovered in apiaries in Devon in August 2001. The NBU undertook a resistance-monitoring programme throughout England and Wales. Pyrethroid resistant *Varroa* mites are now widespread in England and Wales. To access current advice on *Varroa* and it's management please visit BeeBase.

Adult Bee Diseases

The NBU also offers a non-statutory and chargeable service for screening adult bee diseases. The NBU tests for adult bee diseases and parasites such as Nosema species (Nosema apis and *Nosema ceranae*, amoeba (*Malpighamoeba mellificae*) and tracheal mites (Acarine or *Acarapis woodi*) from samples submitted by beekeepers. As these diseases are non-statutory this service is chargeable. For the current cost please contact the NBU or visit the website.

Exotics
Beekeepers must make themselves aware of the potential threats to beekeeping in the UK. The field Inspection team monitors for potential exotics, the SHB and *Tropilaelaps spp*. The laboratory team also routinely screens import and suspect samples submitted for identification by both beekeepers and the field team.

Pesticide Monitoring
The WIIS involves the collaborative work of four separate organisations. It is led by the Chemicals Regulation Directorate (CRD) "http://www.pesticides.gov.uk/", formerly the Pesticides Safety Directorate. They are the 'Competent Authority' for the approval and regulation of pesticides and some other chemicals. Natural England (NE) "https://www.gov.uk/government/organisations/natural-england" manage the Scheme on the behalf of CRD and undertake site enquiries into pesticide exposure and, Fera Science Ltd (Fera) carry out pesticide analysis and, if appropriate, theAnimal and Plant Health Agency (APHA) "https://www.gov.uk/government/organisations/animal-and-plant-health-agency" carry out post mortems on wildlife. At Fera the Wildlife Incident Unit (WIU) "http://fera.co.uk/ccss/WIIS.cfm" will analyse samples for pesticides. and give an interpretation of the result based on information from the agencies involved.

It can also result in changes to label recommendations on pesticide products. It is not provided as a personal service to beekeepers wishing to seek evidence for the purpose of civil litigation but can lead to enforcement action being taken by the enforcer if the misuse or abuse of a product is identified as part of this process. For more information please see BeeBase: https://secure.fera.defra.gov.uk/beebase/index.cfm?pageId=84.

Research & Development
A programme of research and development within the group underpins the Unit's work. They also have long-established links with many European and world wide research centres, universities and the beekeeping industry. The primary aim of our R&D is to improve our understanding of the issues which impact bee health. The NBU also actively supports PhD students, some of which are funded using donations from the beekeeping industry.
For an update on the current R&D work of the unit please see BeeBase.

Extension

The NBU trains beekeepers in several ways: local courses and advisory visits run by the Inspectors, and national courses held at the York laboratory. The NBU annually hosts the National Diploma in Beekeeping residential courses and has also been host to visiting overseas workers and researchers. NBU York based staff also provide training to beekeepers at local and regional beekeeper meetings.

Healthy Bees Plan

The Healthy Bees Plan was published by Defra and the Welsh Assembly Government in March 2009 following consultation with beekeepers and the main Beekeeping Associations. It sets out a plan for Government, beekeepers and other stakeholders to work together to respond effectively to pest and disease threats and to put in place programmes to ensure a sustainable and productive future for beekeeping In England and Wales. The Healthy Bees Plan consists of three working groups that report to the project management board to help deliver the five major objectives of the plan. To view the Healthy Bees Plan, please see BeeBase.

BeeBase

BeeBase is the National Bee Unit website. It is designed for beekeepers and supports Defra, WAG and Scotland's Bee Health Programmes and the Healthy Bees Plan, which set out to protect and sustain our valuable national bee stocks. Our website provides a wide range of free information for beekeepers, to help keep their honey bees healthy. We hope both new and experienced beekeepers will find this an extremely useful resource and sign up to BeeBase. Knowing the distribution of beekeepers and their apiaries across the country helps us to effectively monitor and control the spread of serious honey bee pests and diseases, as well as provide up-to-date information in keeping bees healthy and productive. By telling us who you are you'll be playing a very important part in helping to maintain and sustain honey bees for the future. To register as a beekeeper please visit www.nationalbeeunit.com.

DEPARTMENT OF AGRICULTURE AND RURAL DEVELOPMENT

WWW.dardni.gov.uk

BEE DISEASE DIAGNOSTICS:
Sam Clawson
Agri-Food and Biosciences
Institute (AFBI)
Newforge Lane
BELFAST BT9 5PX
Tel: 028 9025 5289
Email:
sam.clawson@afbini.gov.uk

Training Courses:
Hazel Marcus
Greenmount Campus
College of Agriculture Food
and Rural Enterprise
Tel: 028 9442 6964
Email:
industry.trainingadmin@dardni.
gov.uk

Bee Health Inspections:
Thomas Williamson
Plant Health Inspection Branch,
DARD, Glenree House,
Carnbane Industrial Estate,
Newry, Co Down, BT35 6EF
Tel: 028 3889 2374
Fax: 028 3025 3255
Email:
tom.williamson@dardni.gov.uk

Honeybee Regional Report for Northern Ireland 2014

Bee Health Surveys

A questionnaire survey for Bee Husbandry issues has been circulated annually to beekeepers via beekeeping associations since 2009. The results of the 2014 survey are available as a pdf on the AFBI website (www.afbini.gov.uk). Preliminary results from the 2015 survey show that beekeepers recorded 13% of their overwintering colonies dead and 6% having queen problems. 40% of responding beekeepers reported no losses. The 2015 survey results are currently being processed but will be available on the AFBI website in November.

Bee Health Inspections

The Bee Inspectorate carried out surveys for American foul brood, European foul brood, Small Hive beetle and Tropilaelaps mite. American foul brood remains a problem for beekeepers in Northern Ireland with 7 apiaries found to have the disease by early September compared to 14 apiaries in total for 2013. Inspections were also carried out for European foul brood without any outbreaks recorded. Surveys continued for Small Hive Beetle and Tropilaelaps mite. Apiaries in the vicinity of ports or fruit importers were targeted for Small Hive Beetle inspections using corriboard shelter traps, while apiaries that had imported in the past were selected and hive scrapings examined for Tropilaelaps mite.

190

Adult Bee Disease Diagnostics

Nosema ceranae was first recorded in Northern Ireland in 2010. *N. ceranae* is an emergent pathogen of western honeybees. It is similar to the endemic species, Nosema apis but is considered to produce a more virulent disease than *N. apis*, probably reflecting its more recent association with the western honeybee. In 2014, 172 samples were tested for Nosema, with 39 (23%) positive for a *Nosema* infection. Of those, 22 (56%) contained N.apis only infections. 8 (21%) contained N ceranae only and the remaining 9 (23%) had both species).

Up to September 2015, 141samples of bees had been examined for *Nosema* infections.   21 (15%) were positive for *Nosema* spp. These results are from microscopic examination. PCR determinations have yet to be undertaken which will result in a slight increase in this figure and similar to 2014 findings (21% *Nosema* positive). However, in 2013, 49% of samples were found to be positive for *Nosema*.

  Note, this should not be used as an indicator of prevalence, as samples were not spatially representative of colony distribution in Northern Ireland.

Bee Health Contingency Plan

The Bee Health Contingency Plan is reviewed annually and an updated version was published on the DARD Internet in November 2013.

Strategy for the Sustainability of the Honey Bee

The Strategy for the Sustainability of the Honey Bee was published in February 2011 and aims to achieve a sustainable and healthy population of honey bees for both pollination and honey production in the north of Ireland through strengthened partnership working between Government and Stakeholders. The Strategy confirms DARD's ongoing commitment to help protect and improve the health of honey bees and support the sector in its efforts to sustain and support beekeeping. The Ulster Beekeepers Association (UBKA) and the Institute of NI Beekeepers (INIB) have made a commitment to support the Strategy intentions. The Strategy is aimed at both policy makers and beekeepers, and importantly, identifies the roles

DARD

and responsibilities of the different stakeholders in delivering its aims and outcomes. It seeks to address the current challenges facing beekeepers and provides a plan of action aimed at sustaining the health of honey bees and beekeeping in the north of Ireland for the next decade.

The Strategy for the Sustainability of the Honey Bee can be viewed at: http://www.dardni.gov.uk/strategy-for-the-sustainability-of- the-honey-bee.pdf

Beekeeping Courses at CAFRE

Preliminary Beekeeping Courses are organised and delivered by local Beekeeping Associations affiliated to the Ulster Beekeepers' Association (UBKA) at a range of venues around Northern Ireland. This Intermediate level Beekeeping course consists of three parts, Scientific, Practical, and Apiary Practical delivered over a period of at least two years and leading to the Federation of Irish Beekeepers' Associations (FIBKA) Intermediate Certificate of Proficiency in Beekeeping. Last year we trained 83 people over 7 courses in the Preliminary Beekeeping course and 43 people over 4 courses in the Intermediate Beekeeping course.

If you are interested in a beekeeping course please contact CAFRE Industry training at industry.trainingadmin@dardni.gov.uk or telephone 028 9442 6880

Thomas Williamson
Plant Health Inspection Branch, DARD
Sam Clawson
Bee Disease Diagnostics, AFBI
Andrew Adams
Farm Policy Branch, DARD
Kenny White
Short Course Manager, CAFRE

SG-AFRC

![The Scottish Government]

The Scottish Government

THE SCOTTISH GOVERNMENT AGRICULTURE, FOOD AND RURAL COMMUNITIES DIRECTORATE (AFRC) - RURAL PAYMENTS AND INSPECTIONS DIRECTORATE (RPID)

HEADQUARTERS
Lead Bee Inspector
Stephen Sunderland,
P Spur, Saughton House,
Broomhouse Drive,
Edinburgh, EH11 3XD
Tel: 0300 244 6672
e-mail: beesmailbox@
scotland.gsi.gov.uk

The Scottish Government (SG) is responsible for bee health Policy in Scotland. SG recognises the importance of a strong Bee health programme, not only for the production of honey, but also for the contribution that bees make to the pollination of many crop species and to the wider environment.

Honey bees are susceptible to a variety of threats, including pests and diseases, the likelihood and consequences of which have increased significantly over the last few years.

The Scottish Government takes very seriously any biosecurity threat to the sustainability of the apiculture sector and is working closely with colleagues in Food and Environment Research Agency's (Fera) National Bee Unit (NBU) to enable a more joined up approach to be taken throughout Great Britain on the issues surrounding bee health.

The Scottish Government has invested in the NBU's National web-based database for beekeepers "BeeBase" and actively encourages beekeepers to register onto the system. This service will provide bee health and disease outbreak information and will also assist Bee Inspectors in disease control. BeeBase also provides information on legislation, pests and disease recognition and control, interactive maps, current research areas and key contacts.

Beekeepers have a significant role to play in ensuring disease management and control within their own apiaries are in order as they have a legal obligation to report any suspicion of a notifiable disease or pest to the Bee Inspector at their local SGRPID Area Office. Bee Inspectors are responsible for the operation of The Bee Diseases and Pests Control (Scotland) Order 2007 in their area with duties including:-

- Inspection of apiaries for presence of statutory bee diseases
- Taking and delivering samples to SASA
- Issuing and removal of 'Standstill Notices'
- Issuing of 'Destruction Notices' and supervising destruction
- Informing beekeepers of treatment options for European Foul Brood (EFB), where appropriate
- Granting the option, after taking account of the recommendations of SASA, and carrying out treatment
- Carrying out follow-up inspections after destruction or treatment

SASA

- **Science and Advice for Scottish Agriculture (SASA)** is responsible for providing specialist technical support where duties include:
- Examination of submitted samples suspected of being infected with American Foul Brood, European Foul Brood, Small Hive Beetle (SHB) or *Tropilaelaps*.
- Reporting results on which pathogen or pest is present
- Recommending, in consultation with the Bee Inspector, the most suitable option, destruction or treatment, for each individual case of EFB.
- Where treatment is agreed, ordering supplies of the approved antibiotic
- Provision of a free diagnostic service to beekeepers to identify and confirm the presence of varroa.
- Maintaining technical liaison with NBU and providing technical documentation as required
- Providing training courses and demonstration material as required

SASA (SCIENCE AND ADVICE FOR SCOTTISH AGRICULTURE)
1 Roddinglaw Rd,
Edinburgh, EH12 9FJ

BEE DISEASES,
FIONA HIGHET
Plant Health Section
(0131) 244 8817

PESTICIDE INCIDENTS,
ELIZABETH SHARP
Chemistry Section
(0131) 244 8874

SG-AFRC

✉ ☎

PESTICIDE INCIDENTS

As part of the Wildlife Incident Investigation Scheme (WIIS), SASA undertakes analytical investigations into bee mortalities where pesticide poisoning may have been involved. Beekeepers should send samples of dead bees (200) direct to SASA, Chemistry Section, for analysis. In the case of major incidents, beekeepers are advised to contact their nearest SGRPID Area Office so that an early field investigation can be instigated.

THE FOLLOWING SCOTTISH GOVERNMENT RURAL PAYMENTS AND INSPECTIONS DIRECTORATE (SGRPID) STAFF ARE AUTHORISED BEE INSPECTORS. ALL BEE INSPECTORS HAVE EMAIL ADDRESSES AS "FIRSTNAME.SURNAME@SCOTLAND.GSI.GOV.UK"

EDINBURGH (HQ)
Steve Sunderland
(Lead Bee Inspector)
P Spur, Saughton House,
Broomhouse Drive,
Edinburgh, EH11 3XD
Tel: 0300 244 6672
Fax: 0300 244 9797

GRAMPIAN (INVERURIE AREA OFFICE)
Kirsteen Sutherland
Thainstone Court,
Inverurie, Grampian,
Aberdeenshire, AB51 5YA
Tel: (01467) 626247
Fax: (01467) 626217

SOUTHERN (DUMFRIES AREA OFFICE)
Angus Cameron
161 Brooms Road
Dumfries, DG1 3ES
Tel: (01387) 274400
Fax: (01387) 274440

CENTRAL (PERTH AREA OFFICE)
Steve Sunderland
Strathearn House
Broxden Business Park
Lamberkine Drive
Perth, PH1 1RZ
Tel: 01738 602043

HIGHLAND (INVERNESS AREA OFFICE)
Clem Cuthbert
Jane Thomson
Gordon Mackay
Longman House
28 Longman Road
Inverness, IV1 1SF
Tel: 01463 253 053

SOUTH EASTERN (GALASHIELS AREA OFFICE)
Angus MacAskill
Cotgreen Road
Tweedbank, Galashiels
Scottish Borders, TD1 3SG
Tel: (01896) 892400
Fax: (01896) 892424

SOUTH WESTERN (AYR AREA OFFICE)
John Smith
Russell House
King Street
Ayr
South Ayrshire
KA8 0BG
Tel: (01292) 291300
Fax: (01292) 291301

SCOTLAND'S RURAL COLLEGE (SRUC)

The Scottish Government supports a full-time apiculture specialist (Graeme Sharpe) who provides comprehensive advisory, training and education programmes for beekeepers throughout Scotland on all aspects of Integrated Pest Management, good husbandry (including the control of Varroa) and management practices. SAC also promotes the awareness of notifiable bee diseases and pests.

GRAEME SHARPE,
APICULTURE SPECIALIST,
SAC Consulting, Scotland's Rural College (SRUC),
Veterinary Services
John Niven Building
Auchincruive Estate
Ayr, Ayrshire
KA6 5HW
Tel:01292 525375

WWW.SCOTLAND.GOV.UK/TOPICS/APICULTURE/GRANTS/INSPECTIONS/BEEINSPECTIONS

USEFUL TABLES

BEEKEEPING METRIC CONVERTION TABLES

°CENT	FAHR	INCH	MM	INCH	MM	INCH	MM
0	32	1/25	1	1⁵/₈	42	10	254
5	40	1/12	2	1¹¹/₁₆	43	10¹/₄	260
7	44	1/8	3	1⁹/₂₀	48	11¹/₄	286
30	86	1/16	5	2	51	11¹/₂	292
34	92	1/4	6	3	76	11³/₄	298
38	100	5/16	8	4¹/₄	108	12	305
43	110	3/8	9	4¹/₂	114	14	356
49	120	1/2	12.5	4³/₄	121	16¹/₄	413
54	130	5/8	16	5¹/₂	140	16¹/₂	49
60	140	3/4	18	5³/₄	146	17	431
62	144	7/8	22	6	152	17⁵/₈	448
82	180	1	25	6¹/₄	159	18¹/₈	460
90	194	1¹/₁₆	27	8¹/₄	216	18¹/₄	483
100	212	1³/₈	35	8³/₄	223	20	508
		1⁹/₂₀	37	9¹/₈	232	21¹/₂	546
		1¹/₂	38	9³/₈	239	21³/₄	552
				9⁹/₁₆	246	22	559

INTERNATIONAL QUEEN MARKING COLOURS

YEAR ENDING	COLOUR	REMEMBER
1 & 6	WHITE	Will
2 & 7	YELLOW	You
3 & 8	RED	Raise
4 & 9	GREEN	Good
5 & 0	BLUE	Bees?

USEFUL TABLES

BOTTOM BEE-SPACE HIVES

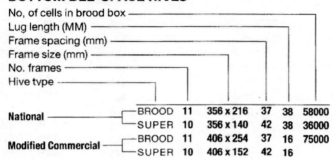

No, of cells in brood box ─────────────
Lug length (MM) ─────────────
Frame spacing (mm) ─────────────
Frame size (mm) ─────────────
No. frames ─────────────
Hive type ─────────────

Hive type		No. frames	Frame size (mm)	Frame spacing (mm)	Lug length (MM)	No. of cells in brood box
National	BROOD	11	356 x 216	37	38	58000
	SUPER	10	356 x 140	42	38	36000
Modified Commercial	BROOD	11	406 x 254	37	16	75000
	SUPER	10	406 x 152	42	16	

TOP BEE-SPACE HIVES

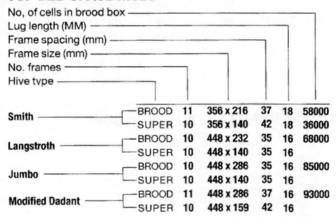

No, of cells in brood box ─────────────
Lug length (MM) ─────────────
Frame spacing (mm) ─────────────
Frame size (mm) ─────────────
No. frames ─────────────
Hive type ─────────────

Hive type		No. frames	Frame size (mm)	Frame spacing (mm)	Lug length (MM)	No. of cells in brood box
Smith	BROOD	11	356 x 216	37	18	58000
	SUPER	10	356 x 140	42	18	36000
Langstroth	BROOD	10	448 x 232	35	16	68000
	SUPER	10	448 x 140	35	16	
Jumbo	BROOD	10	448 x 286	35	16	85000
	SUPER	10	448 x 140	35	16	
Modified Dadant	BROOD	11	448 x 286	37	16	93000
	SUPER	10	448 x 159	42	16	

USEFUL TABLES

CONVERSION FACTORS

TEMPERATURE

Fahrenheit > Celcius (Centigrade)	- 32, x 0.5555 ($^5/_9$)
Celcius > Fahrenheit	x 1.8 ($^9/_5$), + 32

WEIGHT

Ounces > Pounds	x 28.3495
Pounds > Grams	x 453.59237
Hundredweights > Kilograms	x 50.8
Grams > Ounces	⁒ 28.3495
Kilograms > Pounds	x 2.2142

LENGTH

Inches > Centimetres	x 2.54
Yards > Metres	x 0.9144
Miles > Kilometres	x 1.609
Centimetres > Inches	x 0.3937
Metres > Yards	x 1.0936
Kilometres > Miles	⁒ 1.609

AREA

Acres > Hectares	x 0.404686
Hectares > Acres	x 2.47105

VOLUME

Pints > Litres	x 0.5683
Gallons > Litres	x 4.546
Litres > Pints	x 1.7598
Litres > Gallons	x 0.21997

WORD SEARCH ANSWERS

CRAMP	TABER
PHIPPS	BISHOP
JONES	KIRK
CARRECK	HOOPER
WARING	PATTERSON
GOULSON	ROWE
SAMMATARO	DAVIS
SEELEY	OTOOLE
MANGUM	WIDDICOMBE
HORN	MIKSHA
STEVENS	SIMS
ASTON	CONNER
BUCKNALL	KOENIGER
STORCH	SHAW
GREGORY	HAWKER
WEIGHTMAN	HEAF
BROWN	WILSON
ROBSON	LAZUTIN
FLOTTUM	MICHENER
ATKINSON	KRITSKY
SHOWLER	STOREY
MAURER	ROWE
PRESTON	DELAPLANE
WINSTON	ALFORD
BENJAMIN	TURNBULL

Lightning Source UK Ltd.
Milton Keynes UK
UKOW01f1918061215

264203UK00001B/13/P